PENGUIN BOOKS

Weddings and Wives

Edited by

Dale Spender

Weddings and Wives

Penguin Books

Penguin Books Australia Ltd
487 Maroondah Highway, PO Box 257
Ringwood, Victoria 3134, Australia
Penguin Books Ltd
Harmondsworth, Middlesex, England
Viking Penguin, A division of Penguin Books USA Inc.
375 Hudson Street, New York, New York 10014, USA
Penguin Books Canada Limited
10 Alcorn Avenue, Toronto, Ontario, Canada M4V 3B2
Penguin Books (N.Z.) Ltd
182 – 190 Wairau Road, Auckland 10, New Zealand

First published by Penguin Books Australia, 1994
10 9 8 7 6 5 4 3 2 1

Typeset in 11/12.5 Goudy Italien by Midland Typesetters, Maryborough, Vic.
Made and printed in Australia by Australian Print Group, Maryborough, Vic.
Text designed by George Dale

National Library of Australia
Cataloguing-in-Publiciaton data:

Weddings and wives.

ISBN 0 14 023480 2.

1. Weddings – Literary collections. 2. Wives – Literary collections. 3. Australian literature – 20th century. I. Spender, Dale

A820.80354

For Penny,
who knows it all

CONTENTS

Introduction

WEDDINGS WITHOUT WIVES

Many young women still want to have weddings: but very few of them want to be wives.

'I'll be a partner, an equal, a friend,' state many prospective brides. 'But never a wife.'

So passionate are some of the statements there can be no doubt that a number of women recoil at the very idea of being a wife. It's a role, a job, a title – that they definitely do not like. Yet the very same women can have stars in their eyes when they talk about weddings and brides. They will spend much of their time and most of their savings on a spectacle in 'white', which often still features as one of the most important days in a girl's life. But, when asked, they don't seem to find anything strange about wanting the wedding, while resolutely refusing to be the wife.

The belief that you might have been able to take one without the other would have perplexed and perturbed the patriarchs of the past. Up until the nineteenth century – and some would say well into the 1960s – weddings and wives could not be kept apart. But those were the days when women were controlled by marriage: when one man *gave away* his daughter to another man – whom she promised to obey under all circumstances. Those were the days when wifedom was an economic necessity for most women – and the job was for life.

No woman then could escape the pressure of weddings and wives. And no matter how she determines to live, no woman today can simply brush the institution aside. Married, single, divorced, lesbian; mother, daughter, sister, lover; Indigenous, Ethnic, Anglo – women are still invariably defined in relation to weddings and wives, regardless of whether they are for or against.

But if women of the past found wifedom *compulsory* (the term that Cicely Hamilton used in 1909 to describe the arrangement[1]) today's women find it *optional*. And this quiet 'revolution' has been brought about in the last twenty years. Women now actually sum up the pros and cons of being a wife – and clearly many believe it's a low status job, with demeaning 'service' requirements. Few are the contemporary women who do not list all the things they find wrong with being a wife (and this includes those who self-declare that they are still 'happily married'). But if they are constantly critical of the consequences many have very different views about the marriage 'rites'. There aren't the same reservations about weddings as there are about wives.

The ritual, the performance, the very business of being a bride (and brides *are* big, commercial business), is not only still with us, but in many societies is becoming an even more popular public event. The single day of spectacle, of being special, is still high on the list of priorities of many women – be they young or mature, Anglo or Indigenous, or even lesbian or heterosexual.[2]

The testimony that weddings are more of a celebration, a 'rite of passage', rather than an oath of endurance, is not hard to find in most English speaking societies. And 'Susanna' is one of the countless examples of modern times.

Married in April 1993 she separated from her husband six weeks later. Of course she *had* lived with him beforehand – but the marriage changed him dramatically. 'Things that he never questioned before suddenly became big issues once I was *his* wife' she stated. 'I just couldn't believe what I was hearing when he started to say, *'I'm not having my wife go there – or do that'*, so I just had to leave. Men just don't get it,' she added, 'and I'm not the only one who thinks so.'

What about the wedding presents? I asked. What about your parents, his parents, his ego? What about the unbelievable expense of your great day?

'Oh, that's all okay,' Susanna replied. 'I handled him all right. I didn't want any fights. I kept half the presents. And no one wanted them back. They got a good night for their money. And my parents weren't upset either. They said it had been a really great party! They just wanted me to be happy. And mum (and my sister ... *I should have known*!) – well they didn't like him much anyway. So no harm done. It's all okay really. Don't look so concerned,' she said to me. What about the future? I asked.

'Well,' said Susanna, without a trace of irony, 'I'd have another wedding – but next time round I'd make sure I married someone who didn't want a wife. It's just not on anymore.' And off she went to her highly-paid job in real estate, and her prized, independent life.

From the many discussions I have had, Susanna is not atypical. Her mother's generation fought for women's right to wed or not to wed – for a woman to be economically independent and to be able to do her own thing either way. And Susanna's generation has little difficulty in making use of the legacy they have inherited. Unlike their foremothers they don't even pay lip service to male supremacy and they are increasingly vocal about what they see as the 'shortcomings' of men.

But these everyday conversations of a wide spectrum of women are not as yet *public* topics. The extent to which these far-reaching changes in women's lives are absent from research literature, and popular women's culture, is quite extraordinary.

In her update of *Damned Whores and God's Police* Anne Summers comments on the 'shifts', and the 'silence'.[3] Quoting from the Office of the Status of Women she writes that 'Women and their status in Australian society are perceived to have undergone a major and dramatic transformation. The changes made can be described as "revolutionary" and "evolutionary". The women of "middle Australia" generally recognise these changes and tend to embrace their new roles in a positive manner.'[4] But, adds Anne Summers, women are 'generally impatient for the men in their lives to catch up to the new realities, and do their fair share of household and other necessary tasks.'

Hugh Mackay[5] is another social commentator who has labelled women as the pioneers of change, particularly in the private realm, and who states categorically that it's men who have to clean up their act. While he doesn't explicitly advocate that men should give up wanting wives who provide services, this is nonetheless the message that he delivers to men who are not pulling their weight on the emotional, or the domestic front. For Hugh Mackay there's no mystery as to why women don't want to be wives – and why they leave their husbands. Yet these insights about the changes in women's marital lives – and the lag in male performance – are rarely reflected in either serious research studies or in the widely available women's magazines.

Anne Summers points to the 'gap in the literature'. Where once these women's magazines were taken to task for confining women to family and domestic roles, these days they've gone the other way: 'They have largely abandoned their traditional women's service functions of advice on health and other family matters, and have evolved into a rather bizarre mixture of royalty, celebrity and the occult' she states. Some of the magazines directed to younger women 'do address subjects like sex, self-esteem, sexual harassment and the multitudes of day-to-day hassles in any young woman's life'. But this still falls far short of serious analysis of the practical and symbolic transformations in women's role. From the coverage in the majority of women's magazines it would not be possible to gauge that untold women unequivocally maintain that the greatest problem in partnerships with men is their failure to take responsibility for their own emotional states – and for the home.

But it is not just that many of the women's magazines ignore the politics of women's existence. Well might we ask why there is no serious and accessible critique of the range of bridal magazines which seem set to undermine just about every gain that has been made by women in the last twenty years.

The role that advertising plays in women's popular literature – and the implications of the concentration of media ownership – are no doubt related to the dearth of material on matrimonial moves. But it is partly because there are so few data and so little commentary on this aspect of women's (and men's) lives, that *Weddings and Wives* has been undertaken. It was because I could see new lifestyles, and new ways of thinking about relationships, families and commitments, that were not reflected in mainstream social science literature or the media, that I embarked on this project. And why I turned to women writers to describe and explain the revolution.

Some said they were interested but unable to participate. ('I'm too busy trying to meet all the demands of being a wife to have time to write about what's going wrong' one woman tellingly replied.) Another said she couldn't bring herself to write about an experience that was so painful. One sociologist agreed to write about 'wifeliness' and all that it had entailed but then didn't deliver the manuscript. Such are the disappointments for editors.

Because of the influential role she played in exposing the way women were exploited as wives (and because I am full of admiration for her analysis and astuteness), I contacted Germaine Greer, whose response was typically insightful:

Dear Dale (*she wrote*) ...
You are inviting me to contribute to a book on a social revolution

that has taken place over the past thirty years in relation to weddings and wives. I am under the distinct impression that there are more brides traipsing down the aisle in rented or unpaid-off mock virginal finery in 1993 that there have ever been before in the history of the world.

And she quite rightly pointed to the numbers of women in the Solomon Islands – and Japan for example – who have so enthusiastically taken up the western practice of white weddings.

The bridal industry which churns out wedding gear in Japan is 'big business'. But the fact that more women in a variety of countries are adopting the white trappings of the western bridal industry doesn't mean that there hasn't been a revolution. On the contrary, the fact that so many different cultures have seized upon the celebratory ritual alone, can still be an indication of the way weddings retain their popularity – while wives are in decline.

That wives are not what they used to be is the conclusion of most of the contributors to this volume. That it has been a painful process divesting themselves of some of the baggage that traditionally has gone with being 'the wife', is another theme which unites many of the writers. Those who were born and reared before the consciousness raising of the women's movement have often had more difficulty in making the transition. For some of the younger authors wifedom has never been a necessity – just an option – and not a permanent one either.

What does emerge from these accounts is that women are not very sentimental these days about being spouses. In twenty-seven contributions and 416 pages the word *love* barely rates a mention. And extraordinary as it may seem, only one contributor has anything positive to say about the mutual support and companionship of marriage. Where once women were expected to *do it all for love* – to obey, serve, support and smile – they now have very different considerations. There are countless women who will no longer put up with male behaviour they find unacceptable, and there are many women who openly acknowledge that 'quality of life' means – life without men.

When asked why, there was a common chord in the response – as the 1992 market research conducted for the *Bulletin* made clear:

> Australian married and de facto couples consistently agree that a wide range of household chores and family decisions should be shared fairly equally regardless of gender. Yet this is not the reality. Women are being shortchanged, and they are angry about the inequality which persists in their lives. Women tend to initiate family break-ups in Australia – often to the bewilderment of their male partners, who fail to perceive the tension over the gap between ideal and reality in family life.[6]

Most women know what the WET TANK (Women's Economic Think Tank) spells out; namely that the 'situation of women who are sole parents emphasises the fact that children make less work than a husband' and that women without men 'spend less time on cooking and housework' and have 'more time for community activities and friends'.[7] Which is why women are making rational choices about how they spend their time.

Of course there are women who have always been able to observe from the sidelines. These are the women who have chosen to make a commitment to women and who can be disinterested and dispassionate commentators and critics on the fluctuating fortunes of husbands and wives. If however the changes in family groupings continue at the present revolutionary rate – and it becomes optional for women to marry women – then we could find some interesting patterns emerging. Already in New York, for example, gay relationships can be officially registered: and in many employment contexts in Australia they can be unofficially taken into account.

So when 'weddings and wives' lose their heterosexual connotations – which appears more than likely – there will be another opportunity to look at the revolutionary changes that have taken place in social organisations – and socialisation –

and to examine the possible 'arrangements' that couples can make. 'Wife' could not only be again redefined, but the reasons for choosing wifedom could become an open and challenging discussion. Given the history of wifeliness (see this volume page 3) one could be forgiven for asking why anyone would want to become a wife. It's certainly a question that has occurred to most of the contributors to this volume.

For Aboriginal and Torres Strait Islander women the entire tradition of 'weddings and wives' can also be completely irrelevant. But while some have elected to play the 'white' game, others have retained their own cultural features. And this gives them an unusual vantage point when it comes to commenting on changing customs. (See Lisa Bellear and Jackie Huggins, this volume.) But no matter the standpoint, the women writers in this collection all share a common framework. They are products of a society in which women have been defined in relation to men – and where women are now defining their own lives.

This is the lesson that Nadia Wheatley delivers in her satirical treatment of the biblical wedding of the year. Why is it, she asks, that the woman has been led to believe that the wedding day is *her* day when it is brides and their experience that have been written out of history?

Rosie Scott continues with this wedding theme and the negative rituals that are associated with the bride (including those of virginity and sexual innocence). But Debra Adelaide introduces a much more pragmatic note when she describes all the rituals that accompany the wedding breakfast, or reception. As she tells it in 'According to the Book,' there can be little doubt about the priorities for some young women: how they look and what the 'party' is going to be like is much more important when they arrange the details, than who is their partner. Another sign of wanting the wedding without bothering too much about the 'thereafter'.

Jan Owen satirically takes on all the issues that go with finding 'true love' and getting your man as well as the depersonalising process of being 'the bride'; in 'On behalf of myself and my wife ...' she shows how even the modern woman continues to be 'spoken for' on the bridal conveyor belt.

Taking a more lighthearted view of the whole performance, Susan Mitchell with characteristic wit, and wry humour, shows how 'the great day' can so easily become farce – and a fitting introduction for the marital future.

Carolin Baum explores the anguish which goes with choosing the right dress: and the agony which goes with the wrong one.

Lois Ellis and Sara Hardy have written a script which stretches the imagination and plays with traditional imagery: their version of the wedding has its amusing and serious note. And in 'Public Property' Jane Messer goes almost to the ends of the earth to preserve her privacy only to find that she must still deal with the mundane interference that goes with becoming a wife. And she raises one of the most fundamental issues when she states that she not only wants a new role, she wants a new label – '*wife* and *husband* just won't wear' she writes. A modern term is needed for a modern woman's way of life.

The customs of another country are the concern of Yasmine Gooneratne who looks at weddings in Bombay. Even in contexts where marriages have traditionally been 'arranged', we now find wives listing their grievances, setting their own terms – and redefining wifedom in the process.

The Australian Bureau of Statistics indicates that just 'over a third of Australians marry somebody from another culture. Women showed a slightly higher disposition to marry a person born overseas rather than in Australia'.[8] And this helps to explain Pamela Verrall's 'sample'. She interviewed young women for a radio program and writes that 'From these initial interviews the most tantalising issue for me, and I think, one of the biggest changes in weddings in Australia, is the number happening across cultures.' Not that this is the only issue she pursues. Like many of the other contributors Pamela Verrall also has some scathing things to say about the bridal industry!

In her inimitable style, Barbara Jefferis asks – so what's new? Every generation thinks it is having a revolution, she writes –

and she quotes convincing examples from the past. Even the 'blended' family, which is currently being treated as a new arrangement that gives cause for concern, has all been done before: 'The broken marriages, the one-parent families, the complicated step-relationships were very much as they are today. All that was different was the cause – death in earlier centuries – divorce today.'

Lisa Bellear suggests that while the only choice available is that of becoming the wife of a man, then reluctance to tie the knot is most understandable. In this radio script she suggests that there are alternatives to the white, heterosexual model of weddings and wives. And quite a few alternatives for men.

Phryne Fisher, Kerry Greenwood's detective 'flapper' heroine, also has doubts about being a bride; set in the 1920s, 'Marrying the Bookie's Daughter' is a real thriller. It also exposes the double standard and the shameful treatment of women in an earlier period.

The pregnant daughter cast out by the mother is the focus of Sarah Neal's film script 'Daughters – and Dilemmas', which tackles the changing patterns and pressures of marriage. From the grandmother who thinks that being a wife is the only choice to the grand daughter who thinks it is no choice at all, we witness the family tensions that are the price of social revolution.

Dorothy Porter takes women and wives as the centre point of her striking poem 'Wives', while Helen Hodgman's film script 'Blue Skies' provides a stark reminder of the way the beautiful brides can quickly be transformed into wearied suburban spouses.

Bride of Fortune is the title of the opera for which Anna Maria Dell'oso wrote the libretto (with music composed by Gillian Whitehead). It is based on Anna Maria Dell'oso's experiences in an Italian immigrant family. 'A Toast to All You Brides of Fortune' is her personal, poignant and perceptive essay which draws on the same understandings, and is included here; it explores the radical changes that have taken place within an ethnic community. From the fate of a proxy bride to the freedom of a contemporary wife – all in the space of one generation – Anna Maria Dell'oso's chronicle marks a revolution.

For others the experience has been closer to the bone. How could I have been so conned, Lynne Spender asks in 'Down the Aisle – and Up the Garden Path' as she recounts the particular experience of the generation which has tried to keep it all going. She combines the personal and the political as she does her own soul searching: how could she know all the problems that went with being a wife and yet think that for her it would be different. That the disasters wouldn't happen.

But they did.

Marion Halligan is the storyteller extraordinaire. She charts the difficulties, the despair – and the hope – that wives have placed in relationships across generations, while Jackie Huggins analyses the pros and cons of living with a man. In 'Alone Again – Naturally' she wonders about the way twentieth century 'Black-woman-thinking' fits in with traditional Aboriginal culture; what do white weddings have for Black girls?

So bleak and brutal is the picture that Sue Ingleton presents of the relationship between the sexes, that the wonder of it is that women would ever willingly be wives. While not specifically a domestic violence script, her contribution draws on many of the cultural understandings about the exploitation and abuse of women; and no coverage could be complete without this confrontation with the systemic and sexual violation of wives. Kate Grenville also documents the psychological abuse that wives have often had to contend with; in 'Albion the Husband' we encounter a man who calculatingly and calmly sets out to rob his wife of integrity, confidence, judgement. It is a chilling appraisal. And Kaz Cooke demonstrates that one picture can be as good as a thousand words.

The testimony of mother and daughter – Carolyn Quadrio and Lisa Quadrio – makes for a fitting finale. In graphic style Carolyn Quadrio traces the tragedies of her maternal history. The grandmother who as a poor young peasant girl was sent from Greece to become the wife of a middle-aged man she did not know; the mother who had the illegitimate child and never became the wife. Carolyn herself who has put her energies into trying to combine a medical career with the role of wife. And Lisa, the daughter who looks at all that submission and self-denial and says – what was it all for? Lisa who from her position of independence and strength, much of which has been provided by her mother, simply sees weddings and wives as irrelevant. And intends to live happily ever after ...

From biblical times to the new age, this volume records the changing ways of weddings and wives. It is a testimony of the distance women have travelled towards self-realisation. It is a victory even if there are still battles to be won, and obstacles to be overcome. Women who were once exchanged by men, and controlled by men, increasingly set their own terms; these include the right to redefine the role of wife, or to reject it outright.

Understandably many of the contributors to this volume are not only exhilarated by their new freedom, they are angry at the way that women have been treated in the past – and the present. They are in the process of rejecting a centuries-old tradition of wifeliness. And it would be fair to say that the sense of injustice about men not pulling their weight is a subtext in many of the accounts included here. These feelings of resentment and frustration need to be noted. They are a stage in the process of women's liberation; they document the ideas and emotions that are part of many women's lives at the end of the twentieth century.

Wedding and Wives brings together some of Australia's outstanding contemporary women writers. And while all have addressed the common cause of 'weddings and wives', each has her own insights and observations. Together these writers weave some of the new and subtle – and radical – patterns of our society; together they also represent some of the best achievements of writers. Not all have been, will be, or want to be wives. Yet all know the way that women have been drawn into the definitions, if not the institution of marriage. And it has to be said that the verdict is no longer out when it comes to wives. On balance the writers in this anthology are against the role. Which may say something about writers as well as society.

What these stories, plays, scripts, essays, poems, cartoons, have in common is the belief that women have come of age and no longer seek to be subordinate wives. This opens up enormous possibilities ... When you can have as many weddings as you want, to what sex you like, and when no one any longer has to be 'the wife', few would want to speculate on the social arrangements of the next century. But what can be said with certainty is that wives as they have been known – are a thing of the past!

Dale Spender
1994

NOTES

1. See Cicely Hamilton, 1909, *Marriage as a Trade*, The Women's Press, London, reprinted 1981.
2. More often called 'commitment ceremonies' in the United States, a significant number of 'marriages' now take place within the gay community. Some states/countries register such relationships while others give no official status.
3. Anne Summers, *Damned Whores and God's Police*, Penguin, Melbourne, 1994.
4. 'The Women's View: market research study on women's perceptions of themselves and government programs and policies' conducted for the Office of the Status of Women by Consumer Contact, July–August 1992, p. 25: quoted in Anne Summers, 1994, pp. 26–7.

5. See Hugh Mackay, *Reinventing Australia: the mind and mood of Australia in the 90s*, Angus & Roberston, Sydney, 1993.
6. Ben Sandilands, 'The heartland speaks. What we want, what we fear', report of first Australian Social Monitor survey conducted by AMR: Quantum, *Bulletin*, 28 July 1992, pp. 30–44. Quoted in Anne Summers 1994, p. 27.
7. See WETTANK Houseworkshop Bulletin No 1, and Newsletter, October 1993; for further discussion see following section.
8. See Julian Cribb, the *Australian*, 30 October 1993, p. 4.

PART ONE

KAZ
I'd like you to meet my wife
Hi honey. You got a name, or a code number?

I·D·

DALE SPENDER

The Ancient History of Wifeliness

THE 'PROS' AND THE 'CONS'

While today the label and the limitations of being 'the wife' are increasingly shamed and shunned, it is not so long since such status was desired by many a young woman: when the wedding ring could be seen as a badge of achievement; when the wearer could parade her success in 'getting a husband'.

But given that the alternative then was to be branded as a spinster, an old maid, and to be cruelly used by family and society, it is not surprising that women should have sought the promised comfort and safety of holy matrimony. Nor is it surprising that at a time when getting – and keeping – a man was considered to be the occupation of a woman's life, so much of her experience and training should have been directed towards wifeliness.

There used to be a specific code that governed the behaviour of wives. It was outlined in everything from the etiquette columns of the women's magazines to the 'lessons' of popular novels, and real life. *Wifeliness* was held to be an art, and good mothers would try and instruct their daughters in its mysteries and crafts. If managing the home was part of the necessary wifely repertoire, managing the man – as the centrepiece of the arrangement – was the major preoccupation.

Which is one reason that wives were called on for *self-*sacrifice.

The rule that the man must come first has been at the core of all the advice that has been handed out to wives. And many have been the prominent and influential men who have had their own say about the qualities that are required. 'To please, to be useful to us, to make us love and esteem them, to educate us when young and take care of us when grown up, to advise, to console us, to render our lives easy and agreeable – these are the duties … at all times' of the wife, wrote the champion of liberty and equality, Jean Jacques Rousseau[1] (whose reputation remains high in most educational institutions).

Over the centuries, women have found themselves obliged to put the emotional and physical needs of men first – and with no great consideration given to the personal price.

'It has been admitted that marriage is a hard job, requiring constant adjustment,' states Germaine Greer,[2] 'but it is not so often admitted that the husband-provider is the constant – and the variable is the wife!' Jessie Bernard summed up the behaviour expected of good wives in similar style: the husband decrees – the wife complies. 'The tendency for wives to shape themselves to conform to their husbands has been documented and researched in some detail'[3] she writes.

The folklore of wifeliness makes it very clear that the woman must manage all so that the husband can be seen to be 'wearing the pants'. (This is what Virginia Woolf has referred to as 'reflecting a man at twice his normal size.'[4]) The wife's role has been to make him feel good, to make him look important – even at the expense of her own growth, and acknowledgement.

And as personal growth and achievement – and visibility and credit – are now much more the values of the times, it's easy to see how wifeliness has become 'ancient history' and holds little attraction for the present generation of females.

Not that 'massaging male egos' was by any means the limit of wifely duty in days gone by. In more recent years a new job description has emerged – that of *house*wife. And with the title came the sole responsibility for the work of the house – and the pressure to 'hide' both the hard labour involved, and the hard feelings it gave rise to. For not only was the wife supposed to cook, clean, shop, wash, iron etc., *she was supposed to make the whole thing look effortless and untiring!*

What's more – she was supposed to do it willingly, wantingly, fulfillingly. No matter how long it took (or how little time it lasted) she was never to be resentful: she was never to complain.

'No man wants to come home to chaos' warned the agony aunts and mothers-in-law who monitored wifely success and failure. Which was just one reason that the domestic chores had to be done *before* the husband came in to be welcomed and waited on after his long day at 'the coalface'.

But another reason was that no man would want to think that he had turned his wife into a drudge. So not only did she have to look beautiful and as though her hands had never seen housework, it was necessary for her to do all the hard work when he was not around. Or else he might feel uncomfortable. Or even become angry. And one thing can lead to another …

The good wife should always understand that a husband wants to be seen as a reasonable and likeable man – rather than a demanding tyrant. This is why it is important that the housework be kept invisible. Her role is to make the home a haven and to always be on hand; to be admiring, available, attractive. In the words of that caustic critic of wifedom, Cicely Hamilton (1909)[5], this good wife was obliged to combine 'the divergent qualities of an inspiration and a good general servant'. No wonder so many of today's young women think there are better things on offer.

The fact that – until the 1970s – the majority of wives were financially dependent is another explanation of women's self-sacrifice. When Ann Oakley published her ground-breaking book, *The Sociology of Housework* in 1974, 85 per cent of women in Britain were housewives, classified as financially dependent and 'economically non-productive'.[6]

As being a wife – and a housewife – was often the only job open to women, the only way they could 'earn their bread' – it shouldn't come as a surprise that some would try to do the work 'to the best of their ability'. Even if this was at the risk of their physical and mental health (see Jessie Bernard 1972 for further details). But it wasn't always pride in the performance which made them excel as a wife. There's another more insidious explanation for the slavish way that so many husbands have been catered for by their wives.

Apart from the fact that few women would have wanted to risk the ill humour of men who were not pleased with the comforts provided, there was the very real fear among wives that they might be deserted, displaced, discarded. And there was often nowhere else to go. No jobs, no refuges, not even an alternative and acceptable subculture of 'solos'.

'Being a wife is one of the few occupations where experience on the job doesn't increase your value – or lead to a better offer the second time around,' Lynne Spender comments wryly.[7]

In this situation the best insurance that wives had available was to make men dependent upon them. If a husband couldn't look after himself – if he couldn't manage without a wife – then she would stand a better chance of keeping him, and her livelihood. Or so went the rationalisation.

The trouble was – as Germaine Greer was quick to point out – the rationalisation and reality were not the same thing. Although the housewife was supposedly 'an unpaid worker in her husband's house in return for being a permanent employee' there were no guarantees. For 'the lowest paid employees can be laid off and so are wives. They have no savings, no skills which they can bargain with elsewhere, and they must bear the stigma of being sacked . . .'.[8] Many a wife discovered that far from being indispensable – she was interchangeable.

It was exposés like this in the 1970s, of the exploitation of wives, which marked the beginning of the end of wifeliness.

While there had been individual critics of wifedom over the centuries (Mary Astell, Mary Wollstonecraft, and Charlotte Perkins Gilman among them), the women's liberation movement became a chorus of protest and condemnation of the appalling conditions of marital servitude. *Why Be a Wife* campaigns were organised in most western societies and the very name of *wife* was on the way to becoming a four letter word.

And the evidence is that the campaigns were successful. For hundreds of years, women had practised the virtues of wifeliness. For the last twenty, many of them have decided to give it all a miss. They'll keep the wedding – which promises radiance and romance and puts a *woman* first – but the self-sacrifice which goes with being a wife is no longer seen as glamorous, satisfying, or even dignified.

Which is why we are in the unusual position of having a great many more weddings than there are wives.

FROM RITES TO RIGHTS

Cicely Hamilton (1872–1952) always claimed that one reason men denied women access to education and entry to interesting and well paid jobs was because they were frightened that if there were any alternatives available, women would not become wives. Given the choices that women are currently making, it seems that the nineteenth century law makers were probably right.

Wifedom has become an option – rather than an expectation.[9]

Women now have more choices than their foremothers – with financial independence ideally being one of them. In contrast to the time when Cicely Hamilton wrote *Marriage as a Trade* (1909) – and argued that marriage was compulsory for women as there were no other decent jobs on offer – the official rhetoric now is that of *equality of opportunity*: women technically have access to all the education and occupations that men once kept for themselves.

Not much more than a century ago, women were not only denied access to the universities and the professions, they were subjected to many more indignities and constraints. On becoming a wife, for example, a woman lost her legal identity; (when two became one, that *one* was most definitely the husband – hence the loss of her name in exchange for his). The wife also lost her right to own property – while at the same time she was considered the property of the man. The wedding ring, and the title 'Mrs' came to be a symbol of male ownership in the nineteenth century.[10]

It is disturbing to be reminded that at this time an all male parliament and judiciary had passed laws to decree that wives had to be conjugally available to their husbands – on demand. Mary Wollstonecraft (1759–97) referred to wives as legal prostitutes who were required to exchange sexual services in return for their keep; she also said that prostitutes had the better bargain, as they could at least have some say in how long they would work and what they would charge. Wives had no such influence.

The same all-male bodies had defined marriage so that there was no escape for wives. Divorce was virtually unobtainable and any woman who left a marriage was deemed a 'disobedient wife' and could be returned to her rightful owner – her husband. Men also passed a law which was based on the premise that it was reasonable for a husband to beat his wife (and stipulated the width of a weapon and the number of blows permitted). The phrase 'rule of thumb' descends from English common law that said a man could legally beat his wife with a switch 'no thicker than his thumb'. And of course, women had no political power: as men denied them the vote, they could not protest at their treatment through the ballot box.

Which is why it is easy to see women's campaigns – and spectacular gains – of the last one hundred and fifty years, as establishing women's right *not* to be wives.

'The more you learn about ... the legal structure (of marriage)' writes Naomi Wolf[11], 'the less likely you are to call in the caterers. In the nineteenth century when a judge ruled that a husband could not imprison his wife, *The Times* bemoaned, "One fine morning last month, marriage in England was suddenly abolished."'

But one by one the oppressive laws relating to wives have been repealed and revised so that even after the marriage rites, women's rights are now accepted and defined. It is now illegal for a husband to beat his wife, to keep her confined, or to deny her property rights (though this has not stopped such barbaric practices from occurring). 'Rape in marriage' – a concept which could have been barely understood in a context of conjugal rights, is now increasingly being outlawed. Any idea that a husband might *own*, the sexual, physical, material, or mental resources of a wife is systematically being eroded.

One woman who would have seen this as a marvellous victory was that most ill-used of wives, Caroline Norton (1808–1877).

She was an English woman faced with a drunken, violent and foolish husband who made no attempt to provide for the family. Caroline Norton was not able to leave the marriage – partly because this was at a time when fathers were the legal guardians: as women were not considered fit to have the charge of their own offspring, Caroline Norton could not get away from her husband without abandoning her children. Her husband also accused her of 'criminal conversation' – a then euphemism for adultery. Although Caroline Norton was cleared by the courts, it was not much consolation. As a wife she had no legal standing so she could not sue for damages, divorce, or even maintenance. And of course as the all-male legislature had seen fit to consider adultery in males to be comparatively inconsequential, she could not sue on these grounds either. (Because wives who committed adultery could have another man's child, the 'crime' was considered serious, and regarded as sufficient grounds for divorce. But adultery was not seen by men to be such a serious matter in relation to themselves, so a wife didn't have a case just because her husband had committed adultery – she had to have *additional* grounds for divorce! This double standard was eliminated by the 1959 Matrimonial Causes Act.)

And just to ensure that there was no way out for wives,

the law of the land also stipulated that they had no rights to anything they earned, so when Caroline Norton tried to support herself by writing, her husband claimed the income as his own property.

It was men's failure to provide for their wives and families that incensed the nineteenth century women's rights worker, Frances Power Cobbe (1822–1904). While Cicely Hamilton had described marriage as the requirement for women to trade their bodies in return for board and lodging, the fact that there were no guarantees that men would keep their side of the bargain and deliver on food and shelter, was an outrage as far as Frances Power Cobbe was concerned. One of the early campaigners against domestic violence, she denounced the way women were abused in marriage and publicly protested on behalf of the wives who had starved to death because their husbands had denied them 'the necessaries of life'.

Frances Power Cobbe was bitterly critical of the laws men had made to define the duties of the marital relationship. In all the regulations they had set down there was not one word to be found which referred to the duties of the male. Men had made up so many rules (and outlined so many penalties) which applied to wives, but not a word about the obligations of husbands, or about what would happen to them if they failed to meet their responsibilities. Not content to protest in principle, Frances Power Cobbe went public with particular cases which demonstrated in no uncertain terms just how wretched were the conditions of many wives. In her widely distributed pamphlet of 1868 she stated that in Lincolnshire 'a parish surgeon wrote this to the clergyman of the parish who was also a magistrate:-

Dear Sir,
I have today seen Mrs Seymour. I found her in a wretchedly weak state. She is nursing a baby, which office she has not been able to perform effectually from her exhausted condition. Her husband, she says, does not allow her the necessaries of life which he, in his position, could find if he liked. Without some means being taken to provide her with good diet, etc., or to make her husband do so,

she must die of starvation at no very distant period. If you could, in your official capacity, help the poor creature, you would confer a great blessing on the poor woman, and oblige yours faithfully,

J. C. Smallman.

And then she continues:

The clergyman found however, that he had no power as a magistrate to take cognisance of the case, unless the guardians would give the wife relief, and prosecute the husband: and this they declined to do. In vain did the poor half-starved wretch appear before them, and pray to be admitted to the workhouse. She was refused admission on the ground that her husband earned good wages; and so she went home, and after lingering a while, probably fed now and then by neighbours, she died. The husband escaped without any punishment whatever. The jury who tried him (*men* of course!) gave him the benefit of a doubt as to the cause of his wife's death and acquitted him.[12]

This was not the only specific case that Frances Power Cobbe publicised. She drew attention to the plight of women – and the gross gender bias in the law – through the publication of numerous examples of domestic violence. And it was partly as a result of her efforts that in England, in 1878, magistrates were empowered to grant separation orders which afforded wives some small measure of protection from violent husbands.

Even so, the position of wives was so awful that Frances Power Cobbe spent much of her time urging women not to marry. She would have welcomed the day when not only were the conditions of wives legally improved, but when women had the right to refuse to become wives no matter what the circumstances.

Preventing women from dying of starvation and physical abuse at the hands of men were not the only offences that had to be overcome. Wives were also incarcerated; they were locked away in attics (as Charlotte Brontë indicated in her novel *Jane Eyre*, where Rochester kept his 'mad' wife locked away as was the practice). Wives were also locked away in institutions. *Maria: or the Wrongs of Woman* (1798), a novel by Mary Wollstonecraft, is one of the most heart-rending accounts of a wife who has become an 'inconvenience' and who had been imprisoned by her husband.

Most of the nineteenth century women's rights' workers were aware of this appalling way of disposing of unwanted wives and did much to bring about change. In 1861, Susan B. Anthony (1820–1906) defied the courts in the United States when she refused to divulge the whereabouts of a wife whom she had helped to escape from an 'insane asylum' where she had been placed by her husband, despite the testimony of her family that she was mentally stable.

'Could the dark secrets of those insane asylums be brought to light' Elizabeth Cady Stanton (1815–1902) commented, 'we would be shocked to know the countless number of rebellious wives (sisters and daughters) that are thus annually sacrificed to false customs and conventionalisms, and barbarous laws made by man for women.'[13] She too was a sharp critic of marriage (and legal gender bias) and did much to discourage women from entering holy matrimony.

No doubt there were unions where all turned out well and the wife did live happily ever after, but there must have been many marriages then – as now – which were disastrous. The difference was that in those days wives could do almost nothing about it.

It's not hard to see why Cicely Hamilton believed that men had to stop women from doing anything else if they wanted them to become wives. But they also had to prevent the harsh details of abuse and servitude from reaching the delicate ears of young women. As Frances Power Cobbe had boldly declared – no woman in her right mind who knew the full facts about the conditions of service would become a wife.

It was bad form – disloyal and shameful – for a wife to parade any ill use in public. Women had to suffer in silence and many wives 'conspired' to keep maidens ignorant of the potential pain and pitfalls, until the unsuspecting bride herself became 'a member of the club'. And the insidious assumption that any wife who was on the receiving end of male violence was herself to blame, played a powerful part in shaping social values. Because wives were supposed to be responsible for the emotional wellbeing of their husbands, a wife could be seen to have failed in *her* job if *he* resorted to violence. While it was taboo for wives to speak out, or to talk to each other, domestic violence was shrouded in secrecy and shame, with wives as the scapegoats.

Apart from what they could learn from their own personal experiences, the greatest source of information that young women had last century on what happened to wives after the wedding came from novels. Many of them of course provided a totally unrealistic picture of romance and marital bliss (which would have been no less seductive then than it is now) but there were also hundreds, even thousands, of women's novels which were intended to 'educate' women about the duties, dangers, and possible delights of wifedom. One of the most amazing novels in this category is *The Beth Book* (1897) by Sarah Grand; when there was as much secrecy about venereal disease as there was about domestic violence, Sarah Grand took it upon herself to inform young women just how widespread it was in the 'gentleman' class and what an awful fate syphilis was for unsuspecting wives who became infected through their husbands. It's a book that even now is gripping reading.

Charlotte Brontë, George Eliot, and Jane Austen were all concerned with presenting authentic portrayals of women's lives (married and single) and in the absence of formal education for females, they sought to extend and enhance women's values and insights. And while women would have made what they wanted of the stories they read, it would be interesting to know how many changed their minds after reading Jane Austen's *Emma*, for example. (The irony is that while she believes that she will live happily ever after, there are lots of problems in store for the heroine.)

The choice of a husband was no less important in a woman's life than was that of a 'career' for a man. Her income, her daily occupation, her status – where she lived and how she spent her days – would all depend on her husband. He would determine other equally crucial considerations such as whether or not she would be ill used, would be able to have her mother to stay, would be permitted to be an influence with her children etc. In the circumstances it is not surprising to find that many women's novels were concerned with ensuring that women made 'the right choice'.

Reading between the lines of a number of these stories it is easy to find 'tests' that a sensible woman is advised to set a man before she would consent to be his wife. And because they contributed to the awareness and sophistication of women, these works of fiction provided an invaluable service; some of them even began to plant the idea that wives might have rights!

In Australia the three most popular novelists – Ada Cambridge (1844–1926), Rosa Praed (1851–1935) and 'Tasma' (Jessie Couvreur 1848–97) were equally as concerned as their British and American counterparts with the subject of weddings and wives. While Ada Cambridge wrote more than twenty novels, she did tend to favour a particular plot: broadly speaking it was for the wife to realise the day after the wedding that she'd made a terrible mistake which she would have to live with for the rest of her life. The theme of Ada Cambridge's work (and perhaps of her life) was very definitely that there was no fulfilment to be found in the role of wife.

Rosa Praed went further when she not only described some of the difficulties of married life, but questioned whether women had to put up with such unhappiness and exploitation. In one of her most famous novels *The Bond of Wedlock* (1887), which was later adapted for the theatre and enjoyed a great success in London's West End, she raised the issue of wife beating. And she asked whether a woman was bound to her husband for 'better or worse' – or whether ill treatment entitled a wife to break her vows and leave. 'Rites' versus 'Rights' was at the centre of her fiction.

But if Rosa Praed was somewhat ahead of her time, 'Tasma' presented an even greater challenge to the institution of marriage. Her message was that if things got too bad you could always leave. As she herself had done. A divorce in

Australia in 1883 was almost unheard of (and a divorceé almost beyond the pale); but 'Tasma' wrote from personal experience (as did Ada Cambridge and Rosa Praed – who left her husband). The novels of all three authors were very popular – with women.

Reading these novels, wives were likely to 'get ideas' about what was fair and what was not and to draw conclusions about their own experiences. Understandably some developed a sense of grievance and began to think in terms of making changes, which is one reason that novel reading was so often considered a dangerous pastime for women. When medical science decreed that the womb was the origin of women's moods and humours, and women who read novels became resentful and radical, the 'connections' were inevitably made. The physician, Dr Kellog, was stating the obvious and taken seriously when he insisted that novel reading was the greatest cause of uterine disease in young women.[14]

One effect of all this literature about the daily experience of wives was to make the readers realise that if they were abused, distressed, or disappointed, they were by no means alone. It helped to make them critical of the treatment of wives – and to begin to believe that life should afford more options to women. In short, novels were a step along the path to today's choices.

That women now have so many more choices than their foremothers is not the only explanation for the contemporary rejection of wifedom. As important as the sense of injustice that they acquired was the growing sense of self which novels and women's rights' activists implanted, and which led women to believe they were worth more than the value men had placed on them.

Women's movements of the past always fought for women's financial independence regarding it as one of the necessary conditions of women's liberation. But the understanding that freedom was not solely an economic issue was always present. Women had to free their minds, they had to achieve psychological independence and overcome feelings of guilt and self-doubt if they were to become autonomous human beings. And in some ways the history of wives marks this transition from servitude to emancipation.

In comparison to their foremothers, young women today are very aware of their rights. And it is not fulfilment they seek – but a sense of entitlement. They don't think they have to put up with violation or violence; or even with an unfair attitude to housework or childcare. For so many women now, marriage vows are conditional. When earlier generations of women were married, the contract was for life. It was an unconditional commitment – for better or worse, richer or poorer, and until death ended the union. To discover that you had made a mistake, that you had made the wrong choice or got the wrong man, was simply something that had to be borne no matter how wretched your plight. You had had your chance. You had messed it up. Resignation was required as there was nothing more to be done about it.

Today's young women, who are more conscious of their own worth, rarely put themselves in this invidious position. While many believe that 'it would be nice if it lasted for life', most don't like their chances. They 'hope for the best' but 'expect the worst'. And they are being nothing other than realistic when they state that it will all probably end in divorce. And it will certainly end in divorce if the husband doesn't keep his part of the bargain. (Frances Power Cobbe would be overjoyed to hear such sentiments expressed.)

'To put it bluntly,' says Hugh Mackay[15], 'the way we think and talk about weddings is quite different from the way in which we now treat the institution of marriage. We still talk as if it is normal to get married and normal to stay married, but our definition of "normal" is slow to catch up with demographic reality' he writes. 'So many Australian families are now being affected directly or indirectly by divorce and by the redefinition of marriage, that we will eventually have to find new ways of adapting to the increasing diversity of family styles and structures.'

Even 'family names' aren't what they used to be. Changing her name was one of the most powerful symbols that could ever have been devised to indicate that the wife renounced her right to identity and became the property of her husband, and it is interesting to note just how many women today elect to keep their own names (about 80 per cent of the women I spoke to). Not that the symbolism was always the issue: the most common reason given was that there was no point – 'You'll only have to change it back again when you get a divorce,' they said.

The few women to whom I spoke who had decided to change their name on marriage, were relatively young – under thirty, and had not been married before (with one exception). And they all gave the same reason – that it was the husband's wish. 'He would be so hurt,' one woman said. 'He wants the world to know I am his. It's about pride.' Another said she was tired of the arguments: 'It's so important to him, and I guess it is not so important to me. If it keeps him happy and doesn't cost me anything, I suppose I can manage it . . . ' One woman said that her husband and her mother had believed it was the 'right' thing to do. A mature woman, in mid career, who had remarried and changed her name, said that it hadn't occurred to her not to, that she hadn't thought about it being a symbol of male ownership, but that it had been inconvenient – and she wouldn't do it again.

Despite the recognition by many that the marital arrangement could be 'temporary', not all women have the attitude that if it doesn't work out they will get a divorce, and those that do, don't always find it so easy. There's a gap between theory and practice and the current awful statistics on domestic violence reveal that there are still many wives who live in fear and who are physically and psychologically abused.

But ending domestic violence is now official government policy. A legal framework to protect the interest of wives has been established and refuges and counselling services have been set up. No longer can police services publicly adopt the attitude that it is not their business to interfere between husband and wife.

However inadequate the provisions, we have become a society which attempts to deal with domestic violence rather than hide it. If Caroline Norton were today trying to leave her husband she would find herself in such a different position that she could be forgiven for thinking that every reform she had ever envisaged had been accomplished.

The fact that women won't put up with the ill treatment that their grandmothers (and those before them) had to endure, is evidenced by the statistics which show that 40 per cent of marriages now end in divorce, and most divorce proceedings are initiated by women. (And this takes no account of de facto relationships – which are increasingly popular – and which are another expression of women's rejection of official wifedom.)

There is still a long way to go. Wives still work harder, for less money, and are more vulnerable. But they do have the option to leave. And even to try again. There is even some suggestion that serial monogamy – or one husband after another – could be the future trend. (Evidence from women does not always support this however.)

Weddings were once much less important than the serious business of being a wife. Intended, in the British tradition, to mark the exchange of vows in the sight of God, weddings were often small, reverent and private affairs (as were the actual recent nuptials of the Crown Prince and Princess of Japan). There was no 'bridal industry' and none of that showy spectacle associated with today's ritual. But as wifedom has shed some of its strict and sombre overtones, as being a wife has become a role that you could take or leave, the wedding ceremony has emerged more as an event in its own right.

These days a girl can have as many weddings as she wants. She can be a bride as often as she likes. Or as old as she likes. She isn't usually giving an undertaking that she comes to her husband virginal and chaste and that she will stay with him regardless of his domestic habits or his public success or failure. Quite the contrary. She can wear a white dress to her wedding, having spent years living with her de facto. She can be a bride who is obviously pregnant, who is breast-feeding, or who is attended by her own children. She can have a wedding in a park, or a plane, underwater, or in her own backyard.

She can be saving up for and meticulously planning the wedding she is going to have long before she even knows who will be her partner. She can be from a country where there is no tradition of white weddings and where she has purchased a 'package' which includes ceremony, champagne, witnesses and the bridal suite – along with cake and photographs.

And she can write her own contract which sets out everything from his use of the bathroom to the washing of his socks – and the division of property when love has departed.

That she can choose the form her vows will take and the conditions under which she will continue the partnership, speaks volumes for the sense of entitlement and independence she has acquired.

Today a woman can thoroughly enjoy her wedding when she has no intention of being a wife. Or no intention of being a wife who has to put up with behaviour that she doesn't like. And it is this which marks the revolution from rites to rights.

THE ILLEGITIMACY OF ILLEGITIMACY – AND 'SPINSTERHOOD'

It is a standing joke in linguistic circles that no woman could ever have created the concept of *illegitimacy*. (It is just not on that a woman would give birth to a child and wonder whether it was rightfully hers.) But there's no mystery as to where the concept came from or whose interests it served. The sole purpose of decreeing that some children were 'legitimate' and others were not was to protect the property interests of males.

Not that it was usually stated so bluntly. The need for virginity (and marital fidelity) was generally expressed in more romantic terms to the point that it was a widely stated sentiment that a maiden's innocence was a 'gift' that she should bring to her husband. Added to this was a semi-mystical notion that in 'losing' her virginity (another astonishing term if you stop to think about it and again, not one women would necessarily have thought of)[16], a maid was made complete and fulfilled.

'When I was twelve ... Mumsy ... explained to me that my body was a temple that no one must ever touch till I married,' says Eleanor Brent, the heroine of Christina Stead's novel, *Miss Herbert: the suburban wife*. 'She told me my husband would have a golden key to unlock the door' she continues, summing up much of the received wisdom of the decades from the 1920s to the 1950s.[17]

Understandably this idea of a husband with a golden key that works wonders *after* the wedding, and the great spiritual change that it was supposed to represent for new wives, is difficult to appreciate in the present permissive society. But less than a few decades ago there was still a well entrenched belief that chaste young women blossomed when they were transformed into wives, and that husbands played a crucial part in the transformation process. This was all part of the mystique and the lure of wifedom.

In 1909, when Cicely Hamilton wrote her provocative book *Marriage as a Trade*, it was the received wisdom that a woman was 'incomplete' without a husband. 'That is to say,' Cicely Hamilton explains, 'that she is not a woman at all – until man has made her so. Until the moment when he takes her in hand she is merely the raw material of womanhood – the undeveloped and unfinished article.'[18]

Even women who would not or could not becomes wives had their lives framed by their relationship to males; they were the spinsters or old maids. And while the prospect of completeness and fulfilment was used as a sweetener to keep women virginal and entice them to marry, it also served as a stick with which to beat the non-wives. For when she passed from young maid to old maid, a woman ceased to be regarded as chaste, and 'in-waiting' – to be transformed into the bloom of womanhood. Instead she became a pathetic figure of cruel fun and ridicule, taunted with the jibe that she was *unable* to get a man, and that she would become 'dried up', bitter and twisted.

'Compulsory wifedom' Cicely Hamilton called it; 'compulsory heterosexuality' was the term Adrienne Rich was to use more than seventy years later. But regardless of the term, the fact was that those who were not wives, not the property of men, were mocked and marginalised: as Vera Brittain (1896–1970) said – the old maid was 'the cruellest of Victorian institutions.'[19]

In 1857 an article appeared in the British *Saturday Review* which reflected the prevailing values of the period:

> Married life is a woman's profession; and to this life her training – that of dependence – is modelled. Of course by not getting a husband, or losing him, she may find that she is without resources. All that can be said of her is that she has failed in business and no social reform can prevent such failures.[20]

Women who were 'not wives', who had no male protection and no 'reason for existence' in the terms of the time, were referred to as superfluous and redundant. There were even articles in the British press that they should be 'landed in the colonies' where they would soon become decent women once they were turned into wives.

A class of viable single women would have been a threat to the male establishment in a variety of countries. And so the more protest there was from feminists about the lack of options for 'women without men', and the need for decent work and wages (one of the fundamental aims of the nineteenth century women's movement), the more disconcerting this was to many men. There were numerous public expressions of fear that the home and family would be undermined if women were able to set up their own arrangements. Central to male concern was the issue of sexual activity – and inheritance.

If women could reasonably support themselves, what was to stop them from declining wifedom – and yet electing motherhood? And then what would the world be like? According to authorities of the time, it would be the end of the social order as they knew it. There are those today who think they were probably right.

So women were not only directed towards marriage – they were urged to 'save themselves for their husbands'. And the combination of promises of fulfilment for virgin brides, and penalties for failure, had currency until very recently.

Mature women today will well remember all those warnings which equated women's worth with virginity. 'Soiled goods' was a common term for those who 'indulged' before marriage. 'Every man wants to marry a virgin' and 'All nice girls say no' were also ritual incantations that were uttered over young women every Saturday night. But there is no way of knowing how many maids on Sunday morning hoped that *he* wouldn't think *her* a slut, and did deals with their God as they prayed they would not be pregnant. Because such a fate was just too awful to contemplate. Recently I asked a group of nineteen year olds what they thought a *shotgun* wedding was. And while they came up with some wonderfully imaginative ideas and possibilities, not one of them suggested that it was anything to do with being forced into marriage.

Yet in my day, shotgun weddings were all too frequent an occurrence.

Imprinted on my consciousness is the example of my school friend 'Lois': at fourteen years of age she had to leave school and marry the father who was not at all willing to oblige. My class mates felt sorry for the boy (no doubt in those days, I did as well); he was seen as having been 'caught' while she was regarded as a slut, and was openly scorned. As a wife she went to live in a garage at the back of his parents' house; what an awful start for a new life!

At that time it was still considered better to force a young woman to become a miserable wife than to have the stigma of illegitimacy in a family. 'Give the baby a father' was the insistence of the day, as if making her a wife somehow changed the identity or status of the unborn child.

We are much more sophisticated now. And not just because of the mind-boggling leaps in reproductive technology. They may have required us to distinguish between biological and social motherhood and fatherhood, but other dramatic changes have also occurred.

Even as late as the 1960s, the alternatives to becoming a wife were very limited when a young woman was pregnant. Few women were 'brazen' enough to publicly declare their pregnancy, or brave enough to contend with the social ostracism that went with being an 'unmarried mother'. (If you wouldn't think of your own shame you could always be manipulated by consideration of the dishonour it would bring on your family.) 'Going away' and 'keeping it secret' was one approach which could avoid disgrace and spare family and self. But for all those women who went to homes for unmarried 'girls', and who gave their babies up for adoption, the lonely and painful ordeal was often devastating.

And little reference was made to the double standard or to the fact that women's lives were being defined, determined, and destroyed by their relationship to men. It was widely accepted that 'the girl was the one who had to pay' which was a convenient means of placing the onus on *her* to keep *him* from 'having his way'. After all, he wouldn't respect her if she 'let him *do it*'.

Remember all the sayings that used to have such a hold over our minds? That we repeated to each other as we policed each other. Trying to remember what was right and what was wrong ...

I can recall my own sense of disbelief when I found that 'Margaret Mason' was pregnant. She was the 'nicest' girl I knew – the major force in the school's Scripture Union. I reasoned that if it could happen to her – it could happen to anybody. That pregnancy was after me. That it must be a virus that you could 'catch' anywhere. And no one could have been more wary that I was. *I was not going to get pregnant.* In retrospect I think I would rather have been dead. And I am sure that there were many women of my generation who felt the same way.

And how to describe this overwhelming fear of pregnancy to a younger generation. The distance from 'no sex' to 'safe sex' marks a revolution.

Mature women of today, who were subjected to the humiliation of having to become a wife in order to avoid the shame of being an unmarried mother, now watch their own daughters blithely choosing to be no one's wife and to opt for solo parenthood. So dramatic have the changes been that it is almost impossible to bridge the generation gap and to explain to today's young women what it meant to give up your baby for adoption – because there was so much shame associated with being an unmarried mother. All those abusive words which were available – not so long ago – to make outcasts of immoral, 'fallen' women who had babies without being wives.

Yet the same women who endured such terrible treatment in the past, who had to choose between the shame of keeping their baby or the anguish of giving it up for adoption (if the man 'wouldn't "make an honest women" of them'), now see women who *want* to be single mothers! Who know no shame. Who don't necessarily want to involve the biological father. Who will have nothing to do with husbands. Indeed, they can encounter women who expressly state that far from using pregnancy to 'catch a husband', they have no desire to know who the father is – because they don't want to have a future custody suit.

That there are so few babies now up for adoption is an indication of the role that shame and humiliation played in coercing women to give up their babies – and in keeping them in line. A centuries old practice has been transformed as women are now freed from such insidious pressure to be 'pure' and 'in waiting' for a husband. Women themselves now make the decisions about what to do with their newborn infants, and how they will arrange their lives – with or without male partners.

Contraception has also played a big part in women's increasing independence. Women's liberation has been built upon women's ability, and right, to control reproduction. It is not so long since men could jocularly announce that 'barefoot, pregnant and in the kitchen' was the best place for wives, which meant in essence that women could be kept in line when they were economically dependent, confined to the unpaid work of home, and denied contraception.

It isn't an accident that so many men have for so long tried to stop women from having control over their own bodies. During the nineteenth and early twentieth centuries in Britain and the United States, there were men who bitterly resisted any attempts to make contraception available to women – as birth control pioneers Margaret Sanger, Dora Russell and Marie Stopes discovered. Not that this struggle is over: there are still men who pronounce on the conditions of wives (the Pope?) and male politicians who link aid with the absence of birth control – in the interest of keeping women subordinate.

The men of earlier times who opposed every form of independence for women, would feel vindicated if they were now to witness contemporary arrangements. Their worst fears would be realised. Women *don't* have to be wives. Inheritance through the male line is *not* protected. And the very idea that a family might 'die out' because there are only female heirs seems strangely nonsensical to many younger people. With women refusing to marry, to 'serve' – or to take men's names – there is no knowing who is whose any more.

Not that there were ever any certainties of course. It is interesting to note that there is yet still another story to be told, another taboo to be broken, and it is about the extent to which wives 'subverted' the inheritance laws. There is some evidence that about one-third of women patients report to women psychiatrists and counsellors that the paternity of one of their children is problematic: and genetic studies which are based on families often have to be abandoned because the designated father does not match with one of the offspring. So much for protecting 'the male line'.

The old social order *has* ended. And while women have by no means achieved full human rights, the number and nature of their gains since the 1960s is remarkable. To devalue that progress is to detract from women's victories and strengths.

For centuries, the concept of illegitimacy was used as a

weapon to control women. And it no longer applies. While much of the credit for this must go to the women's movement there are also individuals who have made contributions. Anyone who is looking for someone to praise – or blame – when it comes to this transformation, could well nominate Gough Whitlam – and the Labor government of 1972. For in introducing single parent benefits they made it financially possible for women to give birth, without having to give up their babies or become wives. And that was the beginning of the end. By the mid to late 1970s the absurdity of the law on illegitimacy was obvious: laws illegitimising illegitimacy were passed in the various states.

Of course this couldn't have been done unless the climate had changed, and this is where due credit must be given to the women's liberation movement of the early 1970s (and before). Because the cover was blown when women's liberationists (as they were known then) started shouting from the rooftops that virginity and morality were not the same things – that women's worth was not measured in terms of their hymens (if indeed they have them – as Shere Hite (1994) speculates): Protesting women insisted that women were complete in themselves and did not need a man to authenticate their existence or to legitimate the birth of their offspring. The pill, and probably the 'permissive society', also made a contribution.

Some residual practices and prejudices remain. While it is not so common to hear the saying that 'men like to sleep around but only want to marry virgins', there is still a double standard. The responsibility for saying 'no' might not now be placed absolutely on the woman, but evidently some men still think that nice girls don't start off by saying yes.

Besides, some women don't care who men *do* or do *not* want to marry: *they don't want to be wives anyway.*

But no matter the backlash or the conservative pressure, the gains that women have achieved are not about to be lost. It is unlikely that women will be forced back into the state of being nothing without a man: or an outcast if they became a mother – but not a wife.

THE POLITICS OF HOUSEWORK

One reason for the low status of the wife is that the role has had all the connotations of service, sacrifice, and no pay, and one of the major grievances of feminists over the years has been this gross inequality in the sexual division of labour and financial remuneration. That men thought it appropriate to pay themselves for their own efforts but reasoned that wives should work hard for little or no pay, and usually less acknowledgement, is not an admirable way of organising a 'democratic' society: it is not surprising that ultimately there should have been widespread objection and resistance from those who were being left out of the financial arrangements.

There has been no shortage of women over the centuries who have come forward to describe – and denounce – the shocking system of payment (or non-payment) which was designed to make women financially dependent on men. Women were supposed to work for love, not money, and the romantic ideal helped to disguise the dreadful conditions that were women's lot. The prospect of becoming 'one' with a man masked the loss of identity: the suggestion that she would create a mystical place called a home, camouflaged the drudgery of housework. The assurance that the wife was central deflected the concerns about dependency – and defencelessness. The dream of being a romantic couple conquered all doubts.

This was precisely the view of wifedom that Cicely Hamilton determined to demolish in her book, *Marriage as a Trade*. Wifedom is a job, she argued, and the only approved one available for half the population. And as it was a trade – as she pointedly put it – its conditions of employment should be open to investigation. Like those before her who had questioned the hours, the tasks, and the 'rewards' of wifedom, Cicely Hamilton was condemned for her callousness and crankiness. (Her critics predictably argued that she was only against marriage because she couldn't get a man.) But when she conducted her inquiry into the conditions of service and stripped away some of the sentimentality, she found that wives were among the most exploited of workers.

She was shocked but not surprised to find that the marriage market operated in much the same way as any other labour market. Workers were denied any other possible employment – and then forced to compete with each other for any jobs or 'payment' they could get. This was why wages for women were driven down to the lowest point they could go, she argued. Subsistence level. That's what women got for trading themselves – and doing all that work; it was board and lodging, if they were lucky!

Sixty years later Germaine Greer agreed with Cicely Hamilton's analysis of the matrimonial market. She phrased it differently but her findings were the same: a wife was required to sign on to provide free and ever available labour – for life, Germaine Greer protested. And this was such an outrageous proposition that she urged women to refuse to marry – to stop being wives.

Some women have taken her at her word and kept away from marriage altogether. (There has been – at least – a 20 per cent decline in marriage since 1966).[21] Apart from the women who live alone and the women who live with women, it is now the case that de facto relationships are more common than marriage among females in their twenties, which makes weddings a minority practice in the younger generation.

'Australians ain't quite the marrying kind in the way they used to be, considering a 28 per cent drop in the marriage rate over the last twenty years' writes Julian Cribb[22] on the basis of the latest Bureau of Statistics findings. 'When it comes to the crunch we are marrying less often, waiting longer, taking more time off to recover between bouts and are far less inclined towards a religious celebrant.' The 'crude' marriage rate has dropped from 9.1 in every 1000 people in 1971, to 6.6 in 1992. And he adds, 'Not only are young folk less hasty in the rush to the altar, but older souls are showing distinct signs of once bitten, twice shy – remarriage rates too are on the slide.'

But weddings aren't the full story in contemporary society. For even among those who have had their weddings are the women who won't be wives. They have refused the role of wifeliness – that of being unpaid servants in their husbands' households. This might not have been just what Germaine Greer had in mind when she called on women to stop being willing slaves. But keeping the glamour of the wedding while rejecting the drudgery of the wife, is a creative and constructive option which Germaine Greer would certainly admire.

This does not mean by any stretch of the imagination that women have got the division of housework all figured out. But it does mean that what their mothers did for love and duty, they see as mean and unfair. And while it could be said that the dream of a romantic life together has been replaced by the dream of a shared work load, it is still the case that women today expect very different 'domestic labour' arrangements from the ones their mothers tolerated. The post-wife generation has a greater understanding of their own worth, and a greater confidence in their own boundaries.

Any study that has ever been done shows that women still do much more than their share of the housework, and much more of the unpaid work of the family home. But in comparison to where they were twenty years ago – or two hundred years ago – wives are steadily experiencing improvements on the home front – even if it doesn't feel like it because men have not gone far enough in sharing the burden.

The good news is that it is now official. In 1991 the Australian Department of the Prime Minister and Cabinet published figures which showed that men do not do their share of housework, and that their failure to contribute has stayed much the same over the last decades.[23] And this is another indication of what has changed. A century ago, any Prime Minister who had permitted such a survey to be done, and to be published, would not have been in office for very long. Such information which shows men in a very selfish and unsatisfactory light – and which implies that men are in the wrong and women in the right – would have been classed as treason and branded as an act of betrayal in the 1890s.

Every time women have campaigned for their rights in the past, there have been men who have shown their true colours.

Whether it was education, property, divorce or the vote that women called for, the most frequently used male objection was that if women got what they wanted, they would cease doing the housework. In cartoons, editorials, articles and parliamentary speeches, the main argument against women's rights was that they would no longer cook the dinner or look after their spouse. Much of the anti-suffrage literature predicted and portrayed a neglected hearth, husband and home, as the direct result of women getting the vote.

This history of resistance puts men's current 'refusal' to do an equal share of the domestic chores in a different light. This is no new protest we are witnessing – but a last stand.

One of the biggest divides between the sexes has been the expectation that women work in the home – and men do not. (Men have even avoided the housework by using the argument that they are demeaned by doing women's work.) And it is probably true that sex differences would be minimised if the distinction between women's work and men's work were to disappear – and both had paid work and an equal share of home duties.

This could help to explain why – on the average – men have insisted on keeping their house privileges: it is one way they think they can assert that they are men.

Despite male objections, women have won many of their rights. And when they did get the vote it wasn't so much putting an end to housework which preoccupied them (although it has always been high on the list). It was finding a way of giving women money for their work which was a priority for women voters – and Members.

'Wages for wives' (and mothers) in one way or another were almost always on the women's agenda. The introduction of 'Family Allowance' or 'Child Benefit' (and a range of payments under a variety of other names) were all intended to help wives, and their children, to have some financial assistance which would remove them from being totally dependent on their husbands. With the resurgence of the women's movement in the 1970s, the exploitation of housewives was one of the most frequently raised and emotionally charged topics. Most of the thousands of women's groups which sprang up around the globe started with 'speaking bitterness'[24] on the scandalous treatment of wives.

Within academic circles the domestic labour debate as it was called produced some fiery discussions, as theories which related to the oppression of workers were 'massaged' to apply to the oppression of wives. There were even serious campaigns for 'Wages for Housework' as a solution to sexual inequality. The biggest argument against this was that it would reinforce the distinction between women's work and men's work, rather than get rid of it. Husbands would use the fact that women were being *paid* to do the housework as a justification for never lifting a finger themselves and would leave all the work of home and family to the wife. Many women didn't want to be paid a pittance for doing women's work – what they wanted was a new job!

Ann Oakley did her PhD on housework (even though she had trouble convincing the male authorities that *house*work was real work, and that house*work* was a legitimate topic). Her book *Housewife* (1976) was a runaway best seller, and a revelation. It was the first popular book which showed what wives actually did, and what a mammoth contribution they made to the economy. Even though men had not thought fit to include their efforts in any of the nation's measures of work or wealth.

'I don't work. I am just a *housewife*,' which was once a genuine statement of self-effacement, became a 'joke' once women began to recognise the absurdity of the situation. They began to insist that men were not gods to be waited on but part of a family unit and that as such they had *house* responsibilities, and they had to start doing something about them.

Women won when it came to the rhetoric. Few people now would want to argue that the home is the sole responsibility of the wife. There's not the same mileage to be gained for men who scorn women's work and who define their masculinity by their distance from cooking, cleaning, ironing or child-care etc. But if women have been successful in changing the ideas about justice, equality and housework, they still have an uphill battle when it comes to changing the behaviour of husbands.

The reality is that men dramatically over-report their housework efforts. Almost all of them declare they do more than they do. And even where both husband and wife have agreed that the housework is shared, researchers can quickly establish that *her* share is about twice as onerous as *his*.

And it is partly because we are so unused to seeing husbands doing the housework that their behaviour is obvious and that we notice when they do the smallest thing. Also, husbands are likely to draw attention to their contribution.

When they do engage in housework, it is often the more *visible* tasks that husbands elect to do. Like the vacuum cleaning. On Saturday morning. When everyone is inconvenienced. When it is very noisy. And all the furniture is moved. And not put back in the same place again. When not a soul can avoid knowing that it is a man doing the housework. And that he had better be thanked for his efforts.

Even men who have come far enough to admit that it is foolish (and deceitful) to claim that they are *helping* their wives, *when it is their own mess they are cleaning up*, don't assume equal responsibility for the work of hearth and home.

Wives of course, have little or no choice in the matter; not in what is to be done or when they will do it. And in contrast to husbands who are inclined to set aside a specific time for doing the housework (and having it noted), wives are 'on the go' nearly all the time. They wipe hand basins as they walk past, pick up clothes on the way to the bedroom, tidy the kitchen while they talk on the phone, wipe the floor as they listen to a child's homework. It is this habit of integrating so many aspects of the housework with the many other demands, that can make it invisible; it is this which can lead both husband and wife to believe that women don't do as much as they do – and that men do so much more than the time and motion study experts indicate.

And there's also the issue of flexibility. Many of the tasks that women are responsible for can't be negotiated – or postponed. 'It's alright for him to say he'll be half an hour late – and to think he is being wonderful to let me know, and that he'll do the shopping on the way,' a 'working' wife and mother of three complained. 'But I don't have the option of being late. I have to be on time to pick the kids up from childcare. There's no flexibility in my life. Just about everything with the kids has to be done now! I meet their demands. *He still makes demands.*'

It is these very real differences in the way that work is done at the workplace and in the home – and in the behaviour of women and men – that has led the WET TANK (Women's Economic Think Tank) to organise a conference on Housework;

> The world of work is seen as male. Work places are about men producing goods in return for payment and jobs tend to be linear with a beginning, middle and end. Housework is different and female. The worker is home, what is done is not clear, the lines between work and leisure are not spelt out and consumption and production are confused. The time lines are cyclical and erratic. How often is a household task interrupted by another task?[25]

Trying to make men see that there is a legitimate difference between the work men are accustomed to and the work they are being required to undertake becomes a wearying – and additional – burden for so many women. Not that men see it this way. That wives are complaining – and nagging – about the work load, because it is what wives do, is the premise that quite a few husbands operate on. It is another example of the old rhyming slang – 'trouble and strife' equals 'wife.'

While these days you won't find a lot of men going round insisting that they be waited on, the majority of husbands seem to think it is enough to agree in principle that the work load should be shared. You don't actually have to *do* anything about it. And it is this chasm between men's perceptions and women's reality that has proved too frustrating for so many wives; the housework itself might tire them but it is the lack of recognition that drives them mad.

According to the office of the Prime Minister and Cabinet, *When a woman becomes a wife she increases her unpaid work by 60 per cent.* This means that, *women do about 70 per cent of the unpaid work.* That's about twice as much as husbands. *On average wives do approximately 36 hours a week unpaid work. While men on average do about half that amount.*

What's more, it doesn't seem to matter how much work the wife does, paid or otherwise, husbands have a ceiling on *their* contribution. In the words of *Juggling Time: No matter how many hours of paid work a wife does, her husband's contribution remains relatively constant.* It's about 18.5 hours a week; scarcely more than he did before he was married.

But it isn't just that she does twice as much as he does. It's that he gets to do some pretty good things as his part of the deal. Two thirds of his unpaid work is outdoors, and it includes *travel* and *play* (along with the car, the pool, the boat). So golf and footy etc. are on the husband's list of unpaid activities. Wives – in contrast – have lost one hour of leisure time over the last twenty years.

It's not surprising that women are put off. Unlike last century when the details of domestic work were cunningly concealed, women now know the score. Even the office of the Prime Minister is informing them that being a wife is not a good deal. Many women are drawing up their own marital contracts which spell out the domestic responsibilities of the partners. They have no intention of being 'put upon' in the way their mothers were. It's salutary to find how many young women have written their own wedding ceremonies – and how many have included the details about who is to do what! And when and how often! And the problem is that many of the husbands agree. They sign on the dotted line that they will do not just half the load, but half the *shit*work. But then they don't keep their word.

This is where many wives are at the moment. Caught in the double bind of having a husband who solemnly declares that it is right and proper that he should do his share – but who then proceeds to get out of doing just about anything he can. (This approach is called *passive resistance* and the avoidance methods that men use are widely known, and discussed, among wives. 'Feigned helplessness' is one strategy designed to exasperate wives so that women will 'do it themselves' rather than have to keep explaining how it is done. Then there is the ploy of doing something so badly that the woman feels obliged to take over. And of course there's the stalling technique – with men insisting that they *will* do it, but in their own time, to the point where women can no longer stand the dirty floors or the unmade beds that signal their husbands' refusal to accept domestic responsibility. The very fact that women are aware of these tricks suggests that they are wise to men's ways.)

Male sensitivity too often turns out to be mock sensitivity according to Hugh Mackay in his book *Reinventing Australia.* Many men realise that they must at least look as though they agree that the work load should be shared, but at heart they believe that something has gone wrong with their lives, and are both resistant, and resentful – and perhaps even non-comprehending. These changes have been 'forced' on them, without their agreement – and they aren't going to just 'give in' and change their mindsets along with their actions. Women have difficulty decoding this double message. How is it that men can say that they are committed to equality and women's right to self realisation, and at the same time stand by and watch their wives work to the point of exhaustion? How can they claim to be sensitive and behave so insensitively? Why do they think they are entitled to the benefits – but not the burdens?

When one tired and disillusioned wife informed her mother that she couldn't go on, that the resentment as well as the physical burden was just too much, and she was thinking of getting a divorce, her mother's response was quick and cutting: 'Well it will halve your workload, dear, if you get rid of the husband.'

Many wives have decided that if the husbands won't keep their word, they won't keep their husbands. This is one of the reasons that women seek divorce. The problem of housework still features as one of the most common causes when it comes to women wanting men to go. It's the burning sense of injustice, the weariness of protest, and the bafflement that goes with not being able to communicate – as well as the burden itself that incenses so many women. It is the fact that they can still be required to thank men for the little they do – or risk being seen as scolds as well as nags.

Having been a wife, there are many women who readily declare that the job is too hard, and that having tried it once they won't do it again. They can't see the point of the effort.

'MARRIAGE MAKES WOMEN SICK'

Jessie Bernard, a respected US sociologist, was one of the first of the new wave of feminists of the late 1960s to recognise the pressures that were being placed on marriage. The pill and the permissive society, the demands of the women's liberation movement for better material and emotional conditions – particularly for wives – and the shift in employment patterns, all helped to challenge the institution. In her book *The Future of Marriage*, Jessie Bernard took a long and critical look at the myths and realities of 'husbands and wives'.

Her findings were considered scandalous at the time, although today many of her conclusions would be taken for granted. But the most dramatic contribution she made was probably that of putting an end to the idea that two became one on marriage – and that one was the husband. Jessie Bernard made it clear that there were two marriages in every union, his and hers. And – she argued – *his was infinitely better than hers!*

It was a simple strategy to separate the two experiences, but it let Jessie Bernard compare the quality of life of husbands and wives. It wasn't hard to show that it was husbands who were getting the better deal.

This was not, of course, what most people believed in the early 1970s. Everyone knew then that men were reluctant to marry because they had to give up their freedom and assume so much responsibility. That was why women had to 'catch their man' and 'trap them into marriage'.

Don't you believe these myths Jessie Bernard declared. It's husbands who do well out of marriage. It's women who should be wary and who should need to be persuaded.

'Despite all the protestations to the contrary, married life makes husbands happy,' Jessie Bernard wrote.[26] Men thrive on marriage she argued as she compared the health and happiness of husbands with that of single men for whom the risks are so much greater; without a wife to look after them they die twenty years younger.

And husbands knew where their bread was buttered. 'Once they have known marriage they can hardly live without it' Jessie Bernard announced to an increasingly interested audience of women. 'Most divorced and widowed men remarry'[27] she said, resting her case.

Writing more than twenty years later, the psychiatrist Julian Hafner acknowledges that many men still want wifely services and rewards. Commenting on the speed with which divorced men remarry, he says, 'It is not surprising though, that men are more likely than women to remarry early in an attempt to avoid the pain of self-examination and psychological change. But what a newly divorced man seeks from a woman is emotional support and nourishment. He yearns to be nurtured and cared for, until his sense of loss and abandonment becomes manageable . . .'[28] Today, however, there are not as many contenders for the job! It's too hard. And unrewarding. To do it is to risk physical and mental health; and women have been warned.

Jessie Bernard started to plant the doubts about wifedom in women's minds when she revealed that it was not the old maids or spinsters who were likely to suffer from depression, overwork, neglect or lack of appreciation. On every dimension single women were much better off than their married sisters. Even insurance companies admitted as much: actuarial tables reflected the fact that marriage was a health hazard for women.

There could be no denying it as far as Jessie Bernard was concerned: *marriage made women sick.* And in the 1970s she declared that you only had to look at what happened to women when they became wives, to know that the job was debilitating and dangerous:

> If we were, in fact, epidemiologists and saw bright, promising young people enter a certain occupation and little by little begin to droop and finally to succumb, we would be alerted at once and bend all our research efforts to locate the hazards and remove them. But we are complacent when we see what happens to women in marriage ...[29]

The statistics in western societies then spoke for themselves. So many wives were on the sickness list. Among the patients treated for depression (and agoraphobia), the overwhelming number were women.

And of course the term *wife* battering was coined to name another great threat to women's health and safety. And although Jessie Bernard did not deal with domestic violence (another indication of the revolution of the last twenty years) the position was then – as it is now – that the home was the most dangerous place for women.

Jessie Bernard's book left no doubt that the greatest threat to the physical and emotional wellbeing of wives – was husbands.

The low status and powerless nature of wifedom was another contributing factor as far as she was concerned. Stress, and depression can be the outcome for anyone who has a lowly paid, menial, and poorly regarded job – and wives were no exception. No matter how often they were assured that being a wife and mother was one of the best things women could do – it was clear from the way they were treated that wives were not respected.

In the 1970s, Jessie Bernard also speculated that shock might have something to do with the way women's health deteriorated so dramatically after the wedding. And not just because it was a 'come down' to go from the courtship, the romance, the glamour of being a bride – to the demands and drudgery of being a wife. There was also the matter of finding that 'Mr

Right' was not as right and resolute as he was supposed to be.

You have to remember that in the 1970s, few women lived with the men they were going to marry. (The received wisdom was that if you lived with them – they wouldn't marry you, and that you had failed in your quest to catch them.) So quite often the new husband could be something of a stranger to the new wife – who could be dismayed as he daily became more familiar. For women then were not only supposed to 'get their man', he was supposed to be strong, superior, masterful – and to look after them for the rest of their life.

When they found that this wasn't the case, that the manly suitor of their courtship days was an illusion, it was understandable that young wives should go into a state of shock and confusion, Jessie Bernard argued. There was a lot of adjustment called for when a woman realised that instead of a strong and supportive companion she had acquired an emotionally insecure dependent who demanded a great deal of cosseting. This recognition of a husband's weaknesses could also add to a wife's self doubt. Had she made a mistake? Got the wrong man? Done something to him? And if so, what was the best thing to do in the circumstances? Cover it up? Make him look like a good catch rather than a lemon? Should she put all her resources into making him seem desirable thereby keeping up her own appearances of having done well in the marriage stakes?

By identifying 'his and hers' versions of marriage, and raising questions about the health and sanity of wives, Jessie Bernard helped to shape the agenda of the 1970s. In exposing domestic labour as dirty, demanding, despised, dangerous – and daily – she shifted the discussion from romance to exploitation.

The psychiatrist Julian Hafner holds a similar position today; the men who want feminine and submissive – and ornamental wives – are probably in for a bit of a shock, he surmises, because women know a bit more about justice, and fair play, and won't put up with such exploitation anymore. 'In the 1990s, women are less likely to remain with men who treat them as objects,' he states, and 'The men in turn blame them for the marriage break up.' He goes on to say, 'Such men, especially if they are attractive, charming, or wealthy, are frequently able to remarry without having to look at their own contribution to the problems of the previous marriage. But the same difficulties usually emerge in the second marriage and, if lack of insight persists, in subsequent ones.'[30]

Jessie Bernard weighed the evidence for and against and concluded that no one in good conscience could recommend the job of wife. (Being a husband of course, still had a lot going for it.) If women wanted to be happy, healthy, and whole, they should think twice about becoming wives, she advised. And obviously many women got the message.

Twenty years after Jessie Bernard sounded her word of warning, women are renouncing the role of wife. This has not always stopped them from having weddings of course. Nor has it solved all the problems. Women who wed still encounter an increased health risk – but these days it is more likely to be associated with exhaustion than boredom, with being stretched too far rather than too little – and with the demand for independence rather than the demand for submission.

Whereas wives once would have given a great deal for a day out – it is now the case that many of them would give anything for a day at home.

HAVE ONLY WOMEN EVOLVED?

For a very long time the only acceptable job open to women was that of being a wife. And the reason that was generally give for this restriction was that they were women – and could not therefore do the work of men. By the mid-twentieth century this explanation was looking increasingly silly. During the two world wars (and between them) women not only demonstrated that they could do men's jobs, they proved they could do them very well. This was the start of the problem.

It's not news that after the Second World War, women were bundled out of their jobs and sent back home to make way for the men. But this only delayed the inevitable. The traditional argument that was used to get rid of women was that husbands were supposed to be the breadwinners and to support their wives. This did a great deal more than bolster men's importance in the home and keep wives away from the workplace. It became the main justification for *unequal pay*.

Wives didn't need money – they had their husbands to support them. And as non-wives had only themselves to look after – they didn't need much money either. Or so went the explanations for paying men the family wage – though no questions were asked as to whether the men had a family to support of course.

In some cases laws were passed to uphold this arrangement of paying men more, and of making work off-limits to wives. Even in the teaching profession up until the 1960s, women who became wives were expected to resign from their jobs – and to resign themselves to financial dependence on their husbands. So strong was the pressure against 'working wives' that for most women at the time the choices were disturbingly obvious. You could be a wife or have a career. But you couldn't do both!

Women had to make painful choices that were not demanded of men. Work or family: money or marriage: independence or parenthood.

Growing up in the 1950s, I have no trouble recalling the advice of the time. Yes I could be a lawyer – I was told by my parents and teachers. But I wouldn't be able to marry. And it would be such a waste of all that study! For it was simply not on that I might have been able to combine work and husband. (It wouldn't be fair to him, I was informed.)

Unlike husbands, wives could only have half of what was available, which is why it is often said that the 1950s were the worst decade for women, this century. It is also why one of the starting points for women's liberation in the 1960s was the demand for a full share – for wives to have the right to paid work as did husbands. Then came the quest for equal opportunity at the work place, and an end to the husband getting the family wage. There was a call for equal pay for equal work without reference to whether a person was married or supporting children.

Hugh Mackay suggests that this move towards paid work – and *equality* – became a symbol of liberation for the pioneering generation of women who were 'between the ages of 18 and 35 when the Women's Lib [sic] movement found its voice in Australian society in the mid-1970s . . .'[31]

The symbolic behaviour which women chose as an expression of their new-found definition of gender was work: full-time or part-time paid employment outside the home became a central aspiration for this pioneering generation of women. Whereas their mothers and grandmothers had assumed that a career (or even 'a job') would be abandoned in favour of the role of wife and mother, the pioneers of the Seventies and Eighties saw work outside the home as the most potent symbol of their liberation.[32]

It might have been symbolic, and a first step towards ending wifely servitude, but there were other forces which pushed women into the work place as well – economic necessity being the primary one.

It was all very well to argue that husbands were supposed to provide for their wives and families but the plain truth of the matter was that a lot of them did not. So many men defaulted on support for wives and children that the government was obliged to take measures to 'extract' the money from those who were still in receipt of a family wage – but were spending it on themselves. 'Before the Child Support Agency was established' writes Jenna Price in the *Sydney Morning Herald*,[33] 'less than 30 per cent of child maintenance was ever collected.'

Some of the men who did support their wives and children, demanded so much in return that there were wives who decided that the price was too high. All this meant that women needed money – which sent many of them off to find a paid job.

Even husbands who did provide – and who would not have wanted the world to think that they could not keep their wives – began to find it increasingly difficult to survive on one salary. Which led to further pressure – or encouragement, depending on how you look at it – for wives to join the paid work force.

Over the past twenty years the centuries-old pattern of work and wives has changed beyond all recognition, to the extent that anyone in public life who now suggests that women *choose* to work, is likely to look ridiculous. No one would ever suggest that husbands choose to work: they do it because they need the money. And so too do wives.

And if husbands are unemployed, it is seen as a psychological as well as a financial problem. As it is with wives.

But of course these changes in work practices – and in the role of wives – were not just handed to women. They have had to fight battles at home and at work, and there's still a long way to go. To this day there is a male backlash on both fronts. Husbands resent the changes that have been made at home – and they are often bitterly resentful of the changes at the work place. Given the opportunity, there is no doubt that many of them would like to put wives back in their place.

Many of the older men simply don't know how to cope at work with other men's wives, Hugh Mackay reports. They can't come to terms with the idea that women are genuine workers and that they have proper jobs. But that's not the sum total of it:

A more aggressive response to the arrival of large numbers of women in the work force – and one of the most savage forms of the male backlash – is the assertion by some men that the working wife is the primary cause of unemployment. Such men argue that if women had not chosen to use work as their symbol of liberation, young Australians would not be squeezed out of the job market. Men who hold this view, of course, deeply resent the presence of married women at work and find it difficult to take them seriously as colleagues.[34]

Men might be trying to keep things as they were, but women have changed their lives. There can be no doubt that they have been the pace setters, the pioneers, as Hugh Mackay calls them. They have evolved and adapted to the new age. Unfortunately the same cannot be said for many husbands who want to cling to the advantages they enjoyed before there were all these radical changes to the environment.

'New Women & Old Men' is the title that Hugh Mackay gives to his chapter on the remarkable transformations in gender roles that have taken place in the past few years. He readily recognises that few wives live the way their mothers did – while so many husbands want to live like their fathers. And are bitterly resentful that women (and wives) are taking away their privileges. He goes so far as to suggest that male anger and hostility amount to a form of class hatred against women. He explains this as the result of men seeing themselves as 'emasculated' or 'irrelevant or superfluous'[35] as they measure themselves in terms of the past rather than adapt to the conditions of the present. Which is why the question arises – have only women evolved?

Many women certainly feel that men have been left behind. That they are putting their energy into denying change, rather than making creative adaptations. And not just in relation to the avoidance of housework, either.

There is an increasing number of women who see living with men as just too hard. They are often women who have redefined their role as wives – who want to be equal, a friend, a companion, a partner. But whose husbands cannot or will not cope with the challenge, or opportunities. These days women are much clearer about where they are going: it is men who don't know what they want and who are more likely to be confused. They don't know whether to be New Men – or Real Men; as Hugh Mackay says – they often experience 'conflict between the desire to be sensitive and understanding and the desire to avoid being written off as a wimp.'[36] And the base line is that they think they shouldn't be treated like this; they have a grievance against women. And while they can't say it out loud any more, many of them are still likely to believe that it's okay for women to have their liberation – their work, their confidence, their pay cheque – as long as men are not inconvenienced by it. Yet inconvenience, discomfort, threat and uncertainty are bound to be the daily realities for men who have not found their niche in the new scheme of things.

Women are much more at ease with who they are, even if they are too tired to think about it. As girls they could not have imagined the roles they now have as mature women – and they have had to consciously work out their identity – and how the world will be arranged. In general, men do not seem to have undergone such a self-constructing process; and with predictable results.

> What appears to be most significant about this complex quest for the new female identity is that women find it easier to define themselves in relation to a job, or in relation to children, rather than in relation to a man. Men are the complicating factor which confuses the issue, saps the self confidence – and creates the need to explain the inexplicable.[37]

Women set out to achieve self-sufficiency; and it seems they have got just that. Which is why so many of them no longer see the point in being wives.

At a recent meeting to discuss the role of women in parliament, I was confronted with the fundamental nature of the changes that have occurred when I realised that most of the women in the room lived with women. This was not a lesbian event though of course there was a good percentage of gay women present, as there is in any gathering. But what attracted my attention was the fact so many of these women who were living with women had not so long ago been wives.

'It just got to be too much,' a couple of women explained when asked why they had left their husbands and had set up households with other women. 'It wasn't just the housework, it was the emotional work as well,' one commented. 'There just aren't enough hours in the day to make men feel as though they are still the centre of the universe – and the object of your undying interest and attention.'

This fits with some of the latest research findings. If

relationships were left to men, there wouldn't be any, Shere Hite concluded after her survey on the love between women and men. She found that most wives believed that husbands still expected to be related to – while wives were supposed to do all the relating, all the work of keeping communication and emotional channels open. And it was too much after a day's work.

Besides, women wanted some emotional returns, Hugh Mackay agrees:

> ... men who thought that they could get away with relationships (whether in or out of marriage) which were primarily sexual are now finding that women are demanding more sensitivity and equality in the *total* relationship, and that sexual activity is now being placed in a broader context.[38]

'Men just don't reciprocate,' one of the women who shared a 'modified' house with two other women stated. 'At least when you live with women, the workload is *shared*: the housework is shared, and the nurturing is shared. For the first time in my life someone asks me about my job when I get home – and prepares my dinner at least two nights a week – all without needing to be thanked.'

'The success of "the nuclear family" depends on the wife sacrificing herself to create the unit' a woman sociologist explained. 'And women are not prepared to be wives in that way any more. It's women who are setting up new "family" relationships, where their contributions are appreciated. And they are often families without men,' she said, quoting her own life as an example.

Regardless of the sexual arrangements these women were making – (and I didn't ask) – the reality is that there are many women trying this new life style. And not all of them necessarily professional women with careers. Women solo parents are finding that there is a lot to be gained from sharing a household, as are young women students. And while economics undoubtedly plays a part, economic arguments are by no means the ones that are put first.

'I just wanted a bit of peace in my old age,' said a woman who had just moved into a big house with three other women. 'I just couldn't stand the fights about housework and his ego any more.' And she certainly was not alone.

While many younger women are trying to redefine the role of wife – to have the wedding but not the wifedom – many more mature women have given up trying to make changes in the household, or in their husbands' behaviour. But they haven't wanted to live alone so they have formed relationships with other women who want similar arrangements. And it will be interesting to see what new patterns emerge in these new 'families': will we soon have *women with wives*?

Will differences arise when one member of an all female household encounters greater pressure at work or earns more than the other? Will they do fewer emotional and domestic chores – which is what happens with husbands; as Janeen Baxter points out, the more husbands earn the less they are likely to do in the home.[39]

According to some of the women who share with women, sex also played a part in their choice. There are wives who have found, to put it mildly, that men's sexuality is an 'imposition'. Who see it as yet another male need to be met, rather than a contribution to a mutually enhancing relationship. 'It mightn't be the law any more that wives have to provide as much sex as their husbands want,' one ex-wife remarked. 'But what they used to get as a legal requirement, husbands now get by guilt tripping you into it . . .'

There does seem to be consensus among some wives that sex is just another thing you have to do for husbands. Hugh Mackay phrases this in a particular way:

> As she sinks into bed at the end of another day, (the wife) dimly recalls that she used to go to bed for reasons other than restorative sleep. The sex lives of working mothers generally suffer from the effects of fatigue: the proposition that 'you can't be a workhorse all day and a show pony at night' is one which is strongly endorsed by working mothers all around Australia.[40]

But if wives think there is a problem with their sexual relationships with husbands, this tends to pale into insignificance in comparison to the problem that husbands claim to be having with wives.

Again, Hugh Mackay's version of events is interesting. He believes that men resent the way women these days expect 'more out of sex' and are more likely to be assertive about their sexual relationship.

What this means of course is that male performance is being evaluated, and many men don't like it. 'Men who had previously thought perfunctory sex was enough to satisfy their partners,' Mackay explains, 'are finding that their performance is being explicitly criticised by women who now feel sufficiently liberated to take sexual initiatives and to impose sexual standards . . .'[41]

Wives who are doing well in the work place often report that their husbands don't like the image of independence, confidence, self-sufficiency. 'Can't you forget the "power dressing" and be a proper woman in bed' one husband complained to his highly successful wife. 'You were such a nice person before you got into all this women and management stuff . . .' (Meaning – said the *ex-wife* – can't you go back to being sweet and submissive and seeing me as the one who makes you happy!)

Women are working out new styles for themselves and the impression generally gained is that men are reacting, and often in very negative ways. Which doesn't make for happiness or harmony in the home. This atmosphere of hostility and tension is one of the major reasons wives give for getting a divorce and doing without men. Although as Hugh Mackay points out – there are also many men who have decided to do without wives.

> The uneasiness of men . . . has to do with the simple question of a threat to male dominance in an area where males have traditionally assumed dominance. Some men have turned away from relationships with New Women simply because they find it too threatening to play by new rules. Others have assumed that sexual intercourse was

one last bargaining chip in their bid to resist the new feminism, only to be disappointed by the discovery that their wives did not appear to care much, either way; others have quite explicitly retreated from heterosexuality as a defence against women whom they find too assertive and demanding.[42]

One of the demands of the new woman is for quality of life – in her own home. And it is quite mind boggling to find how many women in the mid-age bracket, are up front about the way this means getting rid of the husbands. Not that this is the only basis for women being with women, of course. Many women have never had the slightest desire to have weddings or to be men's wives, and for them much of the struggle between women and men in the private sphere is absolutely irrelevant, if not affirming.

But for those who have been wives the going has often been very hard and it is not surprising that some of them reduce their work load by giving up the husband rather than the paid job.

No one could dispute the fact that on average women today work harder than their mothers or grandmothers. They have *added* more roles and responsibilities to the traditional burdens of wife and mother. And there is some truth in the statement – at this stage – that the only right women have won in the past decades is the right to do two jobs instead of one. It is the right to work harder – to take on the role of breadwinner without losing any of the load of home making and child care.

This is why a number of wives feel cheated; they think that women's liberation feels more like enslavement and they are not convinced that it has been worth the effort.

And they don't always have to tell their daughters that the verdict is still out on whether the new ways are going to be a great improvement. The next generation have too often seen for themselves the costs of trying to be *superwoman*, and are just as determined *not* to follow in their mothers' footsteps as their mothers were determined not to live as their own mothers had done.

But young women today start from a much stronger base than their mothers; they have a sense of worth that puts things in a very different light. For whereas I was told that you couldn't combine a career and being a wife because it was unfair on the husband, many young women now are insisting that you can't combine the two – because it is not fair to the wife.

Just how many women are electing to live without men – or children – because they are in the too-hard basket, is difficult to tell. However, Hugh Mackay writes that 'If present trends in marriage and divorce were to continue, we would ultimately find that Australians who marry once and stay married would be in the minority: they would be outnumbered by those who never marry or who marry two or more times'.

Women have changed their existence. They have wanted it all and have added more activities to their lives. And these changes have led to an unacceptably high work load. Something has to go. But it doesn't have to be the husband: it could be the traditional work of the wife that is eliminated.

At the turn of the last century there were women such as Catherine Helen Spence in Australia – and Charlotte Perkins Gilman in the USA – who were convinced that the greatest institutionalised form of oppression was the unpaid work expected of wives. Until this problem was overcome, they argued, women would never be liberated. And their simple solution was the 'collectivisation' of housework. Both women even wrote novels illustrating how this could be done. Their idea was that women's work had to become *real* work, part of the enonomy, and not some sacrifice made in the name of love. They envisaged communal kitchens, professional cleaning services, and superior child care. And they were mocked for their imaginative solutions.

But a hundred years later, what do we have?

The domestic duties of wives are increasingly becoming part of the paid economy. The very pressure of work has pushed 'working wives' to farm out many of the traditional tasks they once did for no money. Women's work is fast moving into the area of the mainstream economy.

It isn't stretching things too far to suggest that 'take away' is one version of the communal kitchen. It might not be quite what Catherine Helen Spence had in mind, but people are being paid to cook for the family. And this represents a crucial change. Not so long ago if a wife didn't provide the meal, everyone went without. And while husbands have become involved in the preparation of the family meal, most wives have not found this a satisfactory arrangement (particularly if the husband has introduced the rule that he who cooks doesn't have to clean up afterwards). So paying a cook – who can even deliver (as with pizzas for example) is one way of reducing the burden on the wife.

As is paying someone to do the cleaning, and the ironing.

One of the most significant developments in the Australian Labor Party Policy in 1993 was the inclusion of child care in the *Economics* statement, rather than in policy matters relating to women's issues. The 'official' recognition that child care is an integral part of working conditions for parents with dependent offspring, and not just a particular problem of working women, to be solved on an individual basis, is a 'dream-come-true' in terms of the women's liberationists of the 1970s. Child care was always high on the women's charter and the acceptance of it as a *paid job* rather than the invisible work that women do, represents a real shift in economics, and in the role of wives and mothers.

Of course someone has to pay for the child care – and the evidence is that it is women who are footing the bill. (Even where there are joint accounts, the wife is more likely to be paying for services such as housekeeping and child care – while husbands pay the mortgage and the car.) But an increasing number of women think this is okay.

'It takes just about every penny I earn to pay for the child care and the cleaning,' says one 35-year-old woman who has just gone back to work. But she (and many like her) think it is good value. 'It means that I am doing the work I want, while the children are being well cared for and the house is clean. I've just exchanged roles – and I love it.'

And the woman who is doing the cleaning? 'It suits me

fine,' she said. Her daughter was also at child care and she was satisfied with the part-time work. 'I like cleaning,' she said, 'but not ironing. I'm my own boss, and even though child care costs a bit, it's fine with me. And the money makes a big difference in my life.'

So wife A is employing wife B and both employ wife C to do the child care. (And wives who are cleaning, catering, or childcaring etc. are forming their own small businesses – and employing other women.) This makes wives the new generation of employers. It's wives who are hiring cleaners, caterers, cookers, ironers and childcarers. The demand for 'nannies' is unprecedented and the need for 'housekeepers' is growing. It's wives who are creating new jobs as they now pay other wives to do what they did for free until very recently.

There must be some reservations about this development; as is the national trend, the jobs created are primarily low paid, *part*-time, and non-unionised. While the domestic service industry, like the tourist, or 'hospitality' industry, *can* become an accepted service industry with its own professional criteria and career structure, it is still the case that these new jobs are another indication of the division of society into the 'haves' and 'have-nots'. There are many women who are pleased to have these service jobs, and the accompanying conditions, but this is often in preference to unemployment. What we are witnessing for the first time in modern history is a class structure among women – as there has been among men.

Two decades ago wives railed against the way divorce and property laws were so blatantly biased against them when husbands left. And they protested at the fact that a wife's status was that of her husband. The reality was that wives often had a great deal in common; as the 'Why Be A Wife' campaigners could point out, there was usually only one husband between any wife and social services.

But now wives can claim wealth and status in their own right. There is a hierarchy.

This does not detract from the gains that have been made as the unpaid work of women becomes paid work; but it is to point out that as job generators wives are becoming paid *employers* as well as paid *employees.*

'Louise' has just given up teaching, and opened her own agency, Home Care. She has lots of women on her books who want to work and she sees the possibilities as infinite. 'We'll do anything,' she said. 'We can house sit, feed pets, take the garbage out, do child care or take gran to the doctor or the dentist. We can wait in for tradespeople, pick up kids and take them places, clean your house, do your shopping, pay your bills, do your washing, write your letters.'

And wives who have resented unpaid domestic service, seem to find the same work much less onerous and frustrating when they are paid for doing it in someone else's home. 'When I leave the house I'm doing, it looks great with nothing out of place' one woman said. 'It doesn't break my heart to see it reduced to chaos again. Not like when it's your own place ...'

You could say that women are once more leading the way; they are adapting to job share. They are taking the initiative and dividing up their too-many-tasks, and too-long-a-day and paying professionals to do their part. And creating a new domestic industry in the process.

So perhaps wanting the traditional wedding but rejecting the traditional wife-service is not as unrealistic as it may appear. It could be that women have already developed the necessary adaptations for the new environment. Wives are no longer automatically the unpaid employees in their husbands' households. They are becoming the job generators and job sharers of a new age.

MARRYING UP

Cinderella got the prince and ever since, women have been tantalised by the prospect of 'marrying up'.

Women have been urged to 'better themselves' by marriage, and this has generally meant becoming the wife of someone who has greater status and wealth. The basic plot of everything from fairy tales to Mills & Boon romances hinges on the heroine finding, and keeping, Mr Right. Needless to say, 'Mr Right' is invariably older, wiser, taller, stronger – and richer than his bride.

Not that 'a good catch' was all that rare in days gone by. When women had very little, and men had a lot, almost any man could have qualified as 'Mr Right'. As women weren't allowed to own property or to have well paid jobs, then simply by taking on the status of a member of the 'superior sex', any wife was improving her lot. But these days the principle of marrying up doesn't work so well.

We don't have a 'superior sex' in today's terms. And with each move towards gender equality, it becomes increasingly difficult for a woman to find a man she can 'look up to'. Once all things are equal, we will have to accept that up to half the female population will have to 'marry down'; in the words of the vernacular, many women will have to marry 'beneath them'. And it is understandable that they won't see any point to this.

In speaking on *Late Line*,[43] the politician Meredith Bergman stated categorically that less than 10 per cent of men are worth marrying anyway. And no doubt it is the case that if men cannot offer to provide greater wealth or status for their wives, women could well ask – *why would you bother?*

What would a wife get in return for her efforts? There would have to be some trade-off for the risk to her mental health, and all the extra work load.

Women now enjoy increasing independence. As yet, they have not achieved equality but given where they started from, women's gains are remarkable. And now that they have assets of their own they are not so automatically impressed by those of men. Women can be more *choosy*.

'All the worldly goods' which men once bestowed are not nearly so attractive – or substantial – now that women are doing money and status for themselves . . .

Some of these changes are quite measurable. Writing in the *Sydney Morning Herald*, Adele Horin[44] notes that for the first time in history, women now are accumulating more educational resources than men. She was 'stunned' to find that in the last five years 'our young women (have become) better educated on average than our young men.' This certainly is a 'stunning' achievement. Only one hundred years ago women were fighting for the right to be educated at all. Now they are getting ahead, and look like staying that way. (Many wives can testify to the threat that this poses: one of the greatest problems associated with female mature students is the antagonistic response of husbands. There are wives who have had to deal with assault – and sabotage – as they have attempted to upgrade their qualifications. Hugh Mackay reports on the 'husband who put his wife's university assignments into the rubbish bin, instead of posting them'.[45] Such a response is not atypical.)

Adele Horin is interested in the many and significant social 'adjustments' that are going to take place as a result of this change in educational status – although she doesn't specifically mention the hostility of husbands.

More girls than boys are finishing high school. More girls than boys are going on to university. More girls than boys are getting higher qualifications and degrees. (In 1992 nearly 47 000 women finished degrees, compared to only 34 000 men.)

'Traditionally women have "married up" to men older and better educated than themselves,' she comments. 'But there will be fewer well educated men to go around.' And she doesn't shy away from some of the implications for wives: 'women are averse to marrying men with lower qualifications than themselves'. This is the much publicised 'man shortage' for successful career women.

So if men are not better educated – if you can't marry up – then there goes yet another reason for women to become wives. It seems that the attractions of marrying men are fewer and fewer, even if they go unstated. But given that the 'Australian Institute of Family Studies predicts that, by the end of the Nineties, 22 per cent of Australian women will not have married by the age of 35,'[46] the suggestion is that more young women are putting off the wedding, as well as the business of being a wife.

Of course you could argue that these new developments have their down side for men. For if women have had the opportunity to improve their status by marrying up, husbands have had the opportunity to enhance their prestige by 'marrying down.' Men have married women who have served as a foil and who have increased male importance. Wives preferably have been shorter, younger, prettier, 'sillier', and poorer in terms of education, status and wealth. This is how the image of the strong and masterful 'man of the house' has been maintained. And this is why the 'new woman' is seriously undermining the role and authority of the husband.

'It is assumed that wives earn less than their husbands and pity is evinced for men whose wives are more successful than they are,' Germaine Greer wrote in 1970.[47] And in the two decades in between, many money-earning wives have gone to great lengths to hide their own earnings and to bolster the fading glory of husbands.

'I used to have my salary paid into his account so that he could keep his pride and be the money manager,' one woman openly acknowledged at a conference of women in management. 'We even played games, with him making all the decisions, telling me how much I could have and how much I could spend ... and he wasn't even any good at handling the finances. But it just got to be too tiresome,' she added. 'I woke up one day and decided I'd rather keep my money for myself. I had a good job, I really reared the kids ... I did all the housework. For God's sake, I even mowed the lawns. And I just decided that the husband had to go. There wasn't any advantage in keeping him.'

And twenty women participants nodded their heads in empathy and agreement.

Most women earn less than most men. (Women on average earn 67 per cent of male pay.) But the fact that women have *any* money of their own and have been able to increase their choices, has meant that money (and perhaps status) in men don't represent the same 'positives' that they once did.

Traditionally however, women have not just sought to be wives of men who were wealthier and more important: they have also gone for those who are braver, stronger and taller.

And the question that arises is whether women want more even-handed partnerships when it comes to this physical aspect of relationships.

I must admit that I have always been puzzled by women who marry older, taller, stronger, wiser and wealthier men and who then complain that it is unfair because *he* has all the resources. But on the occasions that I have tried to draw attention to this contradiction, I have been met with a comparable degree of puzzlement from some young women.

'But why would you marry him, if he *didn't* have more resources?' one woman student asked me, genuinely bewildered. 'There's no point unless he has something to offer ...'

Older women can also have their own hang-ups to contend with. It seems that old beliefs and values, die hard. Socialised to see men as 'protectors', there can be some difficulty in making the transition to being in charge of one's own destiny. It's not all that unusual to find women sheepishly admitting that they like a man who is masterful, while at the same time they recognise the inconsistencies, and the dangers of such a disposition. The greater size and strength of males does represent a problem for many wives who, from the outset, are aware of their physical vulnerability.

'In the last analysis I have to rely on his good will' said one forty-year-old wife at a self-defence class. 'I have to trust him not to use his strength against me. And that's difficult. The very fact that he's so much bigger and stronger than I am means that it is implicit in our relationship that I'm at his mercy. The threat is always present even when it isn't used. And there's no way I'll even let him make jokes about it. No "games" where he can hold me down or use force in any way. It just isn't funny. I panic.'

Because of our cultural values, our attention is drawn to the sight of a taller woman with a shorter man. We have been 'programmed' to expect that the male will be physically superior, literally someone a wife can 'look up to'. And yet it is clear that for those women redefining the relationship between the sexes, this characteristic of the male can be problematic. Given the horrific statistics on domestic violence and that the most dangerous place for a wife is in her own home, it hardly makes sense for a woman to take as her partner a male who has overwhelming physical superiority.

'Go for someone shorter. If you do want a husband, then "a good catch" has to be one who can't intimidate, threaten or beat you.' That's the advice I give young women who want a profile of the eligible man. 'Stop noticing girls who are with boys who are shorter,' I counsel them. 'It should be the other way around. You should start to ask what does a nice girl see in a big man like that. It's just so *risky*. And you could start congratulating those who can find themselves shorter men. "Lucky you!" you can say to them. "Getting a man who doesn't undermine or challenge your autonomy".'

The code of chivalry – which was about the stronger male, and male protection – never was in women's interest. Even in the seventeenth and eighteenth centuries there were feminists who protested that chivalry was about keeping woman in her place. It was a mark of contempt they argued, and not respect (see Lynne Spender, this volume).

And of course there was a period in the 1970s when men complained that it was no longer possible to be courteous to women without giving offence. This was when women began to think that a place in the work force was more important than a seat on the bus. And behaved accordingly.

With wives making their way on their own, and in their own right, they are no longer in need of chivalry, or a 'protector'. In an information based age where brain rather than brawn is the desirable resource, it could be said that the greater physical prowess of the male has outlived its usefulness. And if some wives now think male size a liability rather than an asset, it is certainly understandable.

So too with having a husband who is older and wiser. Barbara Ehrenreich thinks that women should see their new independence as a freedom, and not as a limitation on the available supply. 'Once you've gotten over the ancient prejudice that a husband should be older, taller, smarter and richer,' she writes, 'then the field is wide open.'[48] And she puts up a very good case for women having younger husbands. (She doesn't mention the matter of life expectancy but if wives were to have *younger* husbands then women who wanted male companionship in their old age – would have countered the problem of husbands normally dying before their wives.)

Currently it seems that mature women are more likely to have younger male lovers than they are to turn the men into husbands. This new pattern is partly because mature women feel that they are invisible to men in their own age bracket. 'Younger men will give them more than a glance but for a man in his forties or even fifties, a woman over 30 is not sexual. Women call these men "duds",' writes Kathy Bail.[49]

Duds are the men who haven't evolved, who are still looking for the stereotype and submissive wife. They are the ones who have missed the boat, who are insecure about their masculinity – and the fallout from the feminist movement. They are the older men who have not been able to make the transition, who cannot welcome the new woman.

But if they don't see such mature women as potential partners, they are still inclined to feel deeply threatened when they find these women with younger men! (Women don't appear to be bothered by other women seeking younger men; in fact they seem to think it is understandable. 'They know the score: they can treat you as a partner rather than as someone who is supposed to make them feel good,' said a prominent career woman who has quite openly chosen a younger man, on the grounds that it makes life easier.)

The belief that younger men are better able to cope with the independence of women is gaining ground among those who *do* want to be wives – and who don't want the abuse and hang-ups of the past. So far from there being a 'man shortage', perhaps it will be the 'remarrying-duds' who will find themselves without partners, who discover that there are no women who want to be their wives!

For women, 'marrying up' isn't the option – or the attraction – that it used to be. 'Marrying down' isn't the answer either.

But if there are to be wives and husbands in the future then they will be very different from the stereotypes we have known. Women, it seems won't settle for less than a relationship of equals. And this means an end to the image of the older, wiser, richer, taller, smarter, stronger – *unemotional* male – as the most eligible bachelor.

It's men who are now on notice as potential husbands.

For centuries marriage has been used to keep women in line. To the point where it is no exaggeration to suggest that the entire patriarchal framework has rested upon the need for women to be willing wives. So we shouldn't be surprised to find in this age of growing gender equality that both male supremacy and willing wives are on the decline. And that those values that have been considered desirable in one sex only – the traditional wifely values of obedience, submission, and dependence, of pleasing a man rather than developing the self – are no longer held up to the next generation as the ideal. Wifeliness as it has been practised throughout the centuries has now become ancient history; the hope is that tomorrow's women will have weddings which celebrate a range of genuine partnerships – rather than reduce half the population to the now discredited status of wives.

NOTES

1. See Mary Wollstonecraft, *Vindication of the Rights of Woman*, (1792), reprinted Penguin, Middlesex, 1978, p.175. Also *Maria: the Wrongs of Woman*, Norton, New York, 1978.
2. See Germaine Greer, *The Female Eunuch*, McGibbon & Kee, London, 1970, p.273.

3. Jessie Bernard, *The Future of Marriage*, World Publishing, New York, 1972, p.39.
4. Virginia Woolf (1929), *A Room of One's Own*, Penguin, Middlesex, 1974.
5. Cicely Hamilton (1909), *Marriage as a Trade* (introduction, Jane Lewis), The Women's Press, London, 1981, p.24.
6. Ann Oakley, *The Sociology of Housework*, Martin Robertson, London, 1974, and in *Housework*, Pelican/Penguin, Melbourne, 1976.
7. Private communication: see also this volume, 'Down the Aisle – and Up the Garden Path', Lynne Spender.
8. Germaine Greer, 1970, p.242.
9. See Hugh Mackay, *Reinventing Australia*, Angus & Robertson, Sydney, 1993.
10. 'Miss' was once the equivalent of 'Master' – and meant a young woman: while 'Mrs' was the parallel of 'Mr' and signified maturity. Single women such as Mary Astell and Harriet Martineau referred to themselves as 'Mrs' when they were past their youth and 'Miss' was wholly inappropriate (it was like calling an adult male, 'Master'). But with the industrial revolution and the increased mobility of women, men required 'evidence' as to which women were 'owned' and which were not: the wedding ring and the title of 'Mrs' were used for the purpose.
11. Naomi Wolf, 'Can you be a feminist and still be attractive to men?', *Cosmo*, October 1993, p.24.
12. For further discussion see Dale Spender, *Women of Ideas – and What Men Have Done to Them*, Routledge, London, 1982, pp.310–17.
13. Dale Spender, 1982, p.222.
14. For the full quote see Dale Spender, *Heroines*, Penguin, Melbourne, 1991, p.9.
15. Hugh Mackay, *Reinventing Australia*, Angus & Robertson, Sydney, 1993, pp.58–9.
16. In her latest report on the family, Shere Hite presents the astonishing information from the women she surveys – that less than 20 per cent of them report the presence of blood or pain with their first experience of intercourse; which leads Shere Hite to question whether women really do have hymens or whether this 'anatomical feature' is another example of male wishful thinking – like the concepts of 'keeping one's self for one's husband' and 'illegitimacy'.
17. See Christina Stead, *Miss Herbert*, Virago, London, 1976, p.8.

18. Cicely Hamilton, 1981, p.20.
19. See *Lady into Woman*, published by Andrew Dakers, London, 1953, and quoted in Jane Lewis's introduction to Cicely Hamilton's *Marriage as a Trade*, reprinted by The Women's Press, London, 1981, p.6.
20. Quoted in Ray Strachey (1928), *The Cause: A short history of the women's movement in Great Britain*, Virago, London, 1978, p.92.
21. Australian Bureau of Statistics figures quoted in Commonwealth Department of Housing, Local Government, and Community Services, International Year of the Family brochure, 1994.
22. Julian Cribb, 'Aussies loiter on the path to marriage', *Australian*, 27 October, 1993, p.4.
23. See Office of the Status of Women survey and publication, *Juggling Time* (selected findings from): *How Australian Families Use Time* (from original research by Michael Bittman), Publications Section, Barton, ACT, 1991.
24. 'Speaking bitterness' was the Chinese term for women's public airing of grievance about inequality.
25. WET TANK, *Houseworkshop Bulletin* No 1 and *Newsletter*, October, 1993.
26. Jessie Bernard, 1972, p.21
27. Jessie Bernard, 1972, p.18
28. Julian Hafner, 'Tyranny of Coupledom'. *Weekend Australian*, June 12–13, 1993, p.20.
29. Jessie Bernard, 1972, p.48
30. Julian Hafner, 1993, p.20.
31. Hugh Mackay, 1993, p.25.
32. Hugh Mackay, 1993, p.26.
33. Jenna Price, *Sydney Morning Herald*, 16 October 1993.
34. Hugh Mackay, 1993, p.97.
35. Hugh Mackay, 1993, p.40.
36. Hugh Mackay, 1993, p.41.
37. Hugh Mackay, 1993, p.49.
38. Hugh Mackay, 1993, p.45.
39. See Janeen Baxter, *Work at Home: the domestic division of labour*, University of Queensland Press, St Lucia, 1993, p.107.
40. Hugh Mackay, 1993, p.31.
41. Hugh Mackay, 1993, p.45.
42. Hugh Mackay, 1993, p.46.

43. ABC TV, 21 June, 1993.
44. Adele Horin, 'Living with the new gender gap', *Sydney Morning Herald*, 13 October 1993, p.12.
45. Hugh Mackay, 1993, p.40.
46. Hugh Mackay, 1993, p.56.
47. Germaine Greer, 1970, p.123.
48. Barbara Ehrenreich, quoted in Kathy Bail, 'The Case of the Invisible Woman', *Independent Monthly*, October 1992, p.7.
49. Kathy Bail, 'The Case of the Invisible Woman', *Independent Monthly*, October 1992, p.7.

PART TWO

The D-I-Y Ceremony

NADIA WHEATLEY

Epistle From Cloud 9

At all times: Always remember that this is your day and that you should have it run as you want it. Keep in mind that it is the most romantic and wonderful day in your life.

'Your Wedding', the *Echo* 27/1/93

Dear Ms Spender,

Word has reached me that you are editing a collection of Women's stories and articles on the subject of Weddings and Wives and so I am putting pen to paper in the hope that you may use my information to set the record straight. What I have experienced personally is a matter that has happened to women throughout the course of history – which believe you me is something which I have been observing since long before you were ever born. That is to put it in a nutshell that women and I in particular have been left out of the history as it has been written down because it was men who did the writing and they only wrote down what their mates did and they were all men too. Are you with me? But enough of grumbling, I will jump straight in and tell you the true facts.

Perhaps I should start by saying that I have seen scores and scores of weddings for even before I died I attended on average one a week as I was eventually a great-great-grandmother with close to four thousand direct descendants at the time of my death, and since then I have witnessed at least a million more weddings of every creed and nationality and race and gender. In fact I guess you could call me a wedding groupie or perhaps a wedding junkie would be more the word. Whether it is a royal princess in the abbey or the humblest stenographer at her local registry office, I like to tune down and watch and cross my fingers and wish her well. But it is not so much the ceremony as the celebration that fascinates me: and again, be it a sit-down spread at the Ritz or a BBQ with BYO at Bondi Beach, I just love to watch the festivities from a distance and I guess it comes from having had such an awful personal experience myself. Not that I am jealous or even envious. But I do have to say that of all the weddings I have known, mine must surely rank as the greatest shemozzle in history. Of course as you probably know it went badly from the start. Later some people (like my husband's uncle and brothers for instance) said it served me right for trying to have ten bridesmaids. *Ten*, they said, *ten*! *Who does she think she is*? Well, I said back (though I didn't say it out loud of course), I had my pride to keep up. I wanted to show that I wasn't just nobody even if I didn't come from such a great famous family like them. Besides, I had a lot of women friends – I still do – and I didn't want to pick and choose and leave anyone out. So all ten of my best friends were happy to do it and I said, *Great, we'll show them*! They made their outfits colour co-ordinated, spent all day braiding their hair and so on, but as you know it didn't work out very well and later some people said ten was too many to organise because half of them got there in plenty of time but the other half were a bit late for the ceremony. Actually this is another case in point about men stereotyping women when they put them into history at all because to call these five late women Foolish (as was done) is as far as I am concerned really offensive. (It was also inaccurate to describe them all as virgins: this was a way of denying the experience of one of them who was as you will see not only married but a victim of her married state. Similarly, it was a denial of me, the way it was written that the ten were going forth to meet the bride*groom*. I mean, if this were the case, that ten virgins were going off to meet a bridegroom at midnight in the darkness – well, if I were the bride in question, I'd have something to say. No, it was obviously *me* they were meeting, but see what I mean about history?) As to the lateness, you've got to understand that there weren't taxis in those days or even public transport despite what they say about how at least Pontius Pilate made the trains run on time – that just isn't true. It was very difficult in those days for women to go out alone at night – difficult and dangerous – and so my ten friends agreed to meet in two groups of five according to which side of town they lived in and to accompany each other for protection against men. Of course what happened was that five met with their lamps full of oil and came to the wedding, and four of the other five met with their lamps full of oil but the fifth one – my dear old friend Sarah who from that day was to be a relative as well as friend, for her mother-in-law was now also my mother-in-law – had a bloody drunk for a husband (so what's new?) and he'd stolen all the housekeeping and gone down the tavern with his brothers and she didn't have any money to buy oil so she borrowed a little from the woman next door but that woman was poor too so there wasn't enough oil and so as Sarah was walking along the dark alleys to the meeting place her lamp went out. She persevered of course. Yes, my dear old friend Sarah walked through the alleys in the pitch dark with potential rapists and broken cobblestones all around her; she walked on (but somewhat more slowly of course under the circumstances) and met up with my other four dear friends Rachel, Naomi, Rebecca and Miriam (I hate how men leave women's names out of history), who of course had waited for her instead of heading on to the party without her, and all this gets described as Foolishness! As far as I personally am concerned, the moral of the story should be Women's Perseverance and Solidarity! But that's me getting on my soapbox again, perhaps. And be that as it may, the other five did turn up in time (their names for the record were Elizabeth, Anne, Ruth, Leah and Hepzibah) and it didn't matter at all that the other five weren't there except for the way my husband's family snooted down their noses and then after my friends arrived and explained, my husband's uncle in his speech made a joke about Five Foolish Virgins and said how they'd all coincidentally been too stupid to buy oil for their lamps – and that was how the story started that was later turned into the Parable. But anyway of course Ms Spender, that is all just a minor and trivial example of what I am saying about women getting written wrongly about if they get put into history at all, because the main bit of my story is at last about to begin. It was actually then, during my husband's uncle's speech, that coming back from relieving myself I noticed that the wine was getting down to the bottom of the six stone jars. *Whoopi-doo*, I thought, *we're saved!* The party had already been in full swing for four or five hours not to mention the fact that some of the men (my husband included as well as his brothers) had been drinking in the tavern before the ceremony, and so I was most relieved to see that the grog was running out. In fact my mother and I in planning the catering had deliberately provided for this event to happen at about this stage. Now I should quickly say that it wasn't that Mum and I were stingy, and it wasn't that we were wowsers either. I personally like a drink. No, it's not the grog in itself that's the problem but the fact that in some cases alcohol and men are a bad combination, aren't they? I mean, some really nice blokes who wouldn't hurt a fly when sober turn into wife-bashers when they're drunk. That is not a biased feminist statement, Ms Spender, but a matter of statistical historical fact which I have been observing for centuries before you were born. Of course at this particular point in time I personally had only four or five hours of my own experience of marriage but that was enough for me to be pleased that the party was nearly over, for not only was my husband looking pie-eyed but his brothers and uncles and so on ... It was a point worth remembering that the House of David into which I had just married and the fame of which my uncle-in-law was currently extolling at great length (And unto Enoch was born Irad: and Irad begat Mehujael: and Mehujael begat Methusael: and Methusael begat Lamech) had – according to the evidence of its own family records – produced the first drunk in history as well as the first murderer. Not to mention the ghastly thing done to Lot's poor wife. So you can imagine my acute anxiety when suddenly I noticed that the waiters who a few minutes before had idly moved in a clump to the courtyard were now scurrying back and forth up and down along the tables, each with a jug in each hand, and now the drone of Uncle's chronicle (And all the days of Lamech were seven hundred seventy and seven years: and he died) was drowned by a splashing and a sloshing and a slurping and a burping such as I was not to hear again until aeons later when I happened by accident to tune down to the last five minutes before 6 o'clock closing in that pub opposite Flinders Street railway station on VJ Day. Where had it all come from, I asked myself then – and ask myself still. Of course as you know, the way it is written down in history it was a certain kinsman of my husband sitting with some of his mates down the back of the room who did it as a miracle. Well. You can believe that or not as you wish, it doesn't affect what I am saying, though I'd like to point out two things, firstly that the notion that it was the kinsman's sainted mother put him up to it seems incredible to me for I have never seen a man's sainted mother suggest that there should be a wholesale piss-up and secondly, if this kinsman was who some people think he was and had the ability to do such a miracle I do not think he *would* have done such a miracle because if he would have had the ability to do the miracle then he surely also would have had the omniscience to know how things were going to turn out and so he wouldn't have let them happen and if he didn't have the omniscience to know how things were going to turn out then he wouldn't have had the ability to do a miracle. Well, that's my opinion. But anyway I am not concerned with cause but with effect. And already I could see blokes looking belligerent, my new brother-in-law who was my dear friend Sarah's husband for one. He really was a nasty drunk despite the considerable prestige of the family he came from, and you could see his eyes glazing over and his chin sticking out and he was spoiling for a fight. He came up to where we were sitting – Naomi and Rachel and Rebecca and Elizabeth and Anne and Miriam and Leah and Ruth and Hepzibah and Sarah and I – and he tried to make out that Sarah had humiliated him – *him!* – by runnning out of lamp-oil and he kept saying she was a really slack housekeeper and he didn't know what she spent all the money on etcetera etcetera. *Oh go and pick on someone your own sex*, I told him (not out loud of course), but that sort of drunk never does. Meanwhile the wine was still flowing fast and furious and Uncle called my husband up to the front and praised him publicly saying, *Every man at the beginning doth set forth good wine; and when men have well drunk, then that which is worse: but thou has kept the good wine until now*, which was tantamount to saying that the wine which my family had provided was cheap and nasty which made my mother and me feel so small. *Bugger them*, we said to each other, and left them to it: my ten girlfriends and my mother and I set off through the courtyard and all the other women followed, those from the groom's family as well, and we all went to our respective homes. After that it was some honeymoon night I can tell you! There I was in a strange room in my mother-in-law's house, and I was as you can imagine absolutely petrified as well as lonely and homesick and miserable. Of course there was many a time I'd seen dogs do it, and roosters, which was bad enough, but my mind kept returning to a time when I'd stayed at my grandparents' home in the country and I'd seen a stallion mount the sweet little donkey who was my special farm pet. As it turned out however when my husband eventually rolled home at cockcrow he just collapsed without taking his clothes off, spreadeagled right across me so that the worst thing to happen – that night at least – was that I got terrible pins and needles in my legs. No, I shouldn't go on about what was wrong with *my* husband that night. I should think myself lucky. Because when my dear friend Sarah's husband – my husband's brother – came home, he progressed from allegations of slackness to accusations of sluttishness: now the reason (he said) that she'd been late was that she was having it off with the lamp-oil vendor! Of course against such charges made by a drunk there is no point arguing so Sarah said nothing, but that did not prevent him from punching her repeatedly in the side of the head in such a way that the bruises would be hidden by her hair. Finally he fell asleep but that did her little good because when he awoke he remembered what he had done and so he naturally began hitting her again because (he said) her existence made him feel guilty for hitting her the first time! Yes indeed, I was fortunate that my husband was of the passing-out variety of drunk. Now I won't go on about the sufferings experienced by other women that night – though I happen to know that there were half-a-dozen rapes-in-marriage as well as a nasty sort of alley rape plus all the other outrages of vomiting and blood-letting that are par for the course when boys will be boys – for I am not concerned here about the nitty-gritty but the portrayal of the event overall. I mean why is it that in all the stories and the pictures of the Wedding at Cana does no one ever think about the bride and her feelings? I mean there I was, fifteen years old and getting married to someone three times my age and who I'd never even spoken to before. As from that night I had to leave my own home and move to my husband's mother's place, where I knew full well I would be the slave and servant not just to my mother-in-law but to all my husband's unmarried brothers and sisters as well. Of course, on marriage such property as I had – down to the very bangles on my wrists – became my husband's property, just as I became his chattel, his breeding cow, his workhorse ... And there I had to sit at the high table smiling fiercely as my husband's uncle blethered on about the privileges that had fallen upon me that day. And meanwhile, when this all gets written up by that mate of my husband's kinsman, for all they always say about weddings being the bride's day, there is nary a word about me! I assure you that I am not saying this because I want to be famous as an individual but simply because this seems to me to be a very typical example of how the whole women's point of view is always left out of history. So what I am hoping Ms Spender is that you or some other woman could use these true facts that I have provided and write up the story properly in your book. Must close now and pop this in the delivery box – Sarah tells me there is a balloon wedding just going up over Canberra so I must tune down and have a look. I personally think that there is no sight in heaven or earth more poignant than the crazed brave radiance of a bride.

Yours with love and sisterhood,

....

P.S. What I want to know when you write back Ms Spender is, why is it always the men who get to write the Bible?

Memo

From: John the Apostle
To: Gabriel Archangel
Re: Delivery of enclosed
Note: In light of dangerous unorthodoxy of correspondent's opinions, obtain standard rejection slip from Penguin Books Australia, enclose, and return to sender.

ROSIE SCOTT

Reinventing the Ritual

One compelling image strangely at odds with the glitz, good humour and sexuality of the 1993 Sydney Mardi Gras was of a lone figure, covered from head to toe in white, drifting down Oxford Street. You could not see the face but it suggested at different times, a muffled woman, a person in mourning, a fugitive and finally and unquestionably a bride. When you looked closer, there was a smear of blood on the breast and trailing soundlessly behind on a long ragged train, was a toaster and iron. What was so fascinating about the figure was the power of its understated message – the fetters of domesticity and materialism, the possibility of violence or even death, the loneliness – they were all immediately recognisable. The bride as metaphor for this dark side of marriage made aesthetic sense, people in the audience reacted noticeably to its sinister overtones.

The startling fact that a bride has such negative connotations along with all the traditional iconography of fertility, sexuality, innocence and hope is a reflection of truly remarkable changes in attitude over the last two decades. As the negative aspects of traditional marriage become even more apparent, so too has the marriage ritual which first set its rigid pattern. Many of the myths underpinning the white wedding have already become historical curiosities to most young women – the submissiveness of the bride for instance, her virginity, the notion that she is afraid of the bridal night, or alternatively, ashamed of the fact of her 'illicit' pregnancy. Thus the symbolic value of the ritual has been greatly attenuated and has very little to do with the real life and aspirations of the couple, especially the woman.

Things are rarely what they seem, and on the most basic level white now rarely stands for virginity, the fertility symbol of confetti is irrelevant to the couples who don't want children, the bride usually has no intentions of obeying her husband or being 'given away' by her father, and to agree to be bonded forever in holy matrimony has rather a hollow ring, given that one in three Australian marriages end in divorce, and very few people go near a church unless they have to.

But the fact is people still want to marry, and continue to do so, however foolish and romantic it might seem. And this being the case, a wedding ritual that has spiritual and emotional relevance seems to me to be a better start to what is a pretty risky enterprise in any case. At its most basic, believing and celebrating the contract you are entering upon means there is at least a chance that both partners have some optimism and commitment; at its most abstract such a ceremony has the capacity to define and possibly sustain a marriage. White weddings for example, possibly because they no longer perform this most important function satisfyingly, have become more and more materialistic as a form of compensation. They have become so clogged with buying and display that the couple are left exhausted and depleted by the ceremony instead of being enriched and affirmed by it. The celebration of love, the sweetness of the moment, its implication for the future is drowned out by the hectic materialism involved, further falsifying a ritual that has little or no relevance to emotional and spiritual dimensions.

The relationship between the meaningfulness and beauty of a ceremony and the ensuing success of the marriage is not exactly the stuff of mathematical certainty, but the redefinition of the whole idea of marriage, that is, equality, mutual respect, and flexibility of roles, has to start somewhere in a way that is significant to both partners. It is evident for example that ceremonies with this kind of full-bodied significance are the threads that hold together the fabric of many non-Western societies. A three-day wedding ceremony with the whole-hearted and robust involvement of an entire community is patently more meaningful that our shrivelled little shuffle at an unfamiliar altar.

There is no doubt though that in the last twenty years people have been trying to change the wedding ceremony to make it more meaningful to them. In this most personal yet universal of rituals, creative adaptation has snowballed. Everyone has read about or seen pictures of skiing, flying, scuba-diving bridal couples, couples standing on top of mountains shouting 'I do' to each other or jumping from parachutes.

In my own family, possibly an atypical microcosm, a white wedding has not been seen for over half a century. In hindsight I realise that most of our family weddings were an attempt to redefine the marriage relationship by reinventing the ceremony. This is not to say of course that they all succeeded. My parents, for instance, married in a registry office just after the war, with only two friends present; they were too preoccupied with saving the world to go through a despised bourgeois ritual that stood for everything they were rejecting. One sister married at dawn in the Auckland Domain. The genuinely lyrical and faintly pagan nature of the ceremony was intensified later on by too much French champagne being drunk too early in the morning, and there are photographs, unfortunately still extant, of the family posing in the middle of a quiet Mt Eden street in various states of Dionysiac disarray. My other sister, dressed dashingly in purple, prudently had none of the family at her registry wedding, and my brother has never married at all though he is a proud father and de facto husband.

My own wedding ceremonies were certainly reinventions, particularly the first, which we made up as we went along.

My girlfriend made my hippie dress and headdress, shopped with me for the ring and put it on my finger herself when the registry official requested it. The best man looked distinctly Dickensian in a second-hand coat and tails that were several sizes too large for him, while the groom, dressed in an old t-shirt and jeans kept very much to the background. My second, a morning ceremony in our garden, under trees I'd planted, was attended by our daughters and conducted by a woman celebrant. The secular service was written by ourselves, and the gourmet breakfast for forty friends and family whipped up by my husband before the ceremony. The celebrant cried, in fact we all did, and it was so moving my father asked her afterwards if she'd do his funeral, to which she gladly agreed, after only a momentary hesitation. As she said, it was a very optimistic, beautiful ceremony considering we'd already been living in sin for fifteen years.

The poem our ten-year-old daughter Bella wrote especially to read at the ceremony is a lovely and idiosyncratic view of weddings and marriage which is worth quoting in full. It is a sign that there is hope, among the younger generation at least, that new ceremonies can replace the stale, sexist symbolism of white weddings, reflect more honest and equal relationships and while they're about it, can also celebrate and affirm, as all good ceremonies do, the life-giving possibility of grace and love in a tired old world.

There was a young fellow of Alice Springs
And he was born in the days of the kings.
He was married, they say, on his wife's wedding day
And his favourite month was May.
He met a young girl called Ms Scott
Who was writing a novel-y plot.
And then one day on the 28th, they got together and said
'I found my pot of gold, now I want my horseshoe
with golden wings and sparkly gems.
I know I love you well.'

DEBRA ADELAIDE

According to the Book

The day before, Ernie polishes the ballroom floor. The floor is hard tallowwood the colour of wild honey, dark and smooth. The room retains all its former glory though balls are rarely held. Huge mirrors either end, wood panelling, red carpet around the perimeter, rosewood grand piano. Half close your eyes and you almost see Ginger Rogers and Fred Astaire. Poetry in motion with a sweep of swansdown and a flick of black tails.

Early in the morning I open the great glass doors to the ballroom. I am dressed in a white shirt and black skirt. My hair is drawn back and up on my head. I feel clean, pure. A priest officiating at a sacred rite. A vestal at the altar. The room is quiet, clean and empty. I breathe in deep the smell of the waxed boards. Years ago I did the flowers and the cleaning at church. It was rare to have it all alone, the church always so full of men in long garments, altar boys, the organist. I would walk in and sit in one of the middle pews for a while, breathing the atmosphere of intense peace. Here's the same air of incipience, something about to be performed, remade, blessed. Here's the very same smell of floor wax, rosewood and old carpets. Here too is the same ritual of polishing, folding, and setting flowers in vases.

Now I have to drag furniture across the gleaming floor. Tables of chipboard and stained plywood, but transformed magically when I throw over the starched white tablecloths that almost reach the floor, and set out the red velvet chairs. When I've laid out all the cutlery and glassware, polished the silver candelabra and cruets, and folded the napkins into fans, it's a dream. Three enormous crystal chandeliers capture the hue of the chairs and carpet, tossing it down again in a ruby glow.

I keep the bridal table for last, like a special morsel to savour at the end of a meal. One long straight table or a horeshoe shape depending on how many in the party. After the cloths are laid I go to the cupboard for the lace and net skirt to pin up the surround. Ruby's special domain: when she left she deliberately reorganised everything, so it takes ages to sort and find all the right pieces. At every wedding there's a spy, someone among the guests who'll report back to her and I want my arrangements to be impeccable, so she'll suffer. I'm repaying her for all the things she did to thwart me when she reigned in the function department. All the times she hid the best cutlery, the serrated steak knives, the scissors. The beautiful old Anthony Horderns' crockery with the hotel crest she tossed out when I planned using it in the dining room.

An hour of pinning, tying and tucking, and I can step back to admire the result. All flowing white net and frills, legs totally hidden from view. With the silverware and the champagne glasses and the shell serviettes it looks spectacular. Almost a pity the bridal party has to come and spoil it. Now for the pièce de résistance: the cake table in front, a small circular one with the same lace and net reaching to the floor, but I place a round mirror on the top instead. The cake comes in and is arranged in its towering glory, a silver cake knife tied with white satin ribbon positioned beside it. The mirror underneath reflects the cake and the bridal table over and over. Even with the plastic bride and groom on top, it looks magnificent. During the day, girlfriends of the bride come just to admire the cake with its flawless icing, intricate, lacy piped patterns, miniature rosettes clustered in the corners. Later we'll take the bottom layer into the kitchen to cut up, after the dessert and before the speeches have ended. This is the part I hate. Plunging the knife through the pure crust into the heart of the cake, ripping away the satin ribbon, crushing the roses, exposing the dry and tasteless interior, the extra marzipan which conceals the hollows and cavities.

The bride herself and some of her helpers arrive to check the tables are right and distribute the place cards. The floral arrangements are brought in; half the time they are too big for the tables and I have to rearrange everything, push aside ashtrays, glasses, remove candles. Then the band comes to set up, dumping speakers, amplifiers, electrifying the room with tortuous feedback before departing to bludge a few beers in the bar downstairs. There's a synthesiser, drums, guitar, a snake pit of leads and wires. Tonight they'll play 'Uptown Girl' and 'Like a Virgin' a dozen times over and the bride'll be living in an uptown world for one whole night.

Satin sheets to lie on ...

This bride's a real fusspot. Hair in curlers, full of authority on the one big day. She's all of twenty, never been married before, but has been envisaging this moment for years. She's peering at the settings, pushing a knife here, a fork there, inspecting a bread-and-butter plate, dusting off a speck of something. Putting her imprimatur on the whole thing. She lays the place cards out with deliberate emphasis, boldly rearranging or making specific requests. A new plate here, this one's chipped. Another ashtray. The place cards she's lettered herself in gold ink, decorating each with a tiny dried rosebud, an idea she had when she was about twelve. I go away to set things out in the bar, clattering loudly. She trips over, gives me back the bridal couple's champagne glasses it took me ages to find (Ruby!). Of course she's got her own, specially engraved for the day with their names and the date.

'I've had these since I was fifteen,' she says proudly.

'Teenage romance, eh?'

'Oh no. We only met last year.'

'So you just got them engraved . . .'

Her glance is scornful. 'No. I had them done then. I've known for years the day I'd get married on.'

I can't help myself. I have to ask it. 'And Steve?'

This time she tosses her head, almost tsking with contempt. 'Oh, I always knew I'd marry a Steve.'

Steve and Janine. 9th Febuary. Forever Love.

'Nice,' I say, handing them back. No point in telling someone so self-assured about a missing 'r'. No one in town can spell, especially the signwriters and trophy engravers, so it wouldn't make any difference. Besides, we've a notice downstairs saying Accomodation, another out the back mentions Correct Dress Atire, so who am I to find fault.

I slam a few more trays of glasses around, clean out the icemaker and she's back again. A table for the gifts. This time I do say something. This wasn't in the book. I could show her, but there's no point so I rearrange the tables to fit it in. I go off to fetch another white cloth and when I return she's standing there frowning, shaking her head and waving her arms about, all bouncing curlers and freshly-painted nails.

'No, not there. There.' I've put it behind the bridal table; she wants it just inside the door.

'That's where the photographer will want to set up his stuff,' I assure her.

'Well there then.' Now I shake my head. That's where the MC will have to be. Ernie appears on cue with leads and microphone and amplifier box.

I know what she really wants. A great mound of silver-wrapped presents right there in front of all the guests the whole night long. Everyone wondering if this is the set of satin sheets or that's the Bohemian crystal from her list at Grace Bros. No, not prominent enough there behind the bridal table. She looks sulky but I point out the impracticality of having it anywhere else.

'Why don't you let the lady put it there, dear?' Mother intervenes.

The lady! The wife. The lady. That's me.

'I'm sure she knows best.'

Bloody oath I do. Oops, the lady wouldn't say that. Mother and I exchange indulgent smiles. Of course I know best. I've tripped over enough tables and chairs doing these weddings to know exactly what's best. For me that is and let's face it, I'm the one who's got to work my legs off running round here all night until after one o'clock.

The bride scowls, waves Silver Rose nails around again. 'All right, all right. Have it your way. Again.' Mother stiffens, lips compress, there's a touch of filial tension here. But then mother smiles and murmurs soothingly, gives me a knowing look. Of course I understand, says the look I throw in reply. It's the bride's day. Indulge her a bit.

I've got this big blue book, my function book. I record everything. It's all here, right down to the way the serviettes have to be folded, and the exact shade. Late in the afternoon I check the lists. Only the hors d'oeuvres to fix, not so soon they'll go soggy, not so late I'm rushed for time. The bride will be having her bath now, preparing to dress. The groom is playing a game of off-season football this afternoon. He'll only just have time to get cleaned up and changed before the ceremony but after the game he'll still be here having a drink with the boys. Buttering biscuits, I fantasise about the service. He arrives late instead of her. Smelling of beer and blood, too much aftershave to disguise the fact he didn't have time to shower. A bruised face, maybe a squashed nose or black eye.

It's not a fantasy. They roll up at six-thirty nearly an hour late, the parents exchanging frowns behind backs. The groom's bursting out of his hired suit a size too small. A frilled shirt front like in the early seventies. Mauve velvet stick-on bow tie toning with the bridesmaids' dresses. And a red face, a cut just below the left eye which is nearly closed over.

And she's straight out of *Modern Bride*, bless her. The Princess Diana influence, though here it's white polyester not ivory silk. The same flounces, puffed sleeves, and sweetly scooped neckline. She's putting on a brave face, all smiles and gracious nods as she passes, forgetting or forgiving our little difference earlier in the day. Postnuptial status lends her a regal condescension. Maybe it's the dress.

Now we have the pre-dinner sherries and hors d'oeuvres. Prunes wrapped with bacon on toothpicks, angels on horseback if you knew the fifties; they asked for them specially. I sneaked in a more contemporary item to the pre-dinner cuisine. Pâté on melba toast squares. But it's the cubes of cheese speared with green cocktail onions, and the angels they really go for. Later it's the seafood cocktail, the roast and veg. There's nothing wrong with our food. I'm proud of my menus. But I'd be happy never to meet a seafood cocktail or pavlova face to face again.

It's a ritual, lacking imagination, but the passport to a timeless world of security. The white dress, though they've been living together. The hired suit, though his own clothes would feel a whole lot better. Coming here months, maybe a year, in advance. Paying a deposit, entering up the details in my book. The cake. Roses or gladioli. Baby's breath. Roast pork, pavlova, and a plastic bridal couple on top of the cake.

The entire predetermined thing. The after-dinner speeches. Telegrams. Jokes about gettin' it in or givin' her a hard time. The one about the bluebird of happiness. The keg of beer. Sugared almonds in net. The garter with its little blue rosette. Paternal posturing. 'I'm not losing a daughter but gaining a son ...' He hopes. Chicken wishbones collected for the last year and painted silver. The second keg of beer. The newly gained son red-faced and inarticulate, the first time he's ever given a speech in his life. He would like to thank youse all.

By the end of the night Janine's pretty crumpled, the white polyester stained with spumante, the veil ripped where one of the flower girls trod on it. The curls obeying the laws of gravity, the mascara smudged. Steve's taken his tie off hours ago. They go around the circle, kiss and shake hands with everyone while the band plays 'Auld Lang Syne' over and over again. Then it's upstairs to the bridal suite where there's a bottle of champagne awaiting them on melting ice. Still in his hired suit, he'll pass out on the bed while she's in the bathroom optimistically donning the satin négligée.

By one o'clock the ballroom's empty. So much for the holy ritual. The vestal's returned to sweep up the confetti and cigarette ash from the floor, gather the twisted and shredded serviettes, collect the lumps of cake icing no one ever eats. The white starched tablecloths have commonwealth country stains of pink wine, maps of beer, mountain ranges of candle wax that won't come out in the wash. The band departed right on midnight leaving a tape playing over and over again. I kick it off because if I hear 'Uptown Girl' one more time I'll scream.

The dream wedding. A few hitches maybe, but all according to the book. Diamond ring. Three-tiered cake with doric columns. Photographic proofs. White dress. A three-piece band. The bouquet pressed and preserved under glass. The glory box, with the very first tea towel she bought on special ten years ago. The velvet album. Silver and white thankyou notes. Three or four bridesmaids. Pavlova. Honeymoon on Hayman Island. The great elaborate ritual to ensure survival. The one planned months, years in advance. Planned even before she knew she was going to marry Don or Rick or Barry. Or Steve. When she was just a girl forseeing a future of joint bank accounts, crock pot dinners, men's shirts on the line.

Satin pillows to cry on ...

'Hey, isn't this one handsome?' yells out Nina over the kitchen noise.

'Who?' I'm preoccupied counting roast potatoes.

'The groom.' She stretches out the last syllable. Emphasis for an idiot.

I push through the swing door and take a look. The groom and his men are all dressed in blue cotton shirts and cream moleskins. Laredo riding boots, Akubra hats. Well they're all from the land, but the bride's wrapped in white from head to foot. I scrutinise them all but can't work it out.

'Which one?' Nina leaves her chocolate mousse and joins me at the door.

'There, in the middle, blond hair.'

'Him?'

'Yeah, what a dish eh?'

I'm stunned. He's a shortarse for a start. And he's got a mouth like a wound. Flat Joh Bjelke-Petersen-lips that spread out in a sore when he smiles. His front teeth are discoloured. Still I can see why he didn't even try to look like a bridegroom. He'd certainly appear a whole lot better on a horse. Taller too.

And she's just gorgeous. Willowy and elegant beneath the yards of froth and net. Beautiful eyes, clear and grey under black brows. But when she talks I know why he wanted to marry her. That soft Edinburgh accent. I'm in love with it, in love with her myself. Imagine living with that all your life. But what's his great appeal?

'Well, what do you reckon?' prompts Nina.

'He's repulsive.'

She's shocked, returns to her mousse.

I gaze at the bride instead. Jean Baird. Jean, Jean, roses are red, all the hills have gone green. I love it. She's twenty-two and her parents called her Jean. They came to Orange six years ago and she went to school with a lot of Sues, Juliannes, Debbies and Mandys. I take the coffee pot from Kim so I can go and fill her cup, listen to that musical accent. Oh, come out to the meadow, Jean.

She doesn't take any notice of course, she's deep in conversation with the best man while Flat Lips massages her palm as he talks to the mother on his left side. They're going to live in the other house on his parents' property and she's going to stay home after she's finished her teaching certificate. Mother nods but looks uneasy. So that's the story. Flat Lips is going to waste that beautiful accent on the sheep in the home paddock. I deliberately slop coffee into his saucer.

Down the end of the table her father looks the most out of place. The fathers usually do, having never worn suits before or given speeches. But this one's different again. He seems comfortable enough in his suit, sitting tall and straight. But there's a wistful look in his eye. He and mother recently separated but reconciled for their daughter's wedding. He's shy, lean, retiring. And that same soft accent! I'm in love with him too.

On my way back to the kitchen I pass the present table. Half the gifts are already unwrapped. Sets of cutlery, boxes of glasses, a coffee pot, the mandatory toaster. An uncoupled auntie pats a pile of matching bath towels and pillowcases, rich cream edged in satin and monogrammed with 'J' and 'T'. Must have cost a fortune.

But, 'Isn't his name Anthony?' I ask, mischief my intention.

'Oh, Jean calls him Tony. Actually ...' the auntie lowers her voice. 'I bought them on special. Three years ago at the sales. Reduced by 60 per cent. How could you pass them up?'

'Luckily she married a Tony then.'

'Oh yes. But then everything works out for Jean.' She glances proudly at her niece, whose head is momentarily bowed over her wedding cake as if saying grace. 'Or she makes it work out,' she adds, a dull note at the edge of her voice. While she talks she fingers the smooth cold satin of the pillowcases.

The next morning Douglas Baird comes down to pay the bill, dressed in khaki cotton, twisting his hat between his hands. He won't stay in a hotel again for years. He's itching to get back home, to the beloved land. All those newborn lambs and the willows down the paddock fondling the river banks with sweeping branches.

But still I'm not happy, can't you see ...

This bride comes in to order the function all on her own a few weeks beforehand. Luckily there's a date available as normally we're booked out months ahead in the wedding season. She doesn't fuss over the details, leaves most of it up to us. Scrutinises the sample menus but makes a quick choice, as if she's in a hurry or doesn't care. Or done it all before.

'This colour serviette.' She points to the aqua blue sample. 'I'm wearing that colour. And having some carnations specially dyed to match. What do you think?'

Aqua blue. It will clash horribly with the ruby red ballroom.

'Beautiful,' I say. She's probably longed for an aqua blue wedding all her life.

On the day they don't go to Cook Park for the photographs like all the other bridal parties. They come straight here from the service. Her dress is knee-length with hat instead of veil. But gloves. And bouquet. Dyed carnations, like she said. Beside her, carrying a tiny basket of flowers, is a six-year-old girl who appeared out of nowhere. She takes the bride's hand.

'Who's this?' asks the groom.

The bride looks at him hard in the face, jaw stuck out slightly.

'Me daughter.'

There are other surprises. Four weeks later when the balance of the bill is still outstanding we send him a nice but firm letter. He comes in to see us, his face crumpled. 'I paid,' he insists. 'In cash too.' The very day after the wedding he reckons. We double and triple check. It's not in the banking, not in the receipt book, not even in my blue book. You can't ask if he's sure since his honesty is so obvious. If he was trying to evade paying the bill he wouldn't be in here arguing about it, he would have just skipped town like all the others do.

'Do you remember when you came in?' I ask helpfully. 'Morning or afternoon? I could check who was on the desk then . . .'

'Oh it wasn't me personally, it was me wife. I gave her the cash to come down and settle up. Don't know what time it would have been, but.'

The scales fall, simultaneously. I look away. He looks away. Mutters something about checking with his wife. He returns the day after, pays cash. 'Sorry about all this.'

I murmur thanks, say nothing. I get the whole story from Shirley anyway who gets it from a regular in the bottom bar. Not only was there the six-year-old daughter but also a previous marriage he didn't know about. Then Bankcard, the Grace Bros account, the phone bill swollen by overseas calls. The ex-husband, in Canada. In a country town the age of chivalry isn't quite dead. He pays them all off but after six weeks she leaves him anyway.

Big long Cadillac ...

This party hasn't got a band, instead pre-recorded music from a paddock-blaster with only one speaker working. The bride's got Dolly Parton bleached hair, a white leather outfit, a complexion like a mandarin. She's up there on the platform belting out 'The Wild Side of Life' off-key and half a bar behind the music but I think from where I am in the bar at the end of the room you catch the worst of the sound effects. Either that or the guests don't care. They're singing along, swaying in their seats, a few of them twirling round the dance floor in their R M Williams boots, their plaid shirts and Akubra hats. Col, the bridegroom, is sixty-two. His third wife. He's dressed in a black Elvis jumpsuit, slashed to the navel, three gold chains adorning piebald chest hair. After the first dance the hair and chains become painfully entangled. I have to find him a pair of nail scissors so he can keep going. Long sideburns, a nose like Barry Manilow met Lionel Murphy, and eyebrows you could scrub a floor with. But Col's rich! The local truck dealer, proprietor of a carrying business, and president of the Orange Country and Western Club.

Three mature cowgirls in fringed jackets come to the bar to order brandy, lime and sodas. Slim's helping me, wearing his steer skull lanyard especially. The cowgirls wink, flashing costume jewellery, tossing back hair with regrowth, telling us what a great catch Col is, ay? Almost made of money. And generous, too. He's already bought Betty a car, a long shiny one, one of those American models with lots of cylinders and tinted windows. Wouldn't you want to be in Betty's shoes, ay? Now Betty's onto a Brenda Lee number, the earlier stuff just being a warm-up, a prelude to a whole string of Country Lady classics. It looks like anyone else'll have a tough time getting the microphone off Betty. The cowgirls nudge each other, faces cracking with smiles that stop somewhere before their eyes. When they glance at Betty their eyes glitter, disappointment and envy bouncing off across the room.

But it's her day, ay? Right. It's her wedding day, let her do whatever she likes. The middle-aged cowgirls sigh collectively, eyeing off the groom now dancing with Betty's daughter, his hand tight across her bum where Betty can't see it. Col's a red-blooded bloke. Pity about Betty's operation ten years ago, otherwise there could have been a few more little Cols bouncing into the world.

All of a sudden everyone screams and hoots. Col – good old Col! – Col's grabbed a lasso and flicked it round Betty, dragging her, microphone and all, towards him in the middle of the dance floor. Someone claims the mike as Betty is hoisted high and twirled around Col's head. The cowgirls laugh, shaking their heads.

Slim is busting with giggles but I poke him quiet. I don't mind this lot. Over by the mirror there's a bunch who've brought along their own picnic dinner. Baskets with red-checked napkins, portions of cold chicken, tubs of potato salad, iced cupcakes and fruit slice. Even thermoses of tea, but some of the older men sneak across to buy a nip of brandy to add to the brew. The Captain's fuming at the insult, we're a quality hotel with a reputation for our catering, do they think this is a day at the races or something? Well they do, some of them. They've got a transistor tuned into the last at Wentworth, in competition with the country karaoke at the other end of the room and the dying bars of 'Queen of the House'.

Anyway, I tell him, they might be hicks but they're friendly and easygoing and won't leave the place full of shit like the overgrown adolescents last week. The ones whose family's wool cheque would pay the national debt, but who climbed up to the rafters to piss on the band at one stage of the evening. I'd have these folks with their picnic hampers a hundred times over, rather than the snotty noses from the local private college.

Tailor-mades upon my back . . .

That was supposed to be the wedding of the year, last week. Sunnyfield Downs marries Maroona Hills. All that money, you think they'd have been able to afford an abortion between the two of them. But instead it's the vintage car limousines, the photographic session amid the wistaria in Cook Park, the pure silks ordered specially from Sydney, the hand-stitched Italian number sent up from Toorak, the honeymoon overseas while college is on holiday and before she starts to show. Seafood flown in on the day from the coast, wines from the Hunter Valley, cheeses and pâtés from a supplier in the city, and general rejoicing because there's not an inch of pavlova in sight, not a single slice of roast lamb or even one green cocktail onion.

But there may as well have been, by the time the oyster shells are hurled across the room like mini frisbees, the croquembouche deployed as hand grenades, the French champagne shaken and sprayed across the groomsmen, and the remainder of the drinks recycled as a shower coming down on the unsuspecting musicians. I catch the best man out across the hall pissing into a pot plant. Reckons he couldn't find the Gents only two doors away but maybe they don't teach them to read at these colleges though you'd think, being an agriculture student, he could distinguish between a potted palm and a urinal.

But still I want you to set me free . . .

Then one chilly afternoon when the wind has shaken the white wistaria over the lawn in the park like an early snowfall, I take the utility and head out of town. We've run out of Quelltaler Hock and none of the liquor stores in town has it so someone must fetch it from the warehouse in Bathurst. 'Can't we serve them something else?' I ask, but the Captain shakes his head and I know he's right. Even my blue book has it down and this evening's wedding is for someone who knows his wines so there's no getting away with another. Not like the time we served bulk port bottled in the kitchen with labels the Captain ran off on the office photocopier. They quaffed it from schooner glasses and asked for more.

'Do you want to get it, or mind the desk?' asks the Captain. He gave Kim the afternoon off and Binge is still on holiday.

This always happens when you're short-staffed. I don't want either since I'm supposed be setting out the bar upstairs but I choose the trip to Bathurst. Anything to get away for an hour or so.

'I'll take Trevor for the run.' There's no need to call him. As soon as he hears the ignition he appears from nowhere and leaps into the back. All the way to Bathurst he stands right on the edge and leans over to lick my ear through the open window while I try and tune in the crackling radio to the local station.

There's this long straight stretch for a while and the wind is roaring through my right ear and the dog is slipping and straining to stay upright when I see this white flag fluttering way ahead. But it's not a flag. In seconds I'm close enough to see it's the wrong shape and it seems to have arms. Arms flapping and waving at the same time as trying to hold billowing folds of white.

I pull up on the gravel as slowly as I can but there's no controlling the dust. She throws back her white veil and peers into the cabin. Then I see she's wearing little headphones, attached to a portable cassette player at her belt. She's got a high brow and complicated hazel eyes.

'I'm only going as far as Bathurst.'

'That will do.'

'Hop in then. You'll crush your gown though.'

'It doesn't matter.' She tosses a small suitcase into the back, gathers up the drapes of her wedding dress and tucks herself into the utility. She's wearing black lace-up shoes instead of satin slippers. Under the veil her hair is long and dark. She smiles, removes the headphones of her cassette player, then throws an arm along the back of the seat to face the wind as I drive away.

'Going far?'

'All the way.'

'Sydney, you mean?'

'Yeah, maybe.' We've both been shouting, with the wind. Then she turns to me. 'I'm marrying Marvin,' she explains, smiling.

Ah. The Ponds advertisement.

'Does he know it yet?'

We laugh, she in a deep full-throated gesture with her head thrown back, me keeping an eye on the potholed road.

'Probably not.'

She flicks open the cassette player.

'What were you listening to?'

Instead of replying she turns my radio off and slips the cassette into the utility's player. A few clicks and whirrs then we're bumping along with the wind whipping our hair, her veil, and the voice of Jeanne Pruett pouring from the speakers.

Satin sheets to lie on, satin pillows to cry on
But still I'm not happy, can't you see ...

She's got a suitcase full of the essentials, she tells me. Lace underwear, Swiss cotton hankies, pearl pink négligée, a silver-backed hairbrush with matching hand mirror. This a family heirloom, she explains. And a grey silk going away outfit with matching shoes.

'But you won't be using your trousseau now,' I say. She must have thought I sounded disappointed.

'Oh, it will all come in handy eventually,' she says reassuringly. 'I mean, I'm all prepared now, aren't I?'

I think about it. The white dress, the veil, the ring, the suitcase in the back. Only one thing lacking, but it seems he's the least of the arrangements.

When I let her off at the railway station she rubs Trevor on the head and accepts a lick. I want to know if she's right for money but she only smiles, shakes her head, waves thanks and goodbye as she disappears towards the platform with that veil lifting up behind in the wind.

On my way back from collecting the wine I pass the station and she's out the front, waving at me to stop.

'I forgot something,' she says twisting at her third finger. 'Give him this will you? He may as well have it back.'

I put the diamond ring in my pocket and turn for the Orange road. Halfway home, I realise I forgot something too.

But it's too far to turn back now, so I switch the cassette player on again and spend the rest of the journey listening to that country gold.

I've found another man who can give me more than you can
Though you've given me everything money can buy . . .

Back at the Hotel Albatross while I park the vehicle I only now realise we won't need the Quelltaler Hock after all. I am sitting at the front desk when the Captain reappears with the news.

Upstairs it's the groom who's devastated. Already in silk tie and Eau Sauvage aftershave, he's come to explain to the Captain. His mother's there, repacking the five tiers of cake. His father is strutting. He's a doctor, a member of Rotary, on the hospital board. He always knew she was flighty, suspect. He never thought she was good enough for his son. The note is waved around like public property. The Captain is too discreet to look. I help mother with the cake, dismantle the floral arrangements, wishing the doctor would go and strut somewhere else, leave us to our women's work. But he wants to nurse his anger publicly and flourishes the note under the Captain's nose. Read it, he insists. Confirm this girl's utter worthlessness.

Neat sloping handwriting. On the back of a florist's card. It could almost be a message of greetings. 'I am going away to be married. Hoping you are not too inconvenienced. Best wishes.' It was returned with a bunch of flowers.

I remember now she was not carrying a bouquet.

'What the hell does the girl think she's doing?' the doctor demands of no one in particular. I feel obliged to offer an explanation.

'She's marrying Marvin.'

'What! Marvin who?'

But I can't answer that one.

'Who is this woman?' The doctor looks me up and down like a curiosity. The Captain steers me to the door, abandoning the atmosphere of puzzled outrage.

Like a fire, the gossip is through the hotel and the town, gathering vigour and detail along the way. She had another man all along. In Bathurst. In Dubbo. In Sydney. She drained their newly-opened joint bank account. She pinched his car, the BMW his rich dad gave him last year. She stole the tickets to Hong Kong meant for the honeymoon. She was already married to someone else. Her family has a history of madness. They lived all alone up there on the ridge, never saw a visitor from one year to the next. She's marrying a bloke called Marvin someone-or-other. The mother was knocked up by her own father. She must be an inbred.

The air's thick with tension you could cut with a wedding cake knife. I return to mind the desk downstairs, then I remember the message. Maybe I shouldn't be laughing but I give the ring to the Captain with instructions and as he heads back upstairs I say I'll put a bottle of the hock on ice.

Someone may as well celebrate.

SUSAN MITCHELL

The Wedding

No one today would understand why my mother and father thought it such a tragedy that I, Sarah, their one and only child should be marrying Timothy. In all other respects he would have been considered a suitable match. Except that he was a Roman Catholic. They insisted on including the word 'Roman' whenever they spoke of it because it conjured up the foreign: the Popery, the incense, the candles, the statues with bleeding hearts and trickling blood.

Not that they were religious in the sense of church going. But church to Jean and Jack meant the Church of Christ. A spare hall, no altar, long pews with no carved adornment and nothing on the walls except a clock and an honour roll of those fallen in the wars. At the far end almost hidden from view was the baptismal bath into which pubescent girls and boys were fully immersed once they had declared Jesus Christ as their Saviour. Both Jean and Jack had been dunked when they were 12 but much to the dismay of Aunt Maureen who unlike the others had never left the Church even though she had left the State, I had never succumbed. Not that I hadn't tried my best to feel the spirit of the Lord come into my heart and fill me with the absolute faith of the convert. I had tried. I had stood steadfastly and earnestly in those plain pews among those plain folk and promised myself that if 'the call' came I would follow it. But to the deep disappointment of my Sunday School teachers, the Church Elders and the despair of my Aunt Maureen I had never felt the urge to leave my seat on a Sunday night. It was always at the evening service that the minister, dressed in a simple, badly cut, double-breasted navy suit, pleaded and implored when persuasion was not enough. Every Sunday night some one in a highly excitable state would succumb and walk down that long aisle to the front where the minister, beaming like an encyclopaedia salesman who had just clinched a deal, grasped both hands in his unless she changed her mind and fled and said, 'Praise be to the Lord, that he has chosen this night to come into your heart, sister'.

I didn't have any sisters or brothers and was convinced that if I had to choose someone as surrogate kin it would certainly not be anyone in the local congregation. Never had I seen such dour people who so consistently talked of the joy that having Jesus in your heart gave you. The women wore no make-up, had faces like blunt axes and haircuts to match. Among my age group I was finally the only one who hadn't been baptised on a Sunday morning, dressed in a plain white surgical robe and a bathing cap. I was the only one who hadn't emerged from that cold white porcelain gasping for air to the sounds of the congregation singing 'Up from the grave he arose', and they were not pleased. I felt their eyes like sharp instruments pricking and prodding me to leave my seat. I stood firm. So firm that one Sunday night the double-breasted navy suit appeared before me and said, 'we are very disappointed in you, Sarah'. And I knew then that I would never return.

Ten years later when Sarah and Timothy had to decide whether they would have a formal wedding and if so where they should have it, the Church of Christ was never a consideration. Nor was the local Catholic Church, Timothy having declared himself an atheist to Jean and Jack who weren't quite sure whether that wasn't in fact worse than being an RC. Both families pleaded with them to at least have a 'proper' wedding even if it wasn't to be in a church. And so it was that in December 1968 in Adelaide, in Jean and Jack's back garden, Sarah and Timothy were to be married by a celebrant. Like most compromises it pleased no one.

Jack had roped off the chooks who normally roamed among the vegetable garden by attempting to camouflage the lot with several layers of striped canvas attached by ropes to tent pegs. He'd had to improvise like this in the desert during the war he told Jean who was expressing her concern that he hadn't rung the proper tent people. It wasn't that he was mean; he just didn't see any point in wasting money on unnecessary frills. And after all, he had paid for a large marquee which he and a few mates had erected while consuming many bottles of beer. Erection, it appeared, was extra. The one thing he didn't mind paying for was the keg. I did have a battle with him over the champagne which he insisted was all just sweet bubbly anyway. He had taken the initiative and ordered a hundred bottles of pink Barossa Pearl.

'Match the bridesmaids' dresses too,' he added in a tone he thought would clinch the argument. My two bridesmaids, Penny and Jenny, had in fact chosen a hot pink shot taffeta which I'd argued might be too 'hot' given the month but they insisted, especially as it would match the pink Sobranies we were all addicted to smoking. Penny said it would also come in handy at the next bad taste ball; after all she *was* a communist, didn't approve of bourgeois celebrations and was a veteran of three anti-Vietnam demonstrations. Jenny was Timothy's younger sister who was still at High School and believed anything Penny said.

My mother had spent the last month with a mouth full of pins. A milliner before she married, she had insisted on making my veil and the pins prevented her from telling me what she really thought about my marriage. But the eyes said what the pinched lips repressed. As Timothy was the eldest of seven his mother, although disapproving, was relieved to get him out of her overcrowded war-service house, and at least they didn't have to pay for the reception. Apart from discussing guest lists and honeymoon arrangements Timothy and I had hardly spoken to each other. Both of us were finishing off the teaching year and had marking, school reports and staff farewells at our separate schools.

The day was suddenly upon us. At six a.m. my father brought me a cup of tea and the news that it was going to be a 'real stinker, well over the forty degree mark'.

'Oh great,' I mumbled feeling a rim of sweat behind the beginning of my hair line.

'Just as well I ordered that extra keg. I bet those Micks will drink till the cows came home, especially when it's free.'

'Yeah, right Dad,' I mumbled, already taking the line of least resistance.

'Cheer up me girl – supposed to be the happiest day of your life.'

'I know, Dad, just give me a chance to make up. Where's Mum?'

'Still in bed. Says she thinks she's got one of her migraines coming on.'

I spent the morning shaving my legs, scraping my armpits, plucking my eyebrows and trimming my pubes. No stray hair was safe. Except for the tresses that would eventually have to be teased within an inch of their lives in order to form the beehive. Penny and Jenny arrived at noon bearing bags of cold champagne and hair spray. As we sipped and teased and sprayed each other's hair, bayonetting the wayward clumps with French pins, I entertained a sneaking suspicion that this might be fun after all.

'Tim's got the most humungus hangover,' volunteered Jenny. 'He was chundering all morning and Mum said she'd have to call the doctor if he didn't stop.'

'Really.'

'Dad said it was just as well the wedding was outside, he could run behind the daisy bush,' she chuckled.

By the time the three of us had finished with our busbies we could have done the Changing of the Guards at Buckingham Palace. My mother had finally risen from her bed and was encased in a mauve silk dress with a matching hat which almost covered the expression on her face.

'Come on, Jean, you're not going to a hanging,' said Jack, looking very jolly in a new suit.

'Do your top button up and straighten your tie,' was my mother's response.

'Jeez, it's a scorcher! Give a bloke a break.'

'Jack, this is your only daughter's wedding,' continued my mother, her voice teetering on the edge of a sob.

'All right, all right, just don't go getting over-emotional. There'll be enough of that when your sisters arrive.'

'Don't you start about my sisters.' The colour of her face was beginning to mirror her hat.

'Come on, you two, give it a rest today, please.'

They both disappeared up the passage mumbling to themselves while my bridesmaids helped me into my dress, which had daisies made from guipure lace appliqued over the bodice. Too much champagne and no airconditioning meant that the entire dress felt as though it was appliqued to my body. Layers of pancake make-up barely hid the fact that our complexions matched the taffeta in the bridesmaids' dresses, not to mention the overflowing ashtray of Sobranie stubs. I was beginning to feel more than a little nauseated.

My father knocked on the door, entered, pronounced us all the most beautiful girls he had ever seen, then asked Penny and Jenny to leave us alone. Closing the door behind them, he hugged me so hard I thought my bones would break. When he finally pulled away I saw tears in the corners of his eyes. He took out a clean white handkerchief and blamed the heat.

'Now listen, sweetheart. Everything's ready. The tent looks a picture. They've done us proud with the flowers. There's enough food to feed the Arabs. Everyone's here, all your mother's sisters, even mad Maureen has flown in from Sydney specially. The Mick rellies look a bit on the rough side and *he* looks like death warmed up.' He paused and lowered his voice.

'But sweetheart, the Holden's out the front, here are the keys. You can still make a run for it. Don't worry about everyone else. I'll get the grog going and they won't even care after a few.'

He was serious.

'Thanks Dad, but I'm determined to see it through. I do love Timothy,' I said with more conviction that I felt.

'I only want what's best for you, Sarah.'

'I know that, Dad. Let's get on with it shall we.'

As we emerged into the dazzle of the three o'clock sun, the University Jazz Band played a barely recognisable version of 'Here Comes the Bride' and, feeling the wet patch already forming in the crook of Dad's arm where I was gripping him, my lobster bridesmaids and I entered the stifling marquee. Timothy was white, clammy and shaky as he took my hand.

'Just try not to throw up,' I whispered through smiling clenched teeth. He did not respond. The celebrant, whom I had never met but Timothy had assured me did most of the university students, was throwing his hands around in a dramatic manner and his lisp didn't help the effeminate rhythms of his syntax.

'Tharah, do you take Timothy to be your lawful wedded huthband?'

Every question was underlined by an exaggerated upward inflection. I could hear Penny sniggering behind me.

'Did you have to get Liberace to marry us?' I hissed. Timothy appeared to be suffering from lockjaw.

My mother's sob punctuated the pronouncement of 'huthband and wife'.

With that our sibilant celebrant grabbed me, brushing his lips on both sides of my face and then repeated the process with Timothy, this time lingering noticeably longer. The band struck up and I heard my father say, 'Anyone for a beer?'

Perhaps it was the heat but no one felt like eating the salmon vol-au-vents, asparagus rolls, potato salad and cold collations which had been laid out on trestles at the back of the marquee. The noise level seemed to rise rapidly. Timothy and I did the rounds of the rellies introducing each other to a series of wet hands and dry lips. I noticed my father doing a roaring trade at the keg and my mother fanning herself with a lace hankie and staring into the middle distance.

A voice at my elbow said, 'Well, Sarah, married but never baptised.' Aunt Maureen, looking more upholstered than usual in a matching floral ensemble, was not smiling.

'Will the kiddies be brought up Catholic or Communist?'

Before I could answer a microphone crackled to life. My aunt Sybil called everyone to attention.

'Timothy's family may not know but Sarah's family has a family song and I and my sisters would like to sing it. Come on girls, join in with me. Out the front here.' And there they were, even my mother. Trained in the choruses of the Church of Christ they made up in volume and trills what they lacked in harmony. They were followed by a red-faced bloke in a fawn polyester suit.

'Tim's family also has a family song. Do you know "When Irish eyes are smiling?" he asked the band.'

It wasn't long before Uncle Bill had pushed his way to the front, grabbed the microphone and was singing 'Three Old Ladies Locked in the Lavatory'. Somewhere in the middle of 'Elizabeth Carter, the most phenomenal farter' my mother swooned against one of the tent poles in either a real or imagined faint. Unfortunately the skills Father had learnt at Tobruk had failed him. Mother collapsed onto the lawn taking the marquee with her as she went. The elaborate arrangement of striped canvas attached to the fence which held the chooks at bay followed suit. The noise and chaos which erupted as the terrified hens squawked and flapped among the guests and the people who were attempting to re-position the marquee was nothing compared to the siren of the approaching ambulance. Aunt Maureen who had gone inside to spend a penny had seen it all through the kitchen window and immediately dialled 999. She always thrived on a crisis.

At ten minutes to seven that evening we were standing on the platform of the Adelaide Railway Station hugging goodbye to those of our friends and relatives who could still stand up and hadn't been admitted to Casualty.

'Just as well the keg was in the shed,' said my father, trying to put on a brave face. My mother was wearing dark glasses and a cloth bandage where once the mauve hat had so smartly sat. Timothy and I were catching the Overland to Melbourne where we would board the *Fairstar* to London and return who knew when. The world was before us.

As I threw my wedding bouquet into the sea of waving hands my mother's mouth opened, suddenly pin free. Her voice soared above the bouquet and the din, 'I'll be dead before you get back.'

CAROLINE BAUM

The Dress

On Julia's first day at the magazine there was a calico sachet of sugar-coated almonds on her desk.

'What's this?' she asked her secretary, slipping one into her mouth and enjoying its pebble smoothness. 'A sample from an advertiser?'

'No, Beatrice got married at the weekend. She brought them in this morning.'

Julia went round to the art director's desk to thank her and introduce herself. 'I'd love to see the photos,' she added.

'You will – they're in the next issue,' laughed Beatrice, with the confidence of a new bride.

There seemed to be a wedding every month in the office. They were announced and celebrated with champagne and a particularly evil chocolate cake called Othello (not the most auspicious choice, thought Julia, but no one else commented on the irony and anyway, the ganache really was excellent, they certainly weren't cheating with gelatine to achieve that mousse texture). Editorial meetings invariably turned into discussions about gift lists, honeymoon locations and, of course, caterers. Anyone would think this was a bridal magazine, thought Julia, as she settled into editing an article on wild mushrooms.

Her secretary came in with an envelope. 'From Susan.'

Julia took the envelope, tearing it open briskly. Why should the editor be writing to her privately, instead of in a memo? She had not been there long enough for a pay rise. Was there some bad news afoot? A takeover? A change at the top? A resignation? She read aloud: 'To celebrate the recent wedding of our art director, Beatrice, who has now joined the ranks of all our senior editorial staff as a married woman, I am giving a small dinner at home on Saturday March 30th at 8 p.m. Wives only. Wear your wedding dress. Photo albums optional. Susan.'

Julia's heart sank.

'Don't forget that as well as choosing your dress you've got to choose Dad's,' Richard reminded Julia on his way to work.

'Do you really think he won't mind?'

'You've already asked and he's said yes. I bet I know just which one you'll pick too – the one with the most gold on it. Just remember, he walks up the aisle ahead of you. You don't want to let him upstage you.'

Julia smiled, enjoying the fact that Richard recognised her tendency to go for the gaudy. It's the Jewish princess in you, he said.

They are to be married in two months, and Richard's father, the Lord Bishop, is to perform the ceremony. He has already shown Julia the cupboard where he keeps his starched surplices, rows of dog collars, purple mantles and sashes and, for high feast days, copes with matching mitres made from his wife's discarded evening dresses. There is a particularly garish, abstractly patterned one, brought as a gift by a visiting African church leader, that reminds Julia of the graffiti she sees on trains, and another edged in the kind of braid Julia has only ever seen on pelmets. But there is one that she thinks will do: it is turquoise silk, edged in gold. With that, his silver crook and knuckleduster amethyst ring, the Bishop will, thinks Julia, dazzle and daunt his audience. She wants him to be as shining as an icon.

'So, have you thought about how I should look?' Julia asks Richard at the end of the day.

'I want it to be a surprise.'

'But anything specific? I'm going shopping tomorrow with Alice.'

'You know what suits you better than I do, you're the best dressed woman I know. What can I tell you?'

'Well, which bits of me do you think I should show off?'

He pauses, looks her over critically. 'Your neck, your shoulders, your waist.'

She is satisfied. They are the very things she had thought of.

'We had the rings made in Florence, where Mark proposed,' said Alice, offering her left hand for inspection. The band of gold is beaten and worked to an antique finish, carved with twisting vines of acanthus and ivy. Julia is impressed by Alice's attention to detail. They have been poring over her wedding album; in each photo she is a radiant Medici bride, her thick Titian hair coiled into a heavy braid, standing at the altar in her bodiced, embroidered, slashed and puffed-sleeve dress of white and gold brocade.

'My mother's dressmaker made it,' says Alice, pointing out the boned seams and the pearl beading along the hem. 'It took eight metres of fabric and six fittings. I copied the design from a Botticelli portrait of a noblewoman. Have you got a theme?'

'Not really,' sighed Julia. 'I just don't know where to start.'

'A theme really helps. Luckily, both Mark and I are mad about the Italian renaissance, so we turned the wedding into a period pageant. Everyone said it was the most original wedding they had been to, and we carried it through, right down to the music and the food.'

Julia wondered what theme she and Richard could share. Their love of opera perhaps? No, too kitsch, turning up as

Carmen (look what happened to her), or Tosca (and her) or Madam Butterfly (not to mention her).

'Richard proposed during the dinner break in *Tristan and Isolde* at La Scala,' says Julia, remembering how, afterwards, they had sat leaning forward in the dress circle box which had cost them a fortune on the black market through the hotel doorman, with tears streaming shamelessly down their faces during the *Liebestod*.

'Mark hates Wagner,' said Alice, rising to make a pot of tea. As for Julia's private passion, Russia, Richard hadn't even been there yet, so it was not as if she could appear looking like a Grand Duchess in a troika flanked by cossacks, wearing a white Siberian fox fur toque and elaborate frogging on a fitted jacket, with balalaikas strumming in the choir stalls. No, not suitable for a summer wedding in Australia to a Sydney architect. If she had wanted that kind of Romanov-style romance, she should have married an émigré white Russian count who intended one day to reclaim a turquoise palace on the Fontanka canal in St Petersburg.

Alice returned with the tea. 'Well, if you want a hand choosing the dress, I'd love to help.'

Julia accepted the offer gratefully, though they hardly knew each other. Alice was the mutual friend of a friend she had left behind in England. After four weeks of playing Scrabble with Richard in a serviced apartment, Julia had rung Alice and they had fallen easily into conversation about how much they missed Marks & Spencer – especially the food and underwear sections. She was the only suitable candidate for Julia's mission in a new city where she had yet to find her bearings, never mind her favourite shops. In London, I would have done this with my mother, thought Julia, and her heart pinched.

She is walking up the aisle on her father's arm, following the bishop. The amethyst in the centre of his mitre, twice the size of the one on his finger, catches the light from the altar candles, The gold thread of the cope sparkles. The bishop is ablaze, incandescent in his magnificence.

'Maybe it's an American custom,' said her secretary, looking over the letter Julia had handed her.

'I don't think so. I think they have something called showers, this is something that Susan has dreamt up all by herself.'

'Isn't it a great idea?' said Stephanie, the recipe editor, now in Julia's office, waving her copy of the letter. 'Thank God I'm only three months gone, I should just be able to fit into mine,' she added, patting her stomach where a bulge has yet to appear.

'Should be a hoot. Wonder what Liza will wear,' she said, rolling her eyes.

Julia remembered Liza's wedding, even though she was not there, was not even on the magazine then. But the event, which had been two years in the planning according to some, took up six pages in the autumn issue and was endlessly referred to as the yardstick by which all other weddings must be measured, confirming Liza's status as style editor.

Julia had studied the photographs closely and felt a stab of envy, more than one stab in fact – not about the money that Liza was patently marrying, not even about the scale or glamour of the occasion, no, it was something else, something harder to define, she thought now, remembering the detail that had most stuck in her mind: Liza had been to Paris and bought two wedding dresses from two of the most expensive designers in the world.

'I wanted to be able to change my mind at the last minute,' she was quoted as saying in the tabloid press.

Julia reaches into the back of the wardrobe, pulls out the pink satin hanger covered with a large white plastic bag. A body bag, she says to herself, untying the ribbon. It is six years since she has seen the dress. She lays it on the bed. She does not recognise it. She goes to the coffee table in the sitting room, reaching under its surface to the concealed shelf for the photo album bound in marbled paper bought in Milan, on the same day as Richard had proposed – over wild mushroom risotto, come to think of it. She opens it, turns the pages slowly. She does not recognise herself.

Alice and Julia start in the dressmaking department, Alice turning the pages of the pattern books, groaning in unison with Julia at the creations for Mills & Boon heroines and Laura Ashley victims. Occasionally Alice hesitates, lingering over a dress that has 'possibilities'.

'Something with detailing in the back is a nice idea,' she says, pointing to two designs, one with a bustle, another with a row of tiny covered buttons running down into the small of the spine. 'It gives the congregation something to look at.'

Julia agrees, but rejects the dresses. 'Too feminine, too romantic for me.' Alice shrugs.

Upstairs, in bridal wear, dresses cling to the walls like shy girls at a school dance. Julia feels the boning in their bodice, strokes the satin sheen of their skirts, but cannot bring herself to try even one on.

'None of them are quite me,' she says, before it occurs to her that Alice is a stranger and has no idea of what 'me' Julia might be referring to. More disturbingly, she has become a stranger to herself and does not know what she is looking for.

Staring past the view of the harbour from her cookbook-lined office, Julia admitted to herself that she realised she had made a mistake on the morning of the wedding.

When Julia had shown the dress to her mother, all she had said was 'Of course we'll pay for it,' like a man offering to pay for an abortion. When her best friend and bridesmaid, Lulu, arrived from London, Julia did not take the dress out of its box, saying only 'I wrote to you about the colour, so that you wouldn't wear anything that clashes.' They had never discussed it, in the six years since.

And then, finally, the last straw, walking up the aisle behind Richard's father, looking, in his finery, as glamorous as sin. She realised that she had let him steal her thunder.

I have engineered my own sabotage, she thought, under the

brim of her pale straw hat trimmed with velvet gardenias. His dress is more beautiful than mine.

Now she would do it all so differently. She would wear a dress as simple as a Greek column, or something a little ambiguous, androgynous even – she smiled, imagining the impact of herself walking behind the bishop, this time in a black tuxedo with satin lapels, hair slicked back, diamond stars in her ears, a white lily in her buttonhole. She looked down at the album in her lap, the photographs of the stranger in the cream lace scattered with seed pearls, her waist sashed in a broad band of ivory silk, with matching full underskirts that rustled as she moved, bare shoulders gleaming in the candlelight. 'Your neck, your shoulders, your waist,' Richard had said and she had agreed and found a dress, that, if nothing else, did fit those requirements.

But she did not want them to see her like that. I am a different woman now, I cannot let them see how I was before, when I had lost myself. I shall tell them the wedding album is in England, with my parents, that's easy enough. But I can't wear the dress.

She thought of Stephanie, whose wedding photos she had already seen, after dinner one evening, when their husbands were still lingering at the table, dicussing the merits of plunger versus filter coffee.

Stephanie had placed the album in Julia's lap, leaning in close, providing a running commentray like the voice-over in a documentary. The album began with some provocative photographs of Stephanie in her underwear, breasts pouting out of an expensive French bra as she stretched out her finger tips for her nails to be painted; over the page, her hair was being piled on top of her head in an artfully disarranged tumble, and a make-up artist ('The best decision I ever made,' said Stephanie conspiratorially, as if Julia could still benefit from this advice) was outlining her lips in pencil.

Further on came pictures of Stephanie dressed – nothing long for her: there was no way she was going to hide any more of that body than was necessary. The dress, an Italian sheath of lavender-coloured lycra, barely grazed the tops of her thighs.

'Not many brides manage to look sexy on their wedding day,' Julia had murmured, closing the album.

Stephanie continued to dress in bum bandages at the office; it was a trademark look they now all teased her about. 'You won't be able to get away with it for much longer,' they warned her, as her pregnancy progressed. At least she's consistent, thought Julia. How would her colleagues reconcile the fake nostalgia of her dress, more like a period costume from a remake of *Gone with the Wind*, with the woman she was today?

She thought of Liza, who had apparently remade herself totally through an act of will, had changed her name from Eliza to the more fashionable Liza, done a cooking course in Venice with Lorenza de Medici and married a lawyer. She thought of the two wedding dresses and wondered how Liza had made her final choice and which dress she would turn up in for dinner.

She went to the bed, picked up the dress, put it on the hanger, slipped it back into its shroud, reached as far into the wardrobe as she could and hung the dress where it had been, undisturbed, for the past six years, found her car keys and went into the city.

'All set for tonight?'

'Of course, I wouldn't miss it for the world,' replied Julia in the bright tone she reserved for Susan.

'You know, I almost wish I hadn't made it wives only – your husband is so divine.'

Julia wondered whether anyone, apart from editors and actors, referred to people these days as divine.

'So's yours,' she replied politely, though it was not what she thought. She had only met Frank once and found him boorish.

'But Frank's not like Richard, he's not interested in talking about food, or books, and I can't get him to come to the opera with me,' sighed Susan.

Julia smiled at the compliment though it was one she heard

over and over again. How is it that I managed to do something as complex as pick the right man, but I couldn't do something as simple as pick the right dress, she asked herself. Stephanie put her head round the door.

'You leaving early?'

'Not planning to – why?'

'Liza is. She's going to the hairdresser before dinner. Have you tried on your dress? I can only just squeeze into mine, I won't be able to eat any dessert, unless Susan makes one of her famous pear souffles.'

'Mine's okay,' said Julia, 'at least, it was when I tried it on last week.'

'Mark was going to give Richard a ring and see if he wanted to have dinner tonight, seeing as we are. I think he was thinking of take away and a video.'

'Richard's away on business, otherwise that would've been perfect,' said Julia.

'Oh well, never mind. Wonder where Susan has parked Frank and the kids for the evening – bet he's not too thrilled at having a hen party at home.'

Julia stood in the drive of Susan's home, making final adjustments. She buttoned her jacket and inhaled the polleny scent of the lily in her buttonhole before ringing the bell. Now I'm ready to walk up the aisle, she told herself, as she saw Susan's shadow appear through the frosted glass panes of the front door, coming to lead her to the altar.

LOIS ELLIS
AND SARA HARDY

Rosie Fingered Dawn

Rosie Fingered Dawn loosely follows a film script structure. The few technical screenplay terms used are explained below:

EXT. exterior.
INT. interior.
POV point of view.
ANOTHER ANGLE a variation of the same shot, from another angle.
A SERIES OF ANGLES the subject of the shot seen from many angles.
MOVING SHOT the camera follows the movement of something or someone through the space.
FAVOURING the camera favours the subject of the shot, i.e. it draws the eye to the person or thing that needs to be focussed on most.
CUT TO used here to indicate the sharp move from one scene to another.
LONG SHOT the subject of the shot is in the distance.

EXT. A ROSY FINGERED DAWN. A REMOTE AIR STRIP, NORTHERN AUSTRALIA

The ground is wet, after a storm. All is quiet, peaceful. Hold. We hear the ROAR *of a twin-engine light aircraft.*

CUT TO:

EXT. THE LIGHT AIRCRAFT

MOVING SHOT

The aircraft gathering speed for take off.

INT. THE AIRCRAFT

ROSIE *at the controls. She is in her twenties, attractive, headstrong, but her face shows signs of stress, fatigue. She has very short, dark hair.*

EXT. THE AIRCRAFT FLIES TOWARDS THE RISING SUN

CUT TO:

INT. DAWN'S BEDROOM

In half light, the blades of a ceiling fan slowly rotate.

ANOTHER ANGLE

DAWN *lies in bed, watching the fan. It's early morning. Dawn's face is reflective. She's in her mid-twenties. She's wide awake.*

ANOTHER ANGLE

Dawn in the bed, AMY, *a dog, is asleep at her feet. Amy suddenly wakes, looks alert. We hear a dull* HAMMERING *sound.*

Dawn, dressed in a robe, opens the FRENCH DOORS *and walks on to the* BALCONY.

EXT. THE FRONT LAWN OF 'MERRIVALE', A PALATIAL HOMESTEAD ON A CATTLE STATION, SOUTHERN QUEENSLAND

From Dawn's POV *we see a group of workers erecting a blue and white marquee. Another group assemble a dance floor. There are stacks of chairs and tables. A general hubbub of preparation to cater for a large gathering of people. A refrigerated truck arrives, its headlights still on.* SUZIE MEADOWS, *the wedding co-ordinator, meets the truck. The sun continues to rise.*

EXT. THE BALCONY

Dawn is leaning on the balcony rail, she looks up into the sky.

INT. THE LARGE KITCHEN OF THE HOMESTEAD

A SERIES OF ANGLES

We follow SHIRLEY *as she moves amongst catering staff who are busy preparing for a wedding. She is in her early sixties, rotund, energetic, excited. She is Dawn's mother. People organise cutlery, glasses, linen, crockery, food, flowers etc. Shirley tries to help but gets in their way. In the far corner, an* ASIAN *man quietly fashions carrots into roses etc. The phone* RINGS. *Shirley answers.*

SHIRLEY: Hallo, yes? ... Who? ... Just a moment. (shouting) Is there anyone here called Dangles? Dangles!

The Asian waves his knife in the air and smiles.

ASIAN: For me I think.

The Asian crosses to the phone as ROY *backs in through the door with a trolley loaded with boxes of champagne. Roy is Dawn's father, late sixties.*

SHIRLEY: Not in here Roy! In the cool room.

ROY: That woman said to bring it in here.

SHIRLEY: Well she's wrong! Cool room. You shouldn't be doing that anyway. Why are we paying all these people!

EXT. BACK AREA OF THE HOMESTEAD

Roy pushes the trolley out of the back door as Dawn walks past on her way to the stables. Amy follows. Dawn wears jeans and a shirt.

ROY: Just as well you're the last of the litter! Never again.

DAWN: It's just a quiet country wedding Dad, just like we said.

They smile at each other, sharing the joke.

ROY: That Meadows woman is looking for you.

DAWN: She's in for a long ride then. Any news of Rosie?

ROY: (shaking his head) She'll be here.

DAWN: Better be.

Dawn walks toward the STABLES *with Amy at her heels.*

SHIRLEY: Dawn! There's an international call for Luke, can you tell him!

DAWN: Mum, it's bad luck to see the groom before the ceremony. Surely Suzie Meadows has told you that!

Dawn laughs as she continues on towards the stables. Roy grins.

SHIRLEY: But it's New York!

CUT TO:

EXT. BUSH LAND, MID MORNING

MOVING SHOT

Dawn gallops on a horse through the bush, one arm around Amy who rides up in the saddle with her.

EXT. THE AIRCRAFT TRAVELS SOUTH EAST, MID MORNING

INT. ROSIE AT THE AIRCRAFT CONTROLS

Rosie looks tired. She blinks to try and wake herself up. She suddenly sings very loudly.

ROSIE: 'The sun has got her hat on,
hip hip hip hooray,
The sun has got her hat on
and she's coming out to play'

CUT TO:

EXT. A ROCK POOL

A large splash as Dawn dives in naked. She swims under

water, then surfaces. Amy guards Dawn's clothes.

INT. THE MAIN BATHROOM IN THE HOMESTEAD

At the basin a HAIRDRESSER *is washing Shirley's hair. Suzie Meadows bursts in.*

SUZIE MEADOWS: Everything is under control.

SHIRLEY: Good.

SUZIE MEADOWS: Except we've lost the bride and there's still no sign of the bridesmaid.

SHIRLEY: What!

SUZIE MEADOWS: Don't worry, plenty of time. Keep smiling!

Suzie Meadows walks out of the bathroom. Shirley grimaces.

INT. ROY'S OFFICE/STUDY

An orderly room with desk, filing cabinet, two-way radio transmitter etc., on the wall is a large framed painting of a champion bull. Prizewinning certificates, awards and ribbons cover the walls and surfaces. We hear the sound of CONSTRUCTION/PREPARATION *on the front lawn. A photo of Roy with a stud bull sits on the desk. The desk is covered with* LUKE'S *things – laptop computer, files, papers, fax machine. Luke is a share market analyst, he's a workaholic, ambitious, successful. He checks with the computer while he speaks on the phone.*

LUKE: But I'm saying sell ... I know that, it's irrelevant ... Look, if I was in your position I'd sell, okay? What more can I say? ... No! It's my wedding day for Christ sake! I'm sitting in the middle of nowhere. That's my advice, Hal, take it or leave it ... Good ... Thanks.

Luke hangs up and immediately dials a number. Rosie's voice comes through on the TWO-WAY RADIO.

ROSIE (VO): This is Romeo Foxtrot calling Merrivale Station, come in, over.

Luke, startled, hangs up, looks at the two-way radio. He tentatively pushes a switch.

LUKE: Hallo? Over.

INT. ROSIE'S AIRCRAFT

ROSIE: It's Rosie here, over.

LUKE (VO): Could this be the camel lady from the north?

ROSIE: Who am I speaking to? Over.

LUKE (VO): The alien from the city – Luke. The bridegroom.

ROSIE: Well g'day. It's the flying brides-maid here, I'll be dropping in on your wedding in twenty minutes. Over.

LUKE (VO): Good, they've been panick-ing about you. You haven't exactly left your- self much time. Over.

ROSIE: Time is an attitude of mind, Luke. Over and out.

CUT TO:

INT. ROY'S OFFICE/STUDY

Luke grins, then picks up the phone, dials the number he wanted earlier.

EXT. THE FRONT LAWN OF THE HOMESTEAD, NOON

The sun is overhead. Dawn, still in her riding gear, walks into the blue and white striped MARQUEE; *she watches the catering staff as they unfurl long white tablecloths. We* HEAR *someone do a sound check.*

VOICE (VO): One two, one two.

Dawn, and Amy, walk out of the marquee. Shirley, her hair only half done, calls to her.

SHIRLEY: Dawn! There you are! Do you know where your father is?

DAWN: No, what's wrong?

SHIRLEY: I need him to meet Rosie, she radioed in about half an hour ago.

DAWN: What?

SHIRLEY: Luke neglected to tell anyone.

Dawn starts to walk quickly. Shirley tries to keep up. Catering staff get in their way.

SHIRLEY: Where are you going?

DAWN: To meet Rosie.

SHIRLEY: But you can't. Suzie Meadows wants you. She's been looking for you all morning!

Dawn breaks into a run, so does Amy. Shirley stops.

EXT. THE AIR STRIP

A dirt runway, rocks, painted white, define the edges. Rosie's aircraft has landed. Painted on its side is a camel and the words: 'Venture Trek'. Rosie sits cross-legged in the shade of a wing, waiting, tired and annoyed. Her travel bag is beside her. In the distance she sees a dust cloud created by a fast approaching vehicle.

INT. THE LAND ROVER

Dawn driving at speed. Amy is on the passenger seat with her head out the window. It's a rough ride.

EXT. THE AIR STRIP

The Land Rover reaches the aircraft and skids to a halt. Dawn and Amy rush towards Rosie.

ROSIE: (with irony) You're late.

DAWN: (without irony) *I'm* late!

Amy leaps into Rosie's arms (an old 'trick' that they both know). Rosie laughs as Amy licks her face.

ROSIE: Hi Amy! Long time no see.

Rosie and Amy enjoy each other as Dawn looks on, stern faced.

DAWN: Amy, get in the car!

Amy does not respond.

Amy! Car!

Rosie lets Amy drop down. Dawn gets back in the car. Rosie gets her bag and slings it in the back of the vehicle and gets in the front seat with Amy. Dawn accelerates before Rosie has closed the passenger door.

EXT. THE FRONT DRIVE OF THE HOMESTEAD

The Land Rover arrives at the homestead. It stops sharply. Dawn gets out immediately, bangs the door and strides past Shirley who comes out to greet Rosie. Rosie eases herself out of the car. She is stiff with fatigue, and frustrated, however she manages to smile at Shirley. Shirley notices Dawn's abrupt behaviour but manages to smile at Rosie. Amy stays with Rosie.

SHIRLEY: Rosie! Rosie.

They hug each other.

ROSIE: Hallo.

SHIRLEY: I'm so upset you had to wait. Coming all this way. You must be very tired. Come in, I'll make you a nice cup of tea and a sandwich – if they'll let me in to my own kitchen!

They walk towards the FRONT VERANDA. *Rosie stares at the activities on the front lawn.*

ROSIE: It's kind of chaotic around here.

Roy comes towards them from the marquee.

ROY: You made it!

ROSIE: Roy!

SHIRLEY: Roy, get Rosie's bags for her. Poor thing, we've got a lot to do.

Shirley hurries inside the house.

ROY: Not before I get my hug.

Roy gives Rosie a hug. Suzie Meadows comes out of the house.

SUZIE MEADOWS: Rosie? At last!

ROY: Uh oh. I'll get your bags. Good luck.

Roy backs off quickly, with a wicked smile.

SUZIE MEADOWS: Hallo, how are you? I'm Suzie Meadows, the Wedding Co-ordinator. Did you have a good flight? Come in, we've got a lot to do.

Suzie Meadows takes Rosie's arm and drags her into the house, Amy follows.

INT. THE LOUNGE ROOM

Suzie Meadows calls down the corridor as she shows Rosie into the room.

SUZIE MEADOWS: Maria! Come on, she's here!

ROSIE: (to herself) Well this room hasn't changed.

SUZIE MEADOWS: We're going to have to move very quickly, but at least you've arrived! Now, there's your fitting, your hair, the ceremony run through, did you bring your shoes?

MARIA *comes in with the bridesmaid's dress. She is Italian.*

Oh good. I hope you haven't put on weight. Gorgeous colour, don't you think? What are we going to do about your hair?

ROSIE: My hair? About the shoes . . .

MARIA: (frantic) Fitting now! Upstairs.

Maria stomps out.

SUZIE MEADOWS: We'd better go up.

Shirley comes in with tea and a sandwich on a tray.

SHIRLEY: Here we –

SUZIE MEADOWS: Not now.

Roy comes in with Rosie's bag.

ROY: Where do you –

SUZIE MEADOWS: Later. Rosie, follow me.

INT. UPSTAIRS BEDROOM

A comfortable room. Rosie, uncomfortable, stands on a table, wearing the bridesmaid's dress, cup of tea in hand. Maria is pinning the waist. Suzie Meadows and Shirley stand watching.

MARIA: Stand straight please for hem.

SHIRLEY: Drink your tea Rosie.

MARIA: Shoes! Where your shoes!

Rosie spills her tea down the dress.

ROSIE: Ah!

Maria storms out hurling Italian invective. Suzie Meadows rushes forward.

SUZIE MEADOWS: Don't panic. Keep calm.

SHIRLEY: Water! Come on, we need cold water!

Suzie Meadows drags Rosie towards the door.

ROSIE: About the shoes . . .

SUZIE MEADOWS: Not now!

CUT TO:

INT. DOWNSTAIRS LIVING ROOM

Luke and DENNIS, *the best man, sit watching cricket on the television. They are relaxed.*

INT. UPSTAIRS, DAWN'S EN SUITE

Rosie lies in the bubble bath, a flannel over her face, very still. Amy is with her. Dawn comes in, she wears a silk underslip, with loose robe over.

DAWN: You really haven't changed have you!

Rosie does not move.

You come late, you forget your shoes, you spill tea all over the dress, your hair's too short – I mean – what's wrong with you!

Rosie slowly removes the flannel.

ROSIE: I was late because I couldn't get clearance to fly because there was an electrical storm. I have no shoes because they just don't sell that kind of thing where I come from. And I spilt the tea because people have been sticking pins in me since I arrived!

DAWN: If you were going to be so irresponsible why the hell did you agree to come?

ROSIE: Well if you're so 'responsible', why did you ask me?

DAWN: Because I wanted to see you!

ROSIE: You didn't have to get married to do that!

DAWN: Leave my marriage out of this!

ROSIE: With pleasure.

There is a KNOCKING *on the door.*

INT. UPSTAIRS CORRIDOR

Suzie Meadows knocks again at Dawn's door.

SUZIE MEADOWS: Rosie – the hairdresser is waiting. And then you must meet the best man. So hurry along. Rosie?

INT. DAWN'S EN SUITE

Rosie makes a face. Dawn FLUSHES *the toilet.*

INT. OUTSIDE DAWN'S DOOR

SUZIE MEADOWS: Oh, sorry. When you're ready then.

Suzie Meadows withdraws.

INT. DAWN'S EN SUITE

Rosie and Dawn stifle their laughter. They smile at each other.

ROSIE: I suppose a fuck's out of the question.

DAWN: What?!

ROSIE: Slip of the tongue. Forget it.

Rosie gets out of the bath, wraps herself in a large towel.

ROSIE: So, how've you been going?

DAWN: Fine.

ROSIE: It came as quite a surprise to hear you were getting married.

DAWN: Did it?

ROSIE: Is that why you stopped writing to me?

DAWN: No ... Yes ... I don't know.

ROSIE: I see!

MOVING SHOT

Rosie, still dripping, goes into DAWN'S BEDROOM, *Dawn follows.*

DAWN: We can't all be free spirits. There are certain family responsibilities that I have to address. It's what I wanted!

ROSIE: I hope you'll be very happy.

DAWN: I will. I am!

Rosie starts to leave.

ROSIE: Well in that case I'd better hurry along.

DAWN: Where are you going?

ROSIE: To get my hair done!

DAWN: Don't go. Not like that.

ROSIE: Like what?

DAWN: Like ... Maybe you should ... take my robe.

Dawn slips off her robe and holds it out. Rosie looks at Dawn in her underslip.

ROSIE: No, this is fine.

Dawn goes to Rosie with the robe.

DAWN: Come on. Have this.

Rosie resists but Dawn coaxes her into the robe. In the process, Rosie's towel drops to the floor. They stand very close.

ROSIE: I um, I'd better go.

DAWN: No hurry.

ROSIE: My hair –

DAWN: It's perfect.

ROSIE: You think so?

DAWN: I know so.

Dawn leans in towards Rosie and kisses her on the lips.

ROSIE: Dawn, are you sure you –

DAWN: Shut up and come with me.

Dawn draws Rosie towards the bed, kissing her all the while. Rosie kisses back. Amy wags her tail.

EXT. THE FRONT LAWN, EARLY AFTERNOON

Some cars have arrived, with more coming. People are gathered in small groups talking. Champagne is being served, a string quartet is PLAYING. *There is an air of expectancy and excitement. Suzie Meadows steers the* CELEBRANT *towards the marquee. Shirley and Roy mingle.*

INT. A LARGE MIRROR, LUKE'S ROOM

Luke splashes aftershave on his face, we hear the cricket COMMENTARY *in the background.*

INT. THE KITCHEN

Dangles, the Asian who cut the carrots into rose shapes, is now preparing strawberries. He takes a particularly large and luscious one and puts it in his mouth.

INT. DAWN'S BEDROOM

Dawn and Rosie make love. Dawn's lips open to encompass Rosie's nipple.

ROSIE: How I've missed this!

Rosie arches with pleasure. They match one another with their passion and longing.

INT. THE HALLWAY AT THE BOTTOM OF THE STAIRS

Guests wander. Friends and relations greet. FAVOUR *Suzie Meadows privately talking with the hairdresser.*

SUZIE MEADOWS: Well why didn't you tell me before? Oh, leave it to me.

MOVING SHOT

Suzie Meadows climbs the stairs and approaches Dawn's BEDROOM DOOR. *She* KNOCKS *sharply.*

INT. DAWN'S BED

Their naked bodies entwined, Rosie and Dawn freeze.

SUZIE MEADOWS (VO): Dawn – are you in there?

ROSIE: Shit a brick!

DAWN: Leave it to me. (calling) Just a moment Suzie!

SUZIE MEADOWS (VO): Is Rosie with you?

Dawn and Rosie stare at each other. Amy barks. Dawn grabs her robe and goes to the door, opens it slightly.

SUZIE MEADOWS: Time's getting on dear – and where's Rosie?

DAWN: She's here. She's wonderful.

SUZIE MEADOWS: Oh, good. But you are behind schedule.

DAWN: We had a lot of catching up to do.

SUZIE MEADOWS: The hairdresser's been waiting.

DAWN: Sorry. We'll be down in a minute.

Dawn closes the door. Rosie is putting on the clothes she arrived in.

DAWN: Where are you going?

ROSIE: I can't stay here after –

DAWN: You're not going anywhere, not without me.

ROSIE: Dawn, you're about to be married.

DAWN: No I'm not.

ROSIE: What are you going to do – walk out on all this?

DAWN: Yes ... will you walk with me?

They look at each other.

ROSIE: Do you like camels?

DAWN: I've always loved camels.

They smile. Amy wags her tail.

CUT TO:

INT. THE KITCHEN

A SERIES OF ANGLES

The bar and catering staff work at speed. An empty tray of champagne glasses is slammed down, a full tray picked up. Drink waiters grab trays, call orders.

WAITER (1): Two gin and tonics, one without ice!

WAITER (2): Brandy lime and soda. Do we have iced tea?

CATERER: No!

The catering staff prepare and dispense trays of finger food. A constant flurry of activity.

MOVING SHOT

Follow Waiter (2) as she goes outside with her tray of drinks.

EXT. THE FRONT LAWN

The height of the sun suggests mid afternoon. There are a lot of people. Children dash around playing tag. The quartet can barely be heard above the NOISE.

MOVING SHOT

FAVOUR Shirley as she moves through the guests and goes down the main hallway and up the stairs.

INT. UPSTAIRS CORRIDOR TO DAWN'S ROOM

Shirley's POV *as she reaches Dawn's bedroom door. She knocks, waits.*

SHIRLEY: Dawn?

Shirley opens the door, walks in.

INT. DAWN'S BEDROOM

Shirley looks around the room.

SHIRLEY: Dawn?

She goes into the EN SUITE, *sees the bath full of water, the bubbles are flat. Without really thinking she plunges her arm into the water and pulls out the plug. The water* GURGLES *down the plug hole. She looks at her wet arm, suddenly puzzled, troubled, comes back into the bedroom. She sees the bridal gown and the bridesmaid's dress lying side by side on the bed. As she crosses to the bed she hears the* DRONE *of a plane. She hurries to the* BALCONY *and looks up.*

EXT. A LIGHT AIRCRAFT OVERHEAD.

CUT TO:

EXT. THE FRONT LAWN

Wedding guests look up at the aircraft.

CUT TO:

EXT. THE AIRCRAFT OVERHEAD, GAINING HEIGHT. THE CAMEL LOGO IS JUST DISCERNIBLE

INT. THE AIRCRAFT

Rosie at the controls, Dawn in the passenger seat, with Amy on her lap, they are singing:

DAWN/ROSIE: 'The sun has got her hat
on
Hip hip hip hooray
The sun has got her hat on
And she's coming out to play'

EXT. THE AIRCRAFT
LONG SHOT

The aircraft flies towards the setting sun.

JAN OWEN

On Behalf of My Wife and Myself

Between the ages of nineteen and twenty-five, I tried getting married twice. The third time I was finally successful. When I look back now I can't understand what women like Liz Taylor have been doing all these years. I have feelings of immense relief that I got it all over and done with in such a short space of time. Imagine dedicating your entire life to the pursuit of marriage? No wonder Liz has battled booze, drugs, diets, surgery and pills for so long – she has been driven to them.

The best thing about getting married is to be finally off the relationship meat market.

It struck me when I finally did get married that this was the beginning of entry into a secret club of women that no one – least of all our own mothers – warned us about. Amidst hopes for the future, belief in togetherness and distinct aversion to loneliness, couples fall in together embarking on journeys to places never dreamed of, or even desired.

I, for one, am now a firm believer in pre-arranged marriages. I am currently in the process of targeting numerous future partners for my daughter and sons in order to help them avoid the time, effort and emotional exhaustion needed to embark on the choosing of a partner. (How long will it last – two to five years?) I've lined up a relay of parners in succession based on their relative maturity at the ages of three, five and seven years of age. Hopefully things will be smooth sailing for my three cherubs from here on. I feel sure they will never quite understand what I have saved them from!

Despite this tremendously time consuming effort, commitment and determination on my part, I sometimes feel I may be attacking this issue from the wrong angle. This has led me to an evaluation of my own experience, although I have strong doubts about the therapeutic or otherwise value of delving back into pre-wedding times.

The first thing that happened to me when I tried to get married was that I picked the wrong person, well twice actually. The first and second lifelong partners I chose were New Zealanders. (You'd think I'd have learnt by the second!) At the tender age of nineteen, the first man and I exchanged words of undying love and desire to spend the rest of our days in harmonious matrimony. (This is what I said – but mostly because I wanted to make an old boyfriend madly jealous, to the point where he would charge in and reclaim me.)

Complicated? I know! It gets worse! The major problem with this strategy was that the old boyfriend never found out I was even going out with anyone else, let alone engaged to be married! Of course no one else realised my true motives either and this is where things began to go astray.

Not long after our engagement announcement and the buying of a not-quite engagement ring, my future partner was required to return to New Zealand. We said goodbye for two whole weeks. Amidst tears we promised to be faithful to each other for ever, made tentative wedding dates and times, booked return air flights. Finally, the fateful day arrived and I sadly waved him off at the airport. To this day I have never heard of or set eyes on him since. I can only presume he's still alive. I have heard, through a mutual friend, that on his return to New Zealand my 'not quite' fiancé had entered the seminary in shock and confusion. He emerged a year later, more or less a whole person and married a devout local girl to whom he was obviously much more suited. I did pause to consider where I went wrong with this particular man, but decided that in light of the limited information available, I should not be at all deterred by this rather over the top recovery program. It could not possibly have been the result of going out with me for only six months. He obviously should never have been allowed out of New Zealand!

My second attempt to get married was a little more serious. I had spent many years on and off with this prospective partner. We had known each other as teenagers and grown up in the same district. This in itself should have been a serious warning sign for anybody with the slightest bit of sense. But not to be deterred, and having a penchant for living on the edge, I proceeded to chart these muddy waters. We broke up for two years during the six we were together. In that period I tried marrying the aforementioned suitor and shopped around, mostly through old boyfriends. Just in case I'd passed over a potential husband without realising.

My criteria were fairly clear. Good prospects for future income, intelligent, thinking, good-looking, nice car and good in bed. For a while there only blondes would do. I had quite a commitment to children with blonde hair and blue or brown eyes somewhere down the track. You can tell that this thinking obviously reflected the deep-felt spiritual and ideological commitment I had to feminist principles during this period of my life.

Not an enormous ask you might say, but an amazingly difficult criterion to fill. I finally came back to the original boyfriend in the belief that the devil you know is better than the devil you don't. I was assisted in my decision making by the fact that it was this boyfriend who had broken up our relationship two years before. I felt it was extremely necessary for me to win him back just to show who was in charge here.

I did. He did. We did. For eighteen months we were engaged. Seeds of doubt crept into my consciousness from time to time. Particularly when my mother, on being informed of our engagement took me aside and in tears said, 'If you ever want out, just tell me and I'll stand by you.' Not a huge vote of confidence there. And this was from someone who really liked the guy! But I couldn't possibly have gone to all this trouble to change my mind at the last minute. Besides the pre-wedding bonanza had begun. The engagement presents started to flow in. I took delivery of the wedding dress I'd found while shopping on a trip to Melbourne which took six months of hard earned cash to get off layby. Then there was the 10 metres of raw silk purchased and carried all round a trip through China for the six bridesmaids. The invitations, the church, the arrangements, the savings program for our first unit together.

All was proceeding well. My doubt had been stubbornly shifted to the recesses of my mind. Until, that is, I unexpectedly met a new man whilst doing some work interstate. As our friendship developed over the next few months, I had a profound sense that I shouldn't have more feelings for the man I was *not* about to marry, than for the one I was!

With a total lack of the style and delicacy with which one should manage this type of dilemma, and just weeks before our long awaited wedding day, I informed my husband-to-be that I wanted to end our relationship. I hung around the city for a week or so to finish off work. Meanwhile my mother consoled my distraught former fiancé, who happened to be living with us at the time. We couldn't possibly share the same house. It was either him or me, but not both! He had nowhere else to go in his distress so as soon as I got organised I was on a plane out of there. Not necessarily a very mature thing to do but there's a lot to be said for the flight part of the fight or flight equation when faced with a distraught former lover. My mother still has a great relationship with my ex fiancé, I've never heard from him since. I can't blame him for never contacting me. Someone like me should never have happened to a guy like him.

I have now been married to the man I left my fiancé for, for ten years. Our wedding was without doubt one of the most exhausting and stressful experiences in our relationship.

In recent times, I've often wondered why women, including friends of mine, who have been with their partners for years, who may even share a number of children, suddenly decide to get married and to become caught up in the wedding bonanza. They insist on having a wedding. Spending money they don't have. Buying a white dress they don't need.

And single women! It never ceases to amaze me how many previously normal, balanced, sane, enlightened, self-aware, single 'twenty' and 'thirtysomethings' totally lose the plot when it comes to getting married. Get them alone with a single, good-looking, trendily dressed mobile phoned male, with obvious prospects, for more than ten minutes, and their entire perspective on the world changes.

Now such an 'eligible' male could be a total disaster area for all we, or she knows (as we observe his eyes sweep the room over her left shoulder, checking out the rest of the talent). But just the possibility that he's not, and that he is therefore a potential lifelong partner, is enough to make her forget everything her mother and any other woman she knows over thirty-five, ever told her. Not only this, chances are if she wins this one, in seven to ten years she'll be back looking all over again. Or he will. It's a modern tragedy that one in three marriages end in divorce and that another one out of two subsequent marriages also fall apart. Now don't get me wrong, marriage as a mindless institution is something I have no time for whatsoever. But marriage as a conscious, sane, thought through choice is something I will entertain. The problem is that just about no one ever gets married under these sensible conditions.

I have a feeling that part of the answer is to be found in the preservation of some form of ritual in our society, which is generally so devoid of meaningful and intimate celebrations and gatherings. Weddings and funerals constitute our last great rituals. Now there's an irony. There's usually the same guest list for both.

I believe I've finally found the secret as to why this marriage thing doesn't work from the beginning. In contrast to the magical six hours of the Big Day it's all … well, so unromantic from there on. I would go further and suggest the problems begin long before the Big Day. The first problem any couple encounters is to do with money. Far from joining your independent incomes together in order to create greater opportunities for all the exciting things you plan to do together, you actually bring your financial dowry like a sacrificial lamb to the slaughter. You begin to discover all you'll need to stage the wedding of the year, and furthermore how much it is going to cost you both. Most parents have opted out of this wedding bit some time ago on the pretext that if you've been living together, then you're big enough to be able to organise (and pay for!) your own wedding. The reality is, of course, they're either still paying off *their* own wedding, or have just hopped on the merry-go-round for a second time. Either way they've got nothing like the sort of cash you're going to need to do a wedding, let alone *the* wedding, of the 1990s.

The checklist goes something like this. The church and the minister all come at a price. Even a couple of innocent bunches of flowers have an exorbitant price tag attached. This is particularly annoying given that you and your partner will never even set eyes on most of the flowers, except in the wedding book at the florist.

I suggest you take a good hard look at those, cut your losses and settle for a few homemade paper roses that you can make out of the *Women's Weekly* circa 1957. Even tracking down one of those collectors items will be cheaper than buying the flowers for your wedding. The other problem with flowers in my experience is that they stay with you forever, through the visual impact of your wedding photos. These photos are generally taken after the flowers have been out of water for a good three to four hours and have got the wilt look down to a fine art.

The major problem is the effect of the flowers on your whole future marriage. They become a constant source of many a financial domestic dispute as your partner fifteen years later, when justifying the securing of a 27-metre yacht on hire purchase, which you'll be repaying for the rest of your married lives, offendedly states, 'Well, what about the time we wasted that absolutely phenomenal amount of money on those (bleep) ... flowers for the wedding?' I think it's best to give the flowers a wide berth, sorry about the pun.

As for me, I decided to wear all the flowers on my head. At least that way I knew where they were and that people were looking at the right thing at the wedding, namely me. And not admiring the flower display behind the minister's left ear.

The next big dollar outlay is the dress. I have indisputable proof that no woman in the entire history of civilisation has worn her white wedding dress again since the big day. Despite this widely known fact, you will still overhear brides-to-be in bridal shops justifying the outrageous price tags of today's wedding dresses by trying to convince themselves, their bevy of bridesmaids and their mother and their mother-in-law, and even the sales assistant (who of all people needs no convincing!) that they *definitely* will be able to wear the dress again. With just a few minor alterations, it will be great as an ordinary everyday number for the office party, or the movies. Furthermore she's prepared to pay $5000 dollars for the privilege of also wearing it on her wedding day.

I'll let you in on a secret. The only women who even come close to wearing their wedding dress again are those who don't wear white! They're not in the least bit romantic, they're just good planners. I have a friend who wore red. I thought this was very creative and practical and yes, she informs me that she has worn it to lots of other people's weddings.

My advice on wedding dresses is to go through the *Trading Post* or to the designer recycled shops in your capital city and you're sure to pick up that once only, soon to be twice only, dress for a quarter of the price you would have expected to pay. Otherwise, hang around the night spots in your city for thirtysomething singles. They've just about all got a once-used white wedding dress locked up somewhere in their closets.

Now the photographs. Wedding photographs have to be the most deceptive and potentially debilitating part of the whole wedding bonanza. The major problem with photos is that they represent this long-term memory of you both. They capture you at the most vulnerable moment of your entire life.

By the big day you are absolutely exhausted, stressed to the max and on the verge of calling the whole thing off. Your partner has been up the entire night before at the great Australian (what did we do to deserve this?) bucks night. You're feeling fairly fortunate that he's there at all. You have run around non-stop in the last week doing all the last minute bits and pieces. (These include finding a new minister because the other one has suddenly been called away to a funeral interstate; and discovering the reception centre has double booked you and you have the nightmarishly impossible task of finding another venue. You decide to go to the gardens with outdoor caterers and hope like hell it's not going to rain.) Added to all this you've been on the compulsory pre-wedding diet for six weeks in order to squeeze back into the dress you purchased on layby two years ago. As a result, your blood sugar levels are dangerously low, you're malnourished, wan and pale. The perfect bride. On top of all this you're then asked to pose and smile for four hours with absolutely no prior training!

Wedding photos, for this very good reason are usually hidden in most Australian homes. The other reason you don't see the photos is that if you're anything like my partner and me, *after* the event the photos don't seem all that much of a priority, especially compared to cooking utensils, a bed and linen or getting the car back on the road. It took us two years to actually pay for the photos. We spent the rest of the time peering at the little passport-size ones we'd chosen to have made up into the official album

By the time you do actually take delivery of the album most of the people, including yourselves, are unrecognisable. Besides, you're certainly too embarrassed to invite all your friends and loved ones around two years after the wedding to have a look at the album. So you hide them in a cabinet never to be seen again. This scenario presumes you're still actually together – in which case the phenomenal down payments you've been making, which amount to a couple of round the world trips by the fourth monthly payment (only twelve to go!) leave you kind of breathless.

It's like a constant reminder of how you felt on your wedding day, especially if the last down payment was two weeks before either of you walked out. You can't exactly say, 'honey, please, let's stay together for the photos!'

My sister and brother-in-law beat the system. They were frantically busy and stressed out before their wedding. When they got the photos back they claimed that they were so bad they bore no resemblance to themselves whatsoever. They threatened to sue the photographer who immediately suggested he do them all over again. No one else ever saw the original photos, but we bought the line and we all turned up to an extremely relaxed post-honeymoon photo session. The photos were sensational. I wish I'd thought of that idea. I think we could begin a new Australian cultural trend here, all couples should postpone their wedding photos until after the honeymoon. Even better, wait for the first two years after the wedding. At least by then you'll have an inkling whether to bother going ahead with them or not.

There's also a growing trend toward using amateur photographers, a sophisticated title for friends and relatives. This is extremely dangerous unless you have a signed, sealed and delivered promise that they will not touch a drop of alcohol on the big day. The Australian phenomeon of F & F (family and friends) 'amateur' photographers arriving early and getting drunk whilst waiting around for the bride and groom to arrive is incredibly common. Your photos end up as blurred images in a sea of bright neon party lights. What's more, the majority of the photos will turn out to be of his or her own girl/boyfriend, and the rest of their group of friends, with about two photos of you, if you're lucky.

I was once the official photographer at our friends' wedding. I was an absolute nervous wreck. I was more stressed than either the bride, the groom or anyone else involved. I had nightmares for weeks before the wedding that I took reels and reels of photos only to find that there was no film in the camera, or that I opened the back of the camera to load another film forgetting to wind it back first. Or that in every photo the couple had those horror movie red eyes jumping off the page. The wedding photos from hell! For three days I waited in terror for the films to be developed. Fortunately, they turned out fine. This may have been because I took fifteen photos of each shot. It took me a long time to recover from the experience though. I've never accepted an assignment since.

Once you have the ceremony worked out down to the very last detail, the next thing you have to do is work out the reception. This is the most contentious issue within the wider family because it hinges on the crucial question of who is to be actually invited to the wedding. Anyone can turn up to the wedding ceremony but only those with *invitations* may proceed on to the reception. This issue can become the cause of family rifts, emotional blackmail, or even downright bribery, taking the passing of a whole generation to be forgotten and *still* never forgiven.

The hot issues in relation to the reception include who has how many places to allocate to whom. For people from big families, this is equivalent to having to pick one of your ten best girlfriends as your bridesmaid. The outcome will be exactly the same. Those not chosen will never, ever talk to you again. The invitation is used as a source of mafia-style corruption within normally quiet – you could say even sedate – suburban Australian families. Your wedding is a fabulous opportunity to heal age-old family rifts. An opportunity for your parents and in-laws to repay favours to everyone from the guy who cemented the front lawn fifteen years ago; to the friends and relatives they didn't invite to their own wedding twenty-eight years ago and who haven't spoken to them since. In the case of still living, now elderly aunts, this is now a pressing problem which, in the short term, may severely limit their chances as beneficiaries to several family bequests. Your in-laws-to-be, if they approve of you as their potential daughter-in-law, will use your wedding to show you off to the entire family, including relatives they've had to locate through the Registry of Births, Deaths and Marriages. On the other hand they may disapprove entirely and demonstrate this by only inviting the couple they play bridge with on Saturday nights, just as a change of venue.

All of this of course, depends entirely on who is paying for what and for whom. Either way you are given the impression that your wedding is fulfilling some sacred family rites of which you had no prior knowledge but for which you alone were born. In the end you're wondering if it actually matters if you and your partner even show up. These torturous discussions about THE INVITATION LIST can go on for days, weeks, even months. They are the very reason that Registry Office ceremonies are so popular and appealing. Nobody gets excited about standing in line for a wedding outside the local Town Hall.

There's one other issue about weddings that concerns me greatly. It's closely related to the well-researched causal link between loss of identity and marriage. In its chronic final stages it is generally characterised by the woman beaming lovingly at her partner, who, whilst giving his speech at the wedding reception, pronounces, 'On behalf of my wife and myself . . .' It's so subtle that most of us have never even realised what's going on. We've missed it altogether. I sincerely hope to begin a revolution now that I am going to expose this conspiracy for what it is. Namely names!

No, I'm not talking about the taking of partners' surnames, although that is also an issue which bears some discussion some other time. I'm talking about the naming of the participants on this small stage of life. It goes on for months and months before the wedding. No longer are you referred to by your own name, but as the 'bride-to-be'. This is particularly evident in those who have a significant commercial investment in your remaining in this role, and who may wish to exercise undue influence on you. The other participants are not immune either. Your partner becomes the 'groom-to-be'. His friends take on a new status depending on whether they are groomsmen or bestmen. Your girlfriend if married, becomes matron of honour (who on earth would choose to be a matron of honour of their own free will?). Meanwhile your nicest, youngest and prettiest girlfriends become bridesmaids; your mother, the mother-of-the-bride; your father, the father-of-the-bride (preferably the old fashioned paying kind!) etc.

There is no doubt, the most exploited person in this process is the bride. She is perceived to be fragile, emotional, and anxious. Is she having second thoughts? Will she last the distance? Why on earth is she having so much trouble choosing the colour for the bridesmaids' dresses? The invitations can only take up so much time, whisper others around her.

All of a sudden you're having a major identity crisis. You can't even remember your real name any more. Your skills in decision making have totally evaporated. Some secret transformation, over which you have no control, has taken place. When you finally emerge from the bridal trail, in rapturous splendour, you feel only enormous relief that your partner has given you a name again. Whatever that name may be – you are no longer a bride-to-be or even a bride. You have finally crossed the matrimonial no person's land. You have become a wife. Good luck!

JANE MESSER

Public Property

One December while holidaying in Mexico, I met a man, and we were married in Oaxaca ten days later (pronounce *wah-ha-kah*). Returning alone to Baltimore in mid-January, to go on with my work at Johns Hopkins University (as we'd arranged), I read in the *New York Times'* Sunday weddings' page (a double-page spread with photos and biogs), about another Australian couple who'd eloped to New York, and married without their family. The photo showed them standing outside the solid registry, happily rugged up in coats and sweaters and scarves; New York is so very cold in January. I understood perfectly why they had escaped, for never in Australia could I have married. All that fuss, that bother, the people crowding round, the chatter.

Not at all ironically, the marriage happened without the thought and consideration that I have given the event since being married. I had tried to think it through, to experience it beforehand in all its complexity – social, emotional, familial, economic – but in my imagination I only got as far as the wedding itself. And being in Mexico, where I had never been before – and finding out only bit by bit, in limited Spanish, as the wedding day approached, what might happen, (a day which shifted, as did its possible locations: at least there wasn't the added question of who I'd be marrying) – I found even the wedding ceremony difficult to imagine. (And it was only going to be a civil ceremony; neither of us is religious.) I'd been to a Sydney Greek Orthodox wedding once, and as a child, had crawled around the feet of a bride at the local church, scraping up the confetti with a girlfriend until shooed away. I knew it wouldn't be like that. But to say I hadn't given it prior thought, is being a little fey, because of course I'd thought about marriage, and rejected the possibility of it for years.

The question had never been who or when to marry, but why would one at all? 'Kids,' me and my home-town Sydney mob would say, 'you might want to marry for the kids,' for somehow that would be safer for them; that is, if you were having any at all. Then too, for those gay friends, with children and without, marriage wasn't often a possibility.

I can count on a couple of knuckles the number of my friends that are married: we're just not the marrying type. And why not? Well, there's the expense, but that's the least of it, that can be got around. No, it's the history of the institution of marriage that we object to, its association with church and state law, the wife as chattel and children as property, the loss of one's name to the man, and all that this means to the patriarchal order, which through our daily habits, and paid and creative work, we are trying to undo. For friends from religious families, it has a special oppressiveness; one friend says that she'd feel conquered by her Catholic parents if she ever got married. Further, there is the fallacy that marriage makes relationships endure when they might not otherwise, in that ungainly sounding de facto state. Perhaps, with tautological logic, it assists some of the couples that believe it will keep them together. But I have an aversion to the idea of people getting married as a way of staying together, as if it was glue, or rope, or a knot too tight and complicated to untie.

In fact, Michiel and I had been involved for many years, so

it wasn't such a rash thing to marry. I was studying and teaching at Johns Hopkins, and he was working on in Sydney. Separation added to the romance of the decision; and it *was* romantic, and exciting, fun, giggly. The combination of that separation and our long past together led to the idea; midway through the separation I felt more connected to him knowing that in a few months we'd be in Mexico. To me, it wasn't only a signal about the future, but an affirmation of the past. Knowing that we'd be holidaying in Mexico, we had found a mythological, memorable location which was also private. (What's more, I'd long wanted to go there, and to see Frida Kahlo's house and paintings.) When we first said yes to each other, I told him via satellite, or maybe optic fibre, 'Don't tell my parents if you think you'll change your mind in the next couple of weeks. It would break their hearts and embarrass them with the family.'

There was a clue. Immediately, what I thought was a private moment between Michiel and myself, had become a contract with other people. But then I had no idea; I missed the clue and spent the next forty days and nights in Baltimore under the illusion that we were celebrating something singular between ourselves, when in fact it was having a huge impact on other peoples' lives. For one, my mother was overjoyed – there really was almost too much joy. It seemed utterly settled; we'd be together happily forever. (I think if Mum had to choose between the two of us, she'd take him.) His parents, divorced from each other but living together again, were much more deadpan about it. He was given sensible, dire warnings, and help with choosing the rings. For those who were thrilled, it was lovely how much pleasure our announcement gave (see how those daggy nuptial expressions creep in), but also a little scary and absurd, because hadn't we been a couple for many, many years anyway?

Oaxaca, where it all happened, is a dry, warm mountain town, a small city really, in central Mexico, just some hundred kilometres south of the capital. Colourful (holidays and marriages ought to be colourful), noisy – the sounds of this city are something of their own. We arrived in Oaxaca by slow bus, one of the many continually honking old buses in Mexico, blessed each New Year's Day at a ceremony for safe travel. (The buses are so old that one of them was sure to have been the same 1925 bus in which painter Frida Kahlo was impaled by a hand-rail, and rushed to hospital from, covered in her own blood and gold dust. She married the muralist Diego Rivera; a troubled marriage made better by having adjacent houses joined by a raised and enclosed walkway, which either spouse could lock.) There are also the huge thumping rhythms of bootleg *mariachi* and pop songs coming from the stalls of deaf tape-sellers; a constant engine-rumble of Brazilian-made VW beetles; the bravura sounds of American tourists, serious, whispering Europeans, and the more melodic Spanish of the indigenous people themselves. Around Oaxaca, the indigenous Mexicans come from about nine local tribes, and have in the past been variously conquerors of and conquered by each other, as well as the Aztecs.

The *zócalo* (a square) was quieter, there being no cars. It was in the city centre, with an interior garden of trees, fountains and pathways, and because it was Christmas, a fenced-off nativity scene sculpted by local children and artists, which people stood and watched like it was TV; and around the garden area, a wide stone path to perambulate along, then the four cobbled streets across which you'd walk to sit beneath the *portales* at one of the cafés or restaurants. Even in winter, the sun was strong, and the shady area beneath the stone *portales* much sought after. Stallholders in the *zócalo* sold glazed fruits, like candied limes stuffed with coconut, or hot fresh corn dipped in grated goat cheese and chilli, flowering cacti, fairy floss, helium *feliz ano nueve* balloons (happy new year), Mexican clothes and other wares of an enormous range made by the Indians in the local towns. We looked for a ring for Michiel, but he was just too big. (People laughed at our 30-centimetre height difference, probably wondering how we 'did it'. Being more homogenous racially, the men and women there are only a centimetre or two apart.) Children sang for money, or sold chewing gum; many other children were in school or working on farms.

Around the *zócalo* in the old city, the buildings were of stone and plaster, painted in glorious colours with soft washes, and there being little neon or electrical advertising, the advertisements were painted straight onto the buildings in a curiously sweet Mexican-Disney style. To the east and north when one looked down a street, there were always the green and dusty mountains to be seen. Women walked the streets freely at all hours, and people were not afraid to look into each other's eyes. (I immediatley felt the change coming from Baltimore, whose inner city is polarised by racial tensions and poverty, and where increasingly people avoid the streets and are silent and subdued in public.) Catholic churches in the towns and along the highways were numerous, and Mexico's religious history complex, but I felt no difficulty with that, taking only a civil ceremony. Oaxaca was a beautiful place to be married in, and the street-living Mexicans good people to be married amongst.

We had met up in Mexico City; I flew in a couple of days early. When Michiel arrived, the hotel receptionist denied I was staying there and booked him into a new room, but I found him by coincidence in the lobby. He was taking his bags to his room, wondering where else I might be in that city of twenty million.

I was prepared with champagne. So was Michiel; when he had told the airline steward he was marrying, the fellow had given him a bottle with serving cloth. (He came with the best present of all – new silk underwear from my mother, lots of it.) I had also collected an obstacle – Béatrice, a young Parisian food science student whose ambition was to work for Nestlé. To save money she intended to sleep on the hotel's roof that night, and was hiding in my room until it got dark enough for her to sneak upstairs. So the three of us drank the champagne, and when she left, with one of our pillows and entreaties to come down to our room if anyone tried to harm her, he brought out two beautiful rings, old English gypsy rings. Mexico City is situated on a high mountain plateau and visitors experience all sorts of ailments with the lower oxygen level – mine that day was swollen fingers. I couldn't get the rings on.

We bused to Puebla, a few hours south. We tried to get married there after meeting a very helpful man at the *tourista oficina*, but the *registro civil* was closed for a couple of weeks over Christmas. It was then that we realised how very very difficult it might be to get married in Mexico. We'd already argued about who had the right documentation (not me, we now thought), and were now faced with the problem that we might be trying to do it at the wrong time of year.

It was a relief to forget about getting married for a few days, and visit other towns, markets and centuries-old Spanish churches built atop of ancient Indian pyramids; not the cones as in Egypt, but flat-topped and stepped. (When the Spanish invaded, they had the Indians take down their pyramids, and used the stones to build Catholic churches. Archaeologists have been reconstructing them.) Sometimes, only for a moment at a time, if we were squabbling we'd say, 'Maybe we shouldn't get married.' Then we would resign ourselves to the idea it wouldn't be possible to do it. We even entertained the plan of flying to flat, suburban San Antonio, near the border, and getting married in the USA.

On our way to Oaxaca we met Arturo, a young local agriculturalist. 'Hello,' he said at the bus station, as I struggled to get us tickets, not understanding that I was to put our names on a waiting list. 'I am not a guide.' We wanted to improve our Spanish and he needed to hear more English, to help him pass the American English-language exam, so that he could take up a graduate offer at the University of Utah. (One day he took us to a *comida familiar* run by friends, and we had the day's special for lunch, a meaty platter including blackened testicles, pig's feet, tripe and grasshoppers, with tortillas and tequila. I returned the favour by telling him about the food he'd get at Utah – pizza subs, coffee with flavours like caramel and raspberry, and ice cream with chocolate-chip cookie dough.)

When we told him what we wanted to do, Arturo proposed that we go out to a dusty little town called Zaachila and bribe the fat, old drunken judge. That way, we wouldn't have to worry about documentation. I dressed up in a suit; Michiel's trousers were white, everyone stared, and the judge, we were told, was out to lunch.

We took up positions on a long stool near the office beneath the *portales*, and watched a group of local farmers renegotiate a loan, emissaries going in and out of an office, conferring with the other men in the street. The cowboy is a Mexican tradition, and many country men wear the hats – this group took their's on and off anxiously as the negotiations continued. Old women crossed the square in front of us, their feet dusty from the walk, carrying food stuffs in bright, striped plastic-weave bags. Every now and then Arturo went back into the *oficina* to see if the judge had returned. The last time, he came back with a look of some concern. 'I can't offer a bribe,' he said, 'the judge is a young woman. It would be an insult.' We went in to look. Here was new Mexico: a professional woman, educated, incorruptible and serious about her work. She sent us back to Oaxaca.

That afternoon, Michiel went to bed. His temperature flew to 40 degrees and stayed there for days, while he sweated the *grippe* out (flu), delirious and unable to walk. In the afternoons I washed out t-shirts, restocked the juices and boiled water, and handed out *aspirinas*. 'Perhaps you'll be well enough to get married tomorrow?' I'd ask.

Just as with marriages held at home, with family, friends and a whole lot of fuss, we were being overwhelmed by detail. The event and its aftermath couldn't possibly be as engrossing as these preparations. In the afternoons, Arturo and I went to see people to find out what we needed to do. We had to have a blood test. The hospital, teeming with people, proved too difficult, so we found a private pathologist, a pleasant Dr Carlos Cordova, who spoke some English and had worked at London University and at Stanford, but was now very interested in Chinese acupuncture and hypnosis. I said we'd be back when the boy was well enough to walk. We found a *notario publico*, very dapper in a cream safari suit, to validate our identities. On the Thursday, I put Michiel into a VW taxi and took him to a doctor to get the requisite medical examinations to say we were not insane or disabled. By now, my descriptions of Michiel's illness were quite sophisticated; I'd even been to the *farmacia* without my dictionary.

We were determined to get married on the Friday. Determined, for now 'there was no turning back'. This event which had begun ethereally, over the fine fibres and pulses of the wonderful American telephone network, was grinding us down with its corporeality. I woke up feeling less than fabulous, and Michiel, though ill, could be said to have improved with the penicillin. Cheerful, and sneezing, we took more *aspirinas*, and put our best clothes on again. Arturo had to work and could not be a witness, and we needed witnesses. All the Americans had left our hotel, so we taxied back to the *zócalo* and cruised the cafés checking people out, looking for two people with whom we wanted to share the brief but special moment. We had to like them. We felt good about a couple of women sitting at a table, so we went over. 'Hi,' I said, 'we're hoping to get married today, and we need two witnesses, and were wondering if you wouldn't mind spending an hour with us witnessing the marriage.' They looked sceptical. They said they had shopping to do, and pyramids to visit. But we re-explained, and Gina and Virginia started to warm to the idea. They were San Franciscans, both technical writers, who'd met each other at Spanish classes and were now the best of friends.

Michiel is quite tall, and so were Gina and Virginia: 190, 182, 177 centimetres respectively. Standing between them in the high-ceilinged stone room of the *Tercera Oficialía*, I felt like a child bride at 162 centimetres. Gina interrupted the official while she read out the ceremony (there's no 'honoor or obey' in it). 'When are you going to say the High Mass?' Gina asked, giggling. Mexico is secular and Catholic, and people have two ceremonies, civil and church. Our judge, Noemy Barrita Chagoya De Sarmiento, was appalled by the Yankee. ('I always wreck everything!' Gina wailed later, back at the *zócalo*, over margaritas. In fact, she couldn't have spoilt it; we were having too good a time.) We went out that night and danced some *salsa* (also 'America's favourite condiment!') with Arturo and friends, but now that both of us had *grippe*, we were too tired for a private celebration. We flew out early the next morning to the Pacific coast, and booked ourselves into a ritzy hotel; part honeymoon, part convalescence. Two days later, we both felt great, but then I accidently swam into the side of the pool. I gashed open my nose and forehead, but didn't break anything. During all of this, the sun blazed down upon us. We had loved being in Oaxaca so much, and were so glad to have celebrated there, that these hiccups tended to be humorous and made for storytelling, rather than catastrophic.

Frida Kahlo had an affair with Leon Trotsky. (She had affairs with quite a few men and women.) The homes that they died in are some streets apart in a leafy suburb of Mexico City called Cóyoacan. She and Diego Rivera were supporters of Trotsky, and helped him settle into his Mexican exile. On our return to the capital before parting again for Sydney and Baltimore, I set off to visit their museum homes alone. Michiel's *grippe* had come back that morning, and on these last days we were tired, and irritable with the city's tremendous pollution; just that morning I'd grumbled that maybe we shouldn't have got married. The taxi took me first to Trotsky's house. It was emptied of all the paintings that Frida had given him. Living under threat of assassination, parts of the house were fortress-like, with solid steel doors and small windows. Yet it was a friendly place, with floors painted in revolutionary red, and parts of walls coloured a bright yellow and blue. Outside in the large garden, I examined some glazed plant holders. They were tiled with broken pieces, from plates perhaps, a montage effect; and some showed small aristocratic scenes: the squire outside a corner of a castle; a lady and her gentleman flirting. I walked on to Frida's house; knocked at the large garden doors. A man opened the door a few centimetres, reluctantly, and told me the place was closed until March. He wouldn't let me have even a quick look at the house with its walkway; I'd so much wanted to see the odd architecture of their relationship. I was very disappointed; I'd only succeeded in one of my Mexican ambitions.

Back in Baltimore, I had a few weeks of feeling that I ought now to be a better person, a 'good' woman. I felt my perception of myself shifting and tugged at, in response to others. Family and peers were ghosts around me, watching and commenting, as though I must now be on my best behaviour. Old clichés took on new meaning: the eyes of the world were upon me. This was a terrifying feeling, and didn't pass until I told a friend, and insisted, 'I am *not* a *good* woman.'

Now that I am back in Sydney, and shacked up with Michiel, I still have objections to the institution, and for new and more personal reasons, which have little to do with my partner ('wife' and 'husband' just won't wear). What other people make of my experience is sometimes at odds with how I feel. The way in which the relationship has become public property within the family is disturbing. Some want to know why I didn't change my name, or say flatly, 'I suppose you'll be having kids/buying a house now.' A cousin has invited me to a shower tea, where I would never have been asked before; five women in the family have given me five tablecloths. The drive to normalise us is very strong with these people. The mob simply congratulated us, with genuine feeling, looked at our wedding photos and Mexican trinkets, and then forgot about it.

Yet still, I'm glad that some people have been made happier, even as I disagree with the reasons (I'd be an ungrateful wretch not to). I acknowledge that I didn't understand that people feel you're signalling to them: 'Making a public announcement of your love for each other!' as a beaming in-law said. Another friend has been helpful in this regard, for when she got married years ago she too felt worn down by the crowds of cheering friends and family. Altogether, Michiel is far less ambivalent, and says that marriage affirms our future and his preparedness for it. I'd taken longevity for granted, and experienced it as a private, interior wish. Such differences between people are to be expected, and encouraged, even as they are precarious.

YASMINE
GOONERATNE

With Garlands Drest: The Oriental Bride

We are guests at a wedding in Bombay, the fabulously rich city that an unfortunate Portuguese princess, Catherine of Braganza, brought in 1661 as dowry to her compulsively faithless husband, England's Charles II. The year is 1983, the month January, Bombay's wedding month. It is the month in which plans can be confidently made for elaborate open air ceremonies, the month in which it never, never rains. In January, we are informed, nothing can possibly go wrong.

Our informant on these matters is a member of neither the bride's nor the bridegroom's families, merely an acquaintance, a 'Hello-ji'. We are Hello-jis ourselves, visitors on our first trip to India. Our objective is the Bird Sanctuary at Bharatpur and (if we are lucky) we will also see tigers at Corbett National Park. And so we are travelling light, our suitcases contain only khaki-coloured jeans and shirts suitable as regards colour, texture and weight for jungle trekking.

But the week we are spending in Bombay has turned out to be Wedding Week, or something very like it, and we have been diverted from our objective by the generous hospitality of Indian friends. In the space of seven days we are guests at six different functions, three of them weddings, the other three being parts of a single marriage celebration that will, when all is complete, link two of Bombay's wealthiest industrial families. Conscious that the clothes we have with us are entirely unsuitable for such splendid festivities, we have hastily equipped ourselves for a different kind of Indian jungle, an urban one.

At one of the functions to which we have been invited, we are privileged witnesses of a traditional marriage ceremony. It is conducted in the centre of a jasmine-decked platform in the ballroom of the Taj Hotel in an atmosphere saturated with perfume and incense, and its rituals are accompanied by the sounds of plucked strings and sonorous chanting. The bride and groom are splendid in gleaming silks, their faces cinematically radiant in the combined flash of cameras and jewels, their shoulders invisible beneath garlands of marigolds and roses.

At the second function connected with this young couple's marriage, we are guests at a small and very elegant cocktail party put on by the bride's parents in one of the city's golf clubs. The party is being held (says our Hello-ji, materialising suddenly at our elbows, glass in hand) chiefly for the college friends of the bride and groom. We know neither bride nor groom at all well, indeed we are seeing both of them for the second time. No problem, says Hello-ji, this is India, this is Bombay.

The third festive occasion, climaxing a week of seemingly non-stop celebration, is something else again. We leave our taxi at the entrance to the Bombay Race Course, step carefully over auspicious designs drawn by artistic hands on a specially constructed floor, and immediately find ourselves walking with twenty thousand fellow-guests upon a magnificent crimson carpet which has been laid over what seems like a kilometre of lush green grass, and stretches all the way from the street to the top of the grandstand steps. There, backed by an enormous mural reproducing the jewelled inlay on Queen Mumtaz Mahal's marble tomb in the Taj Mahal, stand the bride, her groom, and their parents, waiting in line to shake our hands or *namaste*.

As we climb the stairs to greet them, we are swept up in a cloud of perfume. I realise that what I had taken, when viewed from a distance, to be a painted mural on the rear wall of the grandstand is, in fact, not a mural at all but a solid screen of fresh jasmine and rosebuds. The screen, says Hello-ji, has been woven to the bride's design by a team of Bombay's skilled flower-workers in the space of a few hours.

'They've got to work fast, those chappies, to keep the flowers fresh,' says Hello-ji, in the airconditioned interior of whose wealthy papa's private airplane several hundreds of kilograms of blossoms have been specially flown for this purpose from the Valley of Kashmir. He tells us that the bride is a member of a large family, the complicated extensions of which enjoy permanent residence on the various floors of a city skyscraper. Very convenient, Hello-ji adds, for the banks and shops. And of course the arrangement keeps the members of the family together. Living so near – indeed, on top of – one another, it is easy for them to keep in touch.

He kindly parks us on a well-stuffed Chesterfield covered in brocade, and goes away to summon a bearer. The Chesterfield is one of several hundred such sofas dotted about on flowered carpets that have been spread on the grass, under the stars. (It never rains in January in Bombay.) The bearer, impressively equipped with a moustache that resembles the handlebars of a bicycle, arrives with drinks and hot *pakoras*. To be together, and 'in touch' is very important, continues Hello-ji, especially when a marriage is being arranged, for every member of the family has a right to be consulted on every aspect of a proposed alliance, and to have his or her opinion taken into consideration.

Except, of course – traditionally – the bride. She alone knows – or is supposed to know – nothing of the discussions that have been going on at a 'higher level'. She may suspect, she may hope, but she cannot be *sure*: not, at any rate, until her parents tell her what has been decided on her behalf. And then her duty is, simply, to accept.

But do these traditions still apply in twentieth century India? Of course, yes, Hello-ji says. In the villages. But it doesn't apply in this case. Vimla and Ranjit are young moderns. We now learn that the bride and groom have known each other since they were children, and are indeed presently classmates at Cornell, to which campus they will return after the wedding to complete their degrees and graduate.

I relate to Hello-ji a story that used to be told in my homeland, Sri Lanka, of a village wedding in the Kandyan hills. The year is 1817, and the British are just beginning to ease themselves comfortably into their peaceful government of the mountain kingdom they had annexed two years earlier. At the front of a small thatched cottage, a very young girl sits weaving, a basket of grass beside her on the veranda steps. The new British Resident of Kandy, a young Englishman on horseback, with a *sais* in attendance, stops by the verandah, examines the mat, and politely removes his tall hat.

RESIDENT *Sais*, please tell this young lady that I would like to ask her some questions.

SAIS Shall I translate, Excellency?

RESIDENT (who is also Chief Translator to the British Government in Ceylon) That will not be necessary. But please take notes. (in Sinhala) Greetings, Miss. May I ask what you are doing?

GIRL As you see, I am weaving a mat, Excellency.

RESIDENT May I buy your mat when you have completed it?

GIRL It is not for sale, Excellency.

RESIDENT Indeed? What will you do with it, then?

GIRL It is needed for a festivity next week, Excellency. So they say.

RESIDENT And what festivity may that be, Miss?

GIRL The festivity will be a wedding, Excellency. So they say.

RESIDENT And where is it to take place, Miss?

GIRL Here, in our village, Excellency. So they say.

RESIDENT Whose is this wedding, Miss?

GIRL It is my wedding, Excellency. So they say.

Hello-ji finds my story amusing and true (or so he says) to village life in India. And certainly, the gifts provided by fathers of brides in rural India are in striking contrast with the conspicuous opulence of marriage ceremonies among India's wealthy industrialists (many of whom are possessed, in the Johnsonian phrase, of riches beyond the dreams of avarice) This is especially obvious in regions as yet uncorrupted by what Mark Tully calls 'the middle class practice of giving dowries'. One Uttar Pradesh bride (the daughter of a domestic servant) took with her gifts valued at eighty thousand rupees that included the following items: one television set, one scooter, thirty-one cooking pots and pans, thirty-one saris for the women and seven kurta pyjamas for men of the bridegroom's family, five saris and five silver ornaments for the bride, one tin trunk, one wall clock, one wristwatch for the bridegroom, two chairs, one table, one sofa, one bed with bedding, and two thousand five hundred rupees in cash.

In between, the variations are endless: India has the largest and most prosperous middle class in the world, and everywhere in India, whatever the level at which a wedding is taking place, the generosity of the bride's family is a marker of its ability to provide responsibly for its daughters, a public demonstration of its claim to *izzat* or self-respect.[1]

The elderly aunt who had first told me the story of the British Resident and the village bride had thought it delightful, expressive (so she said) of the charming innocence and filial obedience of rural life. I did not. I was nineteen, at university, and becoming aware of some of the pressures that had begun to operate on me and on my sister undergraduates in the area of marriage. I suspected that it made no difference whether we lived in the town or the country. In daytime, and in class, my classmates and I read Keats and Byron. In the evenings, back in Hall, we thought about what we had read, and related it to Life.

Who are these coming to the sacrifice?
To what green altar, O mysterious priest,
Lead'st thou that heifer, lowing to the skies,

And all her silken flanks with garlands drest?

I am not quite sure now just when or how it was I received the distinct impression that, hidden somewhere within the ritual sacrifice Keats describes in his *Ode on a Grecian Urn*, is a reference to a wedding. Perhaps it came out of our discussions, or perhaps it emerged from the *Shorter Oxford* 's definition of a heifer: A young cow that has not had a calf – what could that be but a bride or a very new wife? Perhaps it was an impression born of the several meanings of the verb 'to dress': to clothe, to ornament... or, so much more sinister, to lovingly prepare for the curry pot and the roasting pan?

Perhaps it was connected with the garlands that adorned the 'silken flanks' of Keats's heifer: the poet's emphasis in his *Ode* might well be as much on the beauty and extreme youth of a young woman like the village girl in my aunt's story, as on those of a cow marked out for sacrifice. I now remember how, at the ceremony we witnessed at the Taj, Vimla's mother had placed a fragrant garland of roses around her daughter's neck with the cautious injunction: 'Be unto your husband as Sita, as Savitri, as Sakuntala.' I wonder how (or indeed, whether) Vimla, whose wedding has been surrounded with *motifs* and symbols drawn from time-honoured traditional sources, will apply those heroic models of wifely devotion to married life on an American college campus. I believe she is much more likely to adopt to her requirements the example of Draupadi.

After the staging a few years ago of Peter Brook's dramatic adaptation of the Indian epic poem *The Mahabharata*, and the entry of its images into the Western consciousness through the medium of cinema and television, non-Indianshave become aware, as I am fairly certain they have never been before despite the availablity of the Indian epics in paperback translations, of the heroic personality of the princess Draupadi. This is a royal lady who obediently accepts five husbands at her mother-in-law's bidding, yet challenges the ruling that her life must turn on the fall of dice from the hand of a husband who has already gambled away everything he owns, including his own liberty. Capable of a curse horrific in its implications ('I will not bind my hair,' she says with steely calm to a courtier who has humiliated her before her husbands and the royal court, 'until I have washed it in your blood': a promise she carries out to the letter), she has the fortitude, when offered three boons, to choose freedom for her husband Yuddhisthira and his four brothers, yet refuse anything for herself: 'I will have nothing to do with greed'. Draupadi is celebrated in Indian religious literature (and all ancient Indian literature is religious at its core) as a woman of heroic stature, rivalled only by the three other famous heroine-figures, Sita, Savitri and Sakuntala. Each of these four women possesses mythic status far greater than her beauty: confronted with seemingly unbearable provocation and misfortune, they have the strength to endure. Married though they are to men who prove to be weak, unreliable, forgetful or mistrustful, each treats her husband as a god to be worshipped, and is content to live her life in his shadow.[2]

Is traditional India changing? I ask Hello-ji, who shrugs and helps himself to another *pakora*. I get no reply. And yes, in externals at least, change does seem to be taking place. Shopping for saris that week in the city, I have seen on a stand beside a glamorous plaster model draped in a wedding sari glittering with silver and gold embroidery, a sign that now strikes me as being precisely appropriate to Vimla and her generation: 'For the one day in your daughter's life that she doesn't wear jeans.'

Hello-ji has told us that his brother-in-law is a Scot, and that his sister Amrita had married in Britain, with their younger sister as her bridesmaid. Hello-ji himself, deputising for his unavoidably absent father, had given the bride away. What happens, I ask Hello-ji, when oriental marriages take place away from 'home'? 'All hell breaks loose,' is Hello-ji's curt reply to my question. It is clear that whatever has happened, he doesn't want to talk about it. Later, on another occasion, he does. And this, as far as I can make out, is the way things went:

The time is a fine summer morning in 1960, the place the interior of a car parked outside an English country church. Seated in the car, Amrita, her groom, and her bridesmaid are arguing. They have just completed a rehearsal of the ceremony that is to take place in a week's time. Amrita is showing signs of strain.

AMRITA Yes, but what does it *mean*? The cable just says: 'Five, seven or nine, not four, six or eight. Love, Mother.' Nothing more.

BRIDESMAID She's just reminding you and David that your engagement ring must have an odd number of stones, not an even number. 'Five, seven or nine – *not* four, six or eight.' See?

AMRITA No, I don't see. What does she mean *must*? I've been wearing my engagement ring since the day David and I became engaged, and Mother's telling me how many stones it should have in it? She's telling me *now*? With a week to go before the wedding? (She looks at the ring on her finger. It is made of platinum, and is set with six sapphires.)

BRIDESMAID It's a very pretty ring, Amrita. Don't worry about the cable. Just forget it, Mother'll never know. It's not as if she'll be at the wedding. And you won't be going back home for ages – and then you can always say you forgot and left the ring behind, in the bank or something. Unless David would like to have one of the sapphires removed. Or another one added.

AMRITA Are you crazy? Have you gone out of your *mind*? You're as bad as Mother. I have no intention of altering *anything*. It's my *engagement* ring. It belonged to David's *mother*, and *he* gave it to *me*. And now I suppose you'll tell me there's some weird superstition about even numbers that will doom us to death or divorce.

BRIDEGROOM (Begins to hum wordlessly and starts the car.)

BRIDESMAID Look, forget it. Let's just concentrate on the things we *can* do something about. I'm getting cables from Mother too. The last one told me to place a glass of fresh white flowers on a table where you will see it as you come out of your bedroom ready to drive to church. The one before that reminds me to make sure you aren't greeted by a widow as you come *out* of church . . .

AMRITA Oh, that's just marvellous, isn't it? So when Pat's mother rushes forward – and I know well she will – to be the first to kiss me and congratulate David, *you* are to dash between us and intercept her? Who does Mother think she is? And is this a wedding or a cabaret? Mrs White is one of my closest, *closest* friends, she'll never get over it if I draw back –

BRIDEGROOM Look, have either of you two got any ideas about lunch?

AMRITA What I can't understand is the weird mish-mash of superstitions Mother seems to want us to keep in mind. Am I getting married in a *church*, for heaven's sake, or am I not? Is Mr Harris an Anglican clergyman, or is he some dancing dervish? Just tell me. You seem to be the expert.

BRIDESMAID Well, it's no good taking it out on *me*. I'm merely a receiver of instructions that I'm supposed to pass on to you. In your own interest, Mother says. If you want to ignore them, Amrita, you just go ahead and do that. I'm not responsible. I don't know why

I ever agreed to be the bridesmaid at this wedding, in the first place.

BRIDEGROOM Here it is. 'The Running Footman'. I think I need a drink. *And* lunch.

AMRITA From the moment David and I became engaged and I was foolish enough to write and tell Mother, it's been one set of orders after another. Directives from headquarters. *Don't* do this, *don't* do that, you *must* do this, you *mustn't* do the other . . . Well, you can just tell Mother from me – since you're her interpreter, or transmitter, or whatever it is – that this is *my* wedding – David's too, of course – but *mine*. And no one's going to tell *me* what I can and can't do at my own wedding.

BRIDEGROOM Sherry before lunch, you two? Gin and tonic?

BRIDESMAID I know it's irritating, but you've got to be fair, you've got to look at it from Mother's point of view too. She wants everything to be perfect for you. What she'd like more than anything else in the world is to be here herself, and do everything for you –

AMRITA Well, we have to be thankful for small mercies, Dave, Mother'll be thousands of miles away on the day we get married –

BRIDESMAID – and she's absolutely devastated that she can't be here, so she's –

BRIDEGROOM Running everything by remote control, eh?

AMRITA *Ruining* everything by remote control, more like, it seems to me.

BRIDESMAID Well, all I can say is: I don't care how many cables arrive between now and your wedding day, I absolutely refuse to pass on any more messages. I'll deal with Mother. And I'll tell her everything was done according to her wishes. Whether it was or not.

BRIDEGROOM Thanks. (He looks cheerful for the first time in several weeks.) I appreciate that. Really I do. And so will your sister, when it's all behind us.

BRIDESMAID (in tears) Well, it's obvious to me that the two of you can't see anything but your own –

AMRITA Tell me why we should. Just tell me, that's all . . .

According to Hello-ji, the bride and her bridesmaid were barely on speaking terms by the time the wedding day arrived. Added to which, her mother's insistence on ritual had reduced Amrita to such a nervous wreck that her hand shook while she was painting her nails, and a great stream of crimson nail polish shot out of the container and across the width of the Manipuri silk going-away sari laid out on the bed.

'Bad luck!' Amrita had cried, and burst into tears.

Faced by this crisis, Hello-ji told me, his younger sister had abandoned her pique and removed the ruined sari. She had substituted a dark blue (an old favourite) from Amrita's wardrobe, and calmed the bride down. ('Mother'll never know, not even from the photographs – and anyway, you'd forgotten all about the 'something old' you were going to wear – well, here it is, you've found it.')

As he gave Amrita his arm to lead her up the aisle of the church, Hello-ji told me he felt his sister shaking with fear. 'Poor kid,' he said, 'it must have been terrible for her. Not a happy occasion at all. Everything had become too *tense*.'

'What did you do?' I asked.

' "Well, *baba*", I said, and tucked her arm into mine, "listen carefully now to your big brother. Ready? As one earwig said to the other earwig, Earwig, O." '

I began to laugh.

'Yes, that's what she did too. She laughed. A great big wonderful smile. I don't always say the right thing, but that time I seem to have hit the jackpot.'

Attached to our local newspaper this week is 'Bridal Fair', an advertising supplement devoted to weddings. Presumably February is Wedding Month in Sydney. Brides here can record their memories on video, personalise their wine labels and stationery, frame their bouquets. *Frame their bouquets*? I have moved twice between countries, shedding numerous possessions along the way. I have some souvenirs of my wedding day still with me, but a framed bouquet gathering dust on a mantelpiece or sitting on top of a wardrobe is not one of them.

I wonder whether the concept of a framed bouquet would ever catch on in Sri Lanka. At village weddings and city weddings alike, sprays of coconut flowers are an indispensable part of the decoration of the bridal platform. But – and in this, they clearly symbolise the charmingly naive young girl of my aunt's story, those coconut flowers have to be the genuine article, and they have to be fresh. In an attempt to benefit his country's palm oil industry and its ecology at the same time, a well-intentioned Sri Lankan industrialist once devised a new line in realistic coconut flowers made of plastic, specially designed as wedding decorations. He found few buyers. People just weren't interested.

NOTES

1. For one of the finest detailed descriptions in modern literature of a wedding in rural India, see the chapter 'Ram Chander's Story' in Mark Tully's *No Full Stops in India* (1991). I have taken my list of bridal gifts from this source.
2. Cf. Y. Gooneratne, 'Women in shadow: Silenced voices in literature and culture', in A. Greet (ed.) *Women's Writing in the New Literatures* special issue of *C.R.N.L.E. Reviews Journal* 1 (1990) pp. 1–16.

PAMELA VERRALL

Coming Out Show: Notes for a radio program on weddings and wives

The Coming Out Show began on International Women's Day in International Women's Year 1975. Since then it has encouraged the talents of hundreds of women who have worked on the program either as full-time producers or as occasional contributors. *The Coming Out Show* has also given listeners an opportunity to hear the diversity of voices and opinions that make up this wave of feminism.

NOTES FOR A PROGRAM ON WEDDINGS AND WIVES

Plan, February 1993

AIM: To make 45-minute feature on young women's attitudes to weddings and their notions of wifeliness.

WHY: In looking through our records I find only one entry to do with weddings and that is from June 1975. In this twenty minute piece young women talk about the proposal, the engagement, the dress, and the kind of wedding they want to have. None of them talk about what it means to be a wife. A program about Weddings and Wives is overdue.

WHY FOR RADIO: Whatever we as individuals think about marriage, no woman in this society remains untouched by the potent imagery of 'the wedding'. In audience terms I think this is a winner. There's great sound potential here. Apart from the voices of the interviewees there is lots of music ... popular and traditional; the big TV weddings ... and actuality from the weddings themselves.

HOW: The possible approaches are overwhelming, so I need to start with a period of nothing but research – a kind of semi-structured muddling about in the subject area. What do I know for sure? Not much at this stage other than that I'm looking for women in their twenties who are just about to marry or have recently married.

BUDGET: It won't be an expensive program. It's mainly my time. I'll do the research, the recording, and the editing. The only other expenses are likely to be an actor to do some readings, or some copyright fees if I use film extracts.

GETTING STARTED: Letting people know what I'm doing and picking their brains. Reading whatever I can lay my hands on: academic papers, newspaper articles, women's magazines, bride magazines. And keeping an eye on the TV weddings.

Progress Report, May 1993

I started with two women in their late twenties. One had just got married and the other was about to get married in a couple of weeks. I knew them so I felt more comfortable about questioning them in detail. Both had some doubts about whether they were doing the right thing. Not because of making a commitment to their partner, but because of the social and family expectations that are unleashed by the announcement of a wedding. While many women obviously relish the prospect of being 'the beautiful bride' these women found the pressures to be perfectly beautiful, perfectly prepared and perfectly pleasing to competing interest groups highly fraught. After talking to them I came up with a basic series of questions.

The Questions

MARRIAGE: Did you always think you'd get married? Did you feel any resistance to the idea of getting married? What was your parents' marriage like? What role do you see marriage playing today?

DECISION: Whose idea was it? What factors were influential? Why marry when you can live together? Was there a formal proposal? Did your family play any particular role?

WEDDING: What kind of wedding do you want ... big, small, 'traditional' etc. How important is the ceremony itself? What kind of vows are you making?

PREPARATION: How were decisions made, who did the work, how much did it cost? Were there tensions? What relationship does the wedding have to the marriage? Who is it for?

THE DAY: Was it fun, was it how you'd imagined it? Was it worth it?

WIFELINESS: How do you see yourself as a wife? Do you think you'll be different to your mother? How? Will you change your name? What kinds of decisions have you made about money, housework and children?

To find a potential pool of interviewees I sent out a message on e-mail to women within the ABC asking them for contacts. I specified women in their twenties either just married or in the throes of preparing, and said I was interested in talking to women from a variety of ethnic backgrounds. I got about thirty replies. The most striking and unexpected thing for me was the number of women marrying someone from a different cultural background.

As other general preparation I read papers from the Institute of Family Studies about the current patterns of family formation. I wanted some kind of overview of our attitudes to marriage and cohabitation. I discovered that in 1991 the median age of first marriage was 24.5 years for women and 26.7 for men.

As I haven't been married myself and haven't attended many weddings I feel out of touch with wedding trends and protocol. My local newsagent however, provided me with an astonishing array of *Bride* magazines. I was immersed for hours in 'beauty duty', 'bridal registers', 'honeymoon hotspots' and a breathtaking amount of detail about 'wedding etiquette for the 90s'. It's apparent that the 'serious bride' needs access to a lot of money and time.

As a part of attuning myself to the popular heartbeat of the modern wedding, I also attended the Bridal Expo at Darling Harbour. This ranks as one of the most appalling experiences of my life. I endured a parade of bridal gowns but to music so deafening I feared permanent hearing impairment. I staggered out of Darling Harbour with the firm knowledge that I am not the woman to make a program about the wedding as ultimate shopping experience. I abandoned this line of research.

I have since done long initial interviews with five women. In two cases their partners were present. I thought about including the perceptions of the men but decided this would be an entirely different program. For this one I'll concentrate on the women. I didn't record these interviews but took detailed notes. I didn't want to end up with hours of tape until I was much clearer about who was going to be the focus of the program.

The Interviews

These are some edited comments from the original interviews.

Lyndal has just turned thirty. She grew up on a farm in Victoria and finished a degree in horticulture a few weeks before she married Peter. He is thirty-five and runs a small business from home. They lived together for almost two years before marrying.

WHAT DO YOU THINK ABOUT MARRIAGE GENERALLY?
It's a time when women load huge expectations on each other. There is so much expectation on this one day and event. The wedding isn't really about the relationship or the Groom. It's about the Bride.

HOW DO YOU SEE YOUR PARENTS' MARRIAGE?
I don't think of it as particularly successful, but they've stuck it out.

WHY DID YOU DECIDE TO GET MARRIED?
We were really making a decision about not giving up on the relationship – about making it work. It seemed important to give that decision a public face by standing up and doing it in front of our family and friends. When I first met Peter I was still living in Melbourne, so we really got to know each other in that first year over the phone. We spent a lot of time talking on the phone. That was very important in building the essential dynamic of our relationship – talking and communicating. Then we lived together for a couple of years, so it was much easier to be realistic about the difficulties of loving someone. I didn't feel the same kind of infatuation I'd felt in other relationships, but there was a greater ease and a greater sense of loving.

WAS THERE A PROPOSAL?
Before I decided to move from Melbourne I was looking for some kind of commitment and Peter said he'd marry me. It wasn't what I'd been expecting, so at that time I said 'no' to marriage but 'yes' to coming to Sydney. I was really quite annoyed that he'd asked first – so over the next two years, we'd often propose to each other. We wanted to take some

of the seriousness and tension out of the whole process. I got the chance to propose on lots of occasions and Peter always said yes – I didn't ever go down on my knee though. And he'd often ask me – sometimes I said yes, and sometimes I said no. I enjoyed that – and it was me who finally made the decision about when the wedding would be – that was important. We still propose to each other sometimes – it's a reminder that there really is another person who wants to stick around.

HOW LONG WAS THERE BETWEEN THE ANNOUNCEMENT AND THE WEDDING?

I set the date nine months away to allow for all the preparations. There was the traditional expectation from both sets of parents that the wedding would be somewhere my parents could play host – realistically that meant getting married on the farm. That was good in some ways – it meant my friends got to see this part of my life.

WHO DID MOST OF THE PREPARATION?

I did most of the work and most of the thinking and the organising. This caused some tension between us. There were times when I felt resentful about doing it all. It seemed like I needed to be doing the right thing by everybody with very little support.

The main tension though was with my mother. She had huge expectations and was very critical of a lot of the things I wanted to do. We argued about the fact I wasn't going to change my name, we argued about the fact that I wanted children to come and be involved in the ceremony. There were a lot of arguments. I gave in on some issues like inviting people from the district I didn't know. So instead of the forty I wanted it turned into more like eighty.

And then there were all the things like figuring out how much make-up I was going to wear. I don't normally wear any – but that was fun, trying out different lipsticks and eye shadow and foundation.

HOW DID IT GO ON THE DAY?

We wanted a wedding that was going to be acceptable to all the parents and their friends, but which was different in significant ways.

WHAT WAS TRADITIONAL?

We got married on the farm, we exchanged rings, had flowers, a best man and woman, made speeches and had a cake – those things were all pretty ordinary.

WHAT WAS DIFFERENT?

We went through the ceremony very carefully to eliminate the sexism. The whole bridal party arrived together on the horse and cart rather than me arriving later, I wasn't given away, and the celebrant didn't always address Peter first when we were exchanging vows – we swapped that around.

WERE YOU PLEASED WITH THE WEDDING?

The tension with my mother didn't really let up and I felt this incredible pressure to be the 'beautiful bride'. The most relaxed part of the day was the ceremony – we'd worked out what we wanted to say and practised with a pretend celebrant so that was really enjoyable.

WHAT ABOUT BECOMING A WIFE?

What's hard is the role – and society's expectations that you will give up your sense of self for the relationship. It's expected that your primary role will be about caring for him and taking on the domestic responsibility. Superficially there'd be a lot less struggling if I fitted in with that role. I'd work part time, and get on with the caring and the housework. But we both knew that wouldn't work in the longer term. There are so many hurtful connotations that go with being 'a wife' – I feel pretty uncomfortable with the word.

WHERE DO THINGS GET DIFFICULT?

Money – we haven't decided whether to have a joint account or not. What we have been talking about are the financial arrangements if I get pregnant – how long Peter would support me fully.

And then there's housework. Things go much better when I am relaxed. I try and remember what it's like when I'm trying to do something new – like building things. Then I want to be encouraged, not treated as stupid. So that's how Peter wants to be treated around housework. I'd like to get to the stage where things get done without a lot of thinking about it. For now I accept that things aren't going to be half and half.

Housework and money – they're on the agenda and they'll stay there.

YOU TALKED ABOUT FINANCIAL ARRANGEMENTS IF YOU GET PREGNANT. HAVE YOU ALSO TALKED ABOUT PARENTING?

Because Peter runs a business from home it's very important to me that we take it in turns. It's not just about who does the work – I want to make sure he gets to build a relationship with the child. That's so unusual for men.

WHAT'S CHANGED?

I think our parents' major expectations were satisfied by us getting married, but things with some of our friends are more difficult, especially with those who're cynical about long term relationships. And I know I've got to be vigilant about people not making a whole lot of assumptions – I have to be more active about keeping my own identity.

Julie is Chinese Vietnamese and came to Australia with her family in the early 1980s. She's thirty years old and has been under a lot of pressure from her family to get married. She works in the travel industry. A few weeks ago she agreed to marry Paul. He's thirty-one and works for the police force. They plan to get married later this year.

WHY DID YOU DECIDE TO GET MARRIED?

We've known each other for a couple of years now. We met through work, and over the last six months or so Paul's come down to see me each weekend. He's recently moved to Sydney so we've been spending a lot of time together.

DID YOU THINK ABOUT LIVING TOGETHER?

Paul asked me to move in with him for a while, but I knew the 'gossip' would be too much. We've got to start saving for the wedding though so Paul's moving in with my mother and me in a few weeks time – we'll have separate bedrooms.

DID PAUL PROPOSE?

Yes. I was over at his place having dinner – I was quite surprised and didn't say yes straight away, but I did agree by the end of the night.

HAVE YOU SET A DATE YET?

We're not quite sure but probably in about six or seven months. It'll take us a while to save – I think the wedding will cost around $5000, not including the honeymoon.

HAVE YOU DONE MUCH PREPARATION YET?

Not really – we were thinking of having a small registry office wedding but now we'll probably have a Catholic wedding with about a hundred guests. Paul's a Catholic and his parents want a Catholic wedding. We're just starting to find out about all the different arrangements that need to be made.

HAVE YOU THOUGHT MUCH ABOUT WHAT IT'LL BE LIKE TO BE A WIFE?

In the Chinese culture there's a strong expectation of deference towards the husband. My father made all the decisions when I was growing up, and my mother still defers to him and holds this as the model even though my parents are divorced.

I want a much greater sense of partnership than my parents. I get Paul to help me with things now, like the cooking and the washing. I think it's really important that we share things, that we do things together. I got very angry with him the other Friday night. He went out for a few drinks with the boys and didn't phone me – but I told him, he's not just on his own now. He needs to be thinking about me.

ARE THERE ANY DIFFICULTIES BECAUSE OF YOUR DIFFERENT CULTURAL BACKGROUNDS?

Well, my mother and I and all my relatives speak Cantonese. I've taught Paul a few phrases, but that might be difficult when he moves in with us. He was also brought up as a 'chops and peas man' – so my mother often cooks two different meals – I'm teaching him to use chopsticks and he's beginning to get the hang of it.

I think we might need two TVs – he likes watching sport and I like Chinese videos.

Mary is twenty-one. A couple of months ago she married Huw, who's twenty-six. They decided within two weeks of meeting that they wanted to get married but waited for three months before making the announcement. They're both very committed Christians and both studying at university.

WHY DID YOU DECIDE TO MARRY?

Neither of us thought we'd be getting married when we first started going out. I thought I'd finish university at least, and Huw had written a series of poems called 'Marriage is like death' the year before. He'd seen some of his friends getting married for all kinds of terrible reasons, so he wasn't really feeling very positive about marriage. But then we each realised this was the kind of person we could spend our lives with.

WAS THERE SOME KIND OF FORMAL PROPOSAL?

It wasn't a big thing. Huw did ask me, but it wasn't a big event. It really came out of our discussions. Then we waited for a couple of months before telling my parents, partly because I was only twenty at the time – and I wanted my parents to get to know him a bit first, before we announced we were going to get married.

HOW LONG BETWEEN THE ANNOUNCEMENT AND THE WEDDING?

We worked out we needed a year to let people get prepared and to get things organised but the last couple of months really dragged.

DID YOU HAVE THE WEDDING YOU WANTED?
Yes I did. We wrote our own service, and we had an outdoor afternoon tea for the reception. My mum didn't interfere at all. Her mother had arranged her wedding for her and she ended up with the kind of wedding she really didn't want, so she didn't interfere.

WHAT WERE THE THINGS YOU PUT INTO THE SERVICE?
We really thought about what marriage is for and about our intentions and wrote that down. There were things in the traditional service we weren't sure about. There's a part in the service that talks about marriage as the foundation of society, but I think that society can stand on a firm foundation with single people as well. They're just as important to society as married couples, so we changed that part. We really went through the service – it took hours and hours. I didn't promise to obey him. I wasn't given away. And we changed the part where it goes 'will you take so and so?' We changed that to 'Mary, will you cherish Huw?' and vice versa.

WHAT OTHER KINDS OF PREPARATIONS DID YOU MAKE?
It wasn't that difficult or that expensive because we got so much help from our friends. One friend made my dress and didn't charge me for it. One of the bridesmaids made the skirts. Another friend did my hair and someone else did my wedding make-up. We got help from so many people – it was incredible.

HAD YOU THOUGHT ABOUT YOURSELF AS BEING A BRIDE? WERE YOU FULFILLING THOSE FANTASIES?
When I was younger I'd imagined it would be much more formal – that I'd have a huge train and lace, but I'm glad I didn't have that. When it came to it I wanted something much more simple.

DO YOU THINK OF YOURSELF AS A WIFE?
Not really yet – it feels strange. I think I'm still getting used to it but I do think of myself as belonging with Huw.

DO YOU THINK YOUR MARRIAGE WILL BE LIKE YOUR PARENTS?
I think we've started in a different place. My father came from a generation where you never ever admitted that you had a problem. Having good fights and things like that are some of the things we've been thinking about. My parents have come to that in the last few years but I think we've got a head start.

We haven't had any real fights since we've been married. We had them last year when we were figuring out the way we treat each other and other people. It's really important to me that we be able to talk about everything – that we're interested in what the other's doing – that we don't exclude each other from parts of our lives.

WHAT ABOUT IF YOU DEVELOP A PASSION FOR SOMETHING HUW ISN'T PARTICULARLY INTERESTED IN?
Well, I'm really into music and I'd like to do some more singing lessons. But I think it's about time. If it was becoming more important than the relationship it'd be a problem – but I think it's important not to do everything together but to have some separate areas.

WHAT ABOUT CHANGING YOUR NAME?
I did decide to change my name. I think it's good to be identified together but I think if I'd insisted Huw would have changed his to mine.

WHAT DO YOU WANT TO ACHIEVE IN THE MARRIAGE?
I suppose we want to be a support to each other, and help each other grow as people and Christians. It's about support and friendship. I like coming home to someone who's interested in me and my life.

Lucy is twenty-eight and works part time doing media policy work. A few months ago she married Carlos at the Registry

Office. He's twenty-six, comes from Brazil and works as a cook. They knew each other for a couple of years before they were married.

DID YOU IMAGINE THAT YOU'D GET MARRIED?
Not at all. I'd been very scornful about friends of mine who'd decided to get married. My parents are divorced and there was a lot of trauma involved in their separation. Even though it was years ago now it's neither healed nor resolved. I'd been living for years in a women's share house and I thought I'd continue to live like that.

WHY DID YOU DECIDE TO MARRY?
We'd been going out together seriously for a few months – one day as we were walking down the street Carlos told me he was in Australia illegally. At first I said I didn't mind him being illegal but I wasn't marrying him. I didn't want to get married. It took months before I agreed, but people we knew were getting busted and deported. I wanted the relationship. I just didn't want to get married. But I knew we were going to have to regularise his immigration status.

WHAT HAPPENED THEN?
Carlos went back to Brazil and re-applied for entry. He was back in Brazil for eight months. I found it very hard dealing with the separation, so I went to Brazil for two months, which was good because I got to know his parents and brothers and sisters.

WHAT KINDS OF PREPARATIONS DID YOU MAKE WHILE CARLOS WAS AWAY?
My mother thought making a lot of arrangements would help me cope with his absence. I went into this incredible resistance and blocking. I refused to talk about it with her. She lives up the coast so she'd be ringing me up to organise something or other – there were a lot of phones being banged down. I felt this tremendous pressure from my friends. I was frightened of telling some of them I was getting married. I knew they'd feel

betrayed by that decision. And then there were the others who thought I should be doing it in a particular way.

WHAT SORT OF THINGS DID PEOPLE THINK YOU SHOULD BE DOING?

Most of the pressure was around the dress. I went out with girlfriends a couple of times to buy a dress. It was disastrous. They had all kinds of ideas about what I should buy and the fact that Carlos shouldn't see the dress before we were married. There are all these little detailed rules about how you should get married. I coped by shutting it all out and refusing to make any arrangements at all. I'd been so critical of other people getting married that the whole thing was incredibly confronting.

DID YOU END UP GETTING A DRESS?

When Carlos got back we went to Paddington markets and found what we wanted very quickly and had lots of fun. I bought a purple dress. Carlos bought a tie to go with the suit his parents had given him. And I bought some stockings to match his tie.

WHAT OTHER ARRANGEMENTS DID YOU END UP MAKING?

We did send out invitations about a week before. One of our friends drew it up – so we did at least end up inviting our friends.

WHAT HAPPENED ON THE DAY?

We had it at the Registry Office. I felt this was the only way of keeping it under control. The Registry Office is an incredibly daggy place with plastic curtains, but the ceremony is quick and just involves an exchange of simple promises. We only had a couple of people there. There was my friend Fiona, who was my flower girl, my brothers and mother and one of Carlos's brothers who lives in Australia. Fiona had made these beautiful garlands of flowers that we both wore. We didn't have a special car or anything like that.

WHAT ABOUT THE RECEPTION?

We had it in a park and about thirty people came. Some of our friends decorated the park with signs to show the way, and hung muslin and flowers in the tree branches. It looked really beautiful. Everyone ended up bringing food to share which was great – people had given me such a hard time about this. It'd been the source of a lot of fights with my mother and some of my friends. They said you just couldn't ask people to bring food to a wedding. My mother ended up buying a whole lot of champagne and made a fruit cake with icing, so we did some of the things you're supposed to. My mother actually made two cakes. The other one was to send to people in a couple of months time. When we checked the tin a few weeks later it was infested with ants, so no one got their cake.

SO HOW DID IT GO ON THE DAY?

I really enjoyed myself on the day. I'd had such doubts about what I was doing and resisted to the end, but we ended up having a wedding that was fun.

DO YOU SEE YOURSELF BECOMING A WIFE?

I've made it clear I don't ever want to be referred to as a wife. But it's funny – since we've got married I feel more secure than I've ever felt in my life.

WHAT ABOUT THE CULTURAL DIFFERENCES? DO YOU THINK THERE'LL BE DIFFICULTIES?

There are differences. Even though I've lived in South America and I speak Portuguese, we have very different ways of showing emotion.

Here's something that happened recently that might give you some idea. I'd bought some biscuits from a local shop and they were already well past their use-by date. Carlos came with me when I took them back. The shopkeeper was pretty rude – he couldn't have cared less. Then Carlos butted in saying things like, 'This is my wife ... I love her ... You could have poisoned her ... How could you do this?' I was incredibly angry with him for butting in and so embarrassed by his great declarations of love for me in front of the shopkeeper. We ended up having a huge fight. I think it'll take a long time for us to sort this kind of thing out.

Shanti was married a few weeks ago in a park down by the harbour. She's twenty-nine and came to Australia from Southern India with her family ten years ago. She works as a doctor at the Children's Hospital and has just finished her final exams as a paediatrician. John is thirty. He had a suburban upbringing in Brisbane and is a professional musician. They knew each other for three years before deciding to marry.

DID YOU ALWAYS IMAGINE YOU WOULD GET MARRIED?
I'd always thought I would get married but until I met John I hadn't thought of marrying outside my background.

WHY DID YOU DECIDE TO MARRY?
We knew it had to happen. When John and I started living together my parents gave him a really hard time. He had the wrong hair, the wrong profession and he was the wrong colour. They were incredibly resistant to our relationship. There was a lot of pressure on me too. My parents were offering up alternative partners, using threats and emotional coercion. At one stage they brought in an Indian astrologer. It seemed at times as if the whole South Indian community was involved. It was very unpleasant.

WHAT KIND OF WEDDING WILL IT BE?
We'll be having a Vedic ceremony – it's a ceremony that's over two thousand years old. Now in the good old days Indian weddings went on for seven days – so we've just picked out the parts we want. Our ceremony will probably go for about three hours. It'll be conductd in Sanskrit with a translator. John will be dressed as a traditional South Indian bridegroom and he's asked his sister to be his assistant during the ceremony.

APART FROM BEING A LOT LONGER WILL THE WEDDING BE DIFFERENT IN OTHER WAYS?
Well, for one thing, there's no place in an Indian wedding for anyone to look like a doll. But probably the most important difference is that this ceremony isn't really about vows. The essence of the Vedic ceremony is a series of blessings and a statement of aspirations. I like that because we don't feel we need vows to make a commitment to each other.

WHAT KIND OF PREPARATION WILL YOU BE DOING?
We've just sent out the invitations that we designed ourselves. We want to keep things as simple as possible. We're going to have the reception at the Leichhardt Town Hall. We want it to be a lot of fun, so there won't be any speeches. Basically we want to have a party with all our friends, lots of music, and some Indian dancing.

DO YOU THINK MUCH WILL CHANGE WHEN YOU BECOME JOHN'S WIFE?
My parents will be a lot happier, but I don't think they'll expect too much, except children. From our point of view though I don't expect that too much will change. We don't want our relationship to change. We like to consider ourselves friends and partners and we want that to stay the same. I hope no one calls me 'wife'. The very word contains inbuilt notions of subordination, being at home, keeping the home stable, and waiting.

DO YOU THINK YOU'LL BE A WIFE IN THE WAY YOUR MOTHER WAS?
No, I don't think so, though my mother was and is in many ways very independent. She was never a subordinate or a stay-at-home woman. She's studied and worked since we came to Australia, but even so she was curtailed a lot.

WILL YOU CHANGE YOUR NAME?
I won't change my name. John is going to hyphenate his.

WHAT ABOUT SHARING HOUSEWORK AND MONEY?
We share the housework pretty well but money's been quite interesting. John's had to work through some uncomfortable feelings about marrying someone who's likely to be a much bigger income earner. I think we now realise that at different times we'll have different income levels.

DO YOU THINK THERE'LL BE DIFFICULTIES BECAUSE OF YOUR DIFFERENT CULTURAL BACKGROUNDS?
I don't think so. John shares my love of Indian music and dance so I don't feel I'll have to give up the things that're really important to me. I guess my one regret at the moment is that our children won't grow up speaking Tamil.

I did that interview with Shanti and John a few weeks before the wedding. The next time I saw them was at the ceremony.

The ceremony was conducted in a park down by the harbour. It was the most relaxed and happy wedding I've ever been to. Even though it went on for three hours no one seemed to get bored or fidgety. During parts of the ceremony Shanti and John got to wander around and chat to people. There seemed to be a total absence of striving for perfection. Providing things were generally proceeding in the right direction everyone was happy, though John's father did look rather bemused at one point when he was handed a coconut. After the ceremony people stayed around and ate and then we all dispersed for the afternoon, coming back that night for a great party.

From these initial interviews the most interesting issue is the number of weddings happening across cultures. And it's not just my odd little sample. Soon after I started looking at this I came across a paper that suggests that by the turn of the century 40 per cent of Australians will be the products of such marriages. Given this change I was surprised by the low level of family opposition. It was only in Shanti's case that there was an overt and sustained policy of resistance, but even that was greatly diminished by the wedding itself.

I was also interested in the proposal. My hunch is that men are still expected to do the proposing. I suspect that most women still consider it somehow inappropriate to formally propose. While proposing wasn't a big deal for any of these couples, Lyndal and Peter were the only ones to challenge the formality and the role division in this part of the process.

While there is a lot of pressure to conform to certain notions of what constitutes a 'proper' or a 'traditional wedding,' many couples are experimenting more with the ceremony itself. Even the bridal magazines contain sections on 'Do-it-Yourself Vows.'

And of course weddings still provide families with a marvellous opportunity to go for the throat. Family pathology gets a thorough work-out as wedding preparations proceed, with the mother/daughter relationship as the central drama.

'Wifeliness' generally seems to be in bad odour with many women feeling uncomfortable about the thought of becoming 'a wife'. All the women I spoke to, though, were optimistic about their prospects for constructing new and more equal ways of negotiating the marriage partnership.

And now back to the radio program.

This process has given me the opportunity to focus on what I'm interested in, the ways in which women are going about redefining and renegotiating their position as wife in a cross-cultural context.

I want to focus on three women. Any more and it'll be too difficult to get a clear enough sense of them and this is a topic where listeners will want to get to know each woman in some depth. So I'll go back and talk to Julie, Shanti and Lucy to see if they're happy to proceed. I've got some good sound from John and Shanti's wedding, and if Julie is happy to be involved then I'll be able to interview her a couple of times leading up to the wedding as well as recording sound at the ceremony.

Postscript:

It would be fascinating to drop in again on these marriages in five years time. Will the daily routine negotiations about money, housework and child care continue? How many of these marriages will be intact? How far will these women have gone in creating a different version of wifeliness?

BARBARA JEFFERIS

Money and Maidenheads

I had an aunt who lived nearly ninety years and read more books than almost anyone I've ever known. There were no limitations on her non-fiction reading – pre-history and future predictions interested her equally, as did politics and biography and travel. Fiction, because it was about love and sex and marriage and death and the human heart, naturally formed an important part of her reading. But a novel of which any part was set before 1893 bored her. Like most passionate and uncomplicated people, she knew that the year of her birth was the year in which modernity and sexual freedom began, and the world of the emotions before that time didn't exist for her.

She was wrong, of course. Modernity and sexual freedom began a full generation later, in the year that I was born. It's what we all believe. It began with us, we led the way, and those who come after have only to pick up the torch, and run.

It is one of the tenets of feminism that there has been a three-decade revolution in sexual behaviour. It's true. Of course it's true. But the real question is *which* thirty years are we talking about? Shall we start with the 1940s, which we're asked to believe were full of virgins leaping into marriage beds? or the 50s, where the leaping virgins found that Freud had beaten them to it, and seriously interfered with the ground rules? or the 60s, which were Pill-protected and seemed safeish? Or the 70s where it was discovered there'd been medical miscalculations about some pills and appliances? Or the 80s which effectively sent everyone back to square one? Safe sex had been sex that protected you from pregnancies which would destroy your reputation. By the 1980s it meant protection from a disease which could take your life.

To say that sexual freedom began some thirty years ago is really very patronising. It assumes that whole centuries of women have been dumb, obedient, under-sexed and incapable of by-passing a system that had no bearing on their own wellbeing. You don't need to look any further than the census figures, back to the beginning of this century, to see what the births out of wedlock and the dates of first births after marriage have to say about permissiveness, and it would be disingenuous to think that these unlucky ones were even *half* the number who were gaily courting disaster. But look further. Go back to what Mary Wollstonecraft had to say about the conflict between traditional arranged marriages and the demands of self-fulfilment and self-gratification by both husband and wife in the eighteenth century; or Sir Kenelm Digby who in the 1640s held that breaches of chastity were no greater fault in a woman than in a man; or the unnamed lady who argued with Boswell in 1776 that all real objection to sexual freedom for a married woman was removed if she 'only intrigued when she is with child', since no harm could then be done to property inheritance.

The fact is that women never have valued virginity for its own sake. Only men have valued it, and they have been willing to pay a very high price for it – marriage. Not all men have valued it equally – it wasn't worth more than a very moderate tinker's curse to the labouring classes in other centuries. But the man of property valued it, and its value rose in direct proportion to the value of the property it was being purchased to defend. His bride's virginity guaranteed him safe passage of his goods by primogeniture, so long as the first-born child was male and lived. But the patriarchs wisely backed it up with a double standard operating after marriage. It didn't stop some cuckoos being popped into well-lined nests, but it tended to make the popping harder and the succession safer. Cuckoos were always a problem for men of property. 'We hang a thief for stealing sheep,' said the peevish Dr Samuel Johnson, 'but the unchastity of a woman transfers sheep and farm and all from the right owner.'

What the records tell us – the chronicles and the histories and the letters – is what the upper and the middle classes were thinking about these matters at any given time. Since marriage law had evolved largely to protect property it mattered little what a peasant did since he had no property. Until 1753 when, technically at least, marriage law became the same for everybody, the thing that most annoyed a peasant's betters was for him to desert his woman and her children, so that they then became a charge on the parish funds.

In *The Family Sex and Marriage in England 1550 – 1880* (Weidenfeld & Nicholson, 1977, p. 545) Lawrence Stone says the stages through which English society passed were

> a phase of moderate toleration until the end of the sixteenth century; a phase of repression ... 1570 to 1670; a phase of permissiveness, even licence ... from 1670 – 1810 ... a new wave of repression that began in 1770, was spreading fast by 1810, and reached its apogee in the mid-Victorian period. After about 1870 this wave in turn receded, to be followed by a new period of permissiveness that has perhaps reached its apogee in the 1970s. Both repression and permissiveness eventually generate extremist features, and these slowly turn the pendulum back in the other direction.

Stone believes each of these swings of religio-ethical attitudes towards sexuality lasts about a hundred years.

So *which* thirty years was it we were talking about?

If Lawrence Stone is right about the repressive swings and the permissive roundabouts it's not hard to guess where the pendulum is now. If we had apogees in 1870 (repressive) and 1970 (permissive) we are at the beginning of the downswing now, with a possible twenty years to go before we are into a recognisably more restrained society, and perhaps fifty before the brakes are hard on.

Women's history, since it has until very recently been written by men, has never been anything more than a footnote to the main text, squashed down at the bottom of the page in very small type. One essential piece of women's history which has been profoundly distorted by its condensation is the history of marriage. Because, in this century and the last, the Christian church in most of its disguises has been saying that marriage is a Christian sacrament, that monogamy is God's will and that legitimate birth and female chastity are the rocks on which Christian society is built, we have been asked to believe that these are age-old laws which underpin our civilisation. It would really be safer to argue that they are 250-year-old laws which underpin patriarchy. (My bookish aunt told me that monogamy meant having one husband too many. I was too young to be sure she was joking, and found it morally and mathematically confusing.)

In England, where our initial ecclesiastical and legal systems began, bigamy was not a civil offence until 1603. The marriage we know, and are now so rightly dismantling, grew from parliamentary law imposed in 1753 on church law which had itself been imposed on layman's law dating back to the Dark Ages. In England, in the early and late Middle Ages, a marriage was a civil contract made between families; it had very little to do with anyone else, and was designed to protect property in the male line and make some rudimentary provision for the woman if she was widowed, deserted or divorced.

The medieval church held that laymen were making a botch of marriage law, worrying too much about rents and taxes, and too little about illegitimacy, adultery, fornication and incest.

Progressively, from the 1300s, the church had been moving in on marriage, insisting that it must be monogamous and indissoluable, that bastards must be excluded from property inheritance, and that adultery and fornication must be punished, and the prohibited incest degrees extended in every possible direction. The civil courts, with their minds on mortgages, had been notoriously lax about morals. The church, therefore, took over the patriarchal and property-orientated precepts of the civil courts, and added sexual prohibitions which were in savage contrast with the layman's view that marriage was private, and primarily about money. This growing church control over the rules didn't extend to control over the ceremony.

The ways in which marriages were celebrated usually depended on family or local custom. The central part of most rituals was a simple exchange of promises before witnesses, followed by cohabitation. Marriage was not elevated to the status of a sacrament until 1439 and the Catholic church didn't demand the presence of a priest to make a marriage binding until 1563, after the Reformation.

A convenient place for this marriage ritual was at the church door. It was a means of giving a little more solemnity to the bargain being struck. 'At the church door' meant exactly what it said – the happy couple didn't cross the doorstep and didn't bother the priest who had better things to do with his time, and left marriages to his clerk. Marriages celebrated like this were binding, but by no means indissoluble.

The very rich could buy their way out in the church courts; the very poor could put a halter on a wife's neck and sell her in the marketplace. This (the last case was recorded in England in 1887) was taken to free the husband of all responsibility and allow both of them to marry again. So the very rich and the very poor had their escapes; and there was bigamy, too. Bigamists might be presumed to go to hell, but they didn't go to gaol, and the best thing to do with an unworkable marriage was to walk away from it, and make another. Lord Hardwicke's Marriage Act of 1753 ended the church's ineffective policing of marriage laws; it put control into the hands of the civil courts, made only the church ceremony (not the spousals or promises) binding and enforced entry of all marriages in the church register. Until written records were kept there was no way of proving that the unhappy couple and their witnesses were lying, if they said no marriage had ever taken place. So the Act practically finished bigamy as a convenient way out.

Through all these centuries of no laws and disputed laws and church laws the great sufferers had been the middle classes. They were the ones for whom a bad marriage remained a life sentence. They couldn't afford the costly petitions and bribes of the rich man's divorce and they daren't risk the remote chance of being caught out by the church in the poor man's illegal divorce. Respectability and the look of things bound them, and led to the forging of the iron bonds of the Victorian age.

While it is true that women have never valued their own virginity, they have, as mothers, had to trade in a marketplace where it commands a very high price. Until this century marriage was the only career open to women – unless you count governessing, domestic service or prostitution, all of which have disadvantages. All a good and loving mother could do for her daughters was to educate them for marriage – that is, teach them nothing but domestic skills and the social graces.

In 1675 Mrs Woolley, who had herself been a governess and the wife of a free-school usher, said in a pamphlet '… most in this depraved age think a woman learned enough if she can distinguish her husband's bed from another.' In the 1730s the second Duke of Argyll forbade his daughters to learn French because 'one language was enough for a woman to talk in.'

Competition was always stiff in the marriage market. Males were more delicate than females, and more readily wiped out by the plagues of those centuries, as well as by the normal hazards of early life; in addition primogeniture meant that younger sons couldn't, at worst, ever marry at all and might, at best, have to wait until they were in their late thirties to do so. And the dissolution of the monasteries in the middle of the sixteenth century meant that families suddenly lost a haven for unwanted daughters.

What we lose sight of is the shortness of marriages in other centuries, and the interminable length of Victorian marriages when divorce was nearly impossible and medical science was pushing the expectation of life up and up. The average duration of marriages in the seventeenth century was less than seventeen years. The common marriage age was 25 for women and 27 for men; the child-bearing years were 18 – 40. The average time between births was thirty months and the couple who had six children could expect two or three of them to die before they were fifteen. Very few adults had two living parents, so the problem of what to do with grandma was rarely a pressing one. Marriages were contracted late, and broken early. The broken marriages, the one-parent families, the complicated step-relationships were very much as they are today. All that was different was the cause – death in earlier centuries, divorce today.

At first glance it might look as though the sudden passion of the very young today for white weddings with all the trimmings, or wild weddings with knights and dragons and dungeons, is the first touch of the brakes, the first sign of disenchantment with freedom without all the fuss of marriage. But the facts don't bear that out. Today's weddings are often more for *fun* than for ever. Or perhaps the public acknowledgement of commitment is an attempt to give their partnership permanence in the same way as it's easier to become a non-smoker if you tell everyone you're doing it. In both cases you look a bit foolish if you don't bring it off.

In fact, it's more likely an attempt to achieve Andy Warhol's fifteen minutes of fame, and to stretch it into the best part of two hours. For that time, and for that time only, the bride has the leading role in the duo *bride and groom*. Afterwards, it's downhill all the way – it's man and wife, male and female, Darby and Joan, he and she, sir and madam, boys and girls, kings and queens, brothers and sisters, lads and lasses, grandfathers and grandmothers. She's going to run the gamut of those, but for this one day she comes first. She's the bride. She has top billing.

The old-fashioned marriage was an insurance policy, the

wedding itself being the premium the bride's father paid to guarantee that the woman was protected and provided for for life. The modern bride may pay for the wedding herself, or split the cost with the groom, or persuade an indulgent father to do the paying, but she is usually wise enough to clean up the text so that she's no longer a piece of property being passed from the ownership and control of one man to another. And she's against re-branding, seeing the name change as a patriarchal ploy to remind her that she has no existence in her own right, but only as someone possessed and protected by a man.

So what have the changes been in the last thirty years? Pre-marital and extra-marital sex has been around for a very long time. The only change there is that it's more acceptable to talk about it. If we recognise that the permissiveness applies to the talk rather than to the sex, then the changes are two – because normal adolescent sexuality can be talked about by normal adolescents, fewer of the timid ones are frustrated by their own fears, or by parental or church strictures. The second change is in abortion – not the number, but the ambience. There's no reason to think the rate has gone up, and indeed improved birth control should have reduced it. But at least it's more easily available and a lot more comfortable than when the law said it was your absolute duty to add to the world's gross over-population, whether you wanted to or not. Two things should be remembered about abortion. No one has ever had an abortion for fun. And no one who wants an abortion for good and carefully thought out reasons suffers the fearful guilt and nightmare traumas promised them by press beat-ups.

The other change is in parental attitudes to marriage. It's no longer hard for the middle-aged to admit their young are living in irregular relationships and that their grandchildren are ... um ... technically ... well ... um ... that bit is hard for some; for others it has no meaning at all. But let's not fool ourselves that, as a society, we're enlightened and free from hang-ups. We may have changed the form (though the young are rushing back to something mirroring the old one) but we haven't yet made much impression on the relationship. Women who have decided not to marry are sometimes surprised to wake up eight or ten years later to the discovery that if you have a house and a mortgage and a couple of kids and a car and a dog and a parrot and two television sets, walking out is not one jot easier than if you'd tied the knot with bell, book and candle.

Way back in 1903, the bridegroom Jack Tanner in Shaw's *Man and Superman* said at his wedding to Ann Whitfield,

> What we have done this afternoon is to renounce happiness, renounce freedom, renounce tranquillity, above all, renounce the romantic possibilities of an unknown future, for the cares of a household and a family. I beg that no man may seize the occasion to get half drunk and utter imbecile speeches and coarse pleasantries at my expense.

He was speaking for both of them.

Today, couples making their promises in someone's backyard, on a bungee-jumping platform, in a diving bell or in the lion's cage at a circus, might say the same. The commitments are huge, the changes are small, bigamy and the nunnery are to all intents out, and no matter what comes of what you're doing now, thirty years on you'll believe it began with you, and all that your children and grandchildren had to do was to take the torch, and run.

Cheer up. The course is strictly circular. They'll pass you on the way as they head back into the dark jungles of repression.

LISA BELLEAR

Reluctant to Marry

This is a radio play – the setting is in an inner city suburban house late Friday evening and moves to a local Brunswick hotel the next day for a poetry reading. There are five characters:

SALLY: A indigenous feminist lesbian in her thirties who is having a relationship with Vicki. As the oldest sibling, Sally feels responsible for the way her brother and her immediate friends behave both in private and public. She occasionally expresses her fears and concerns, and this leads to tension between herself and those who are at the receiving end of her barbed comments. Sally means no ill will.

VICKI: A white woman in her late thirties; although Vicki appears quiet, she is a mediator between Sally's occasional outbursts and the people who are affected by this. Vicki is a feminist and works as a film projectionist.

RONNIE: Sally's brother, a poet. He is trying to behave in a more respectful manner to Aboriginal/Torres Strait Islander women; although there is a degree of scepticism as to his sincerity, he believes that he is ingenuous.

LILLA: In her early thirties, shares a house with Vicki and Ronnie. Indigenous, feminist and poet. Falls in love with women, but never quite manages to convert fantasy into reality.

CARLA: In her late twenties, indigenous feminist and actor. Hoping to get a break and to be taken seriously as an actor. Was involved with Ronnie, and although she still loves him, prefers to remain friends.

LILLA Alright then, I'll get the damn thing. Ronnie, you home?

RONNIE Depends.

LILLA Sally?

SALLY I'm not home, well, only if it's . . .

RONNIE Mum! . . . Ha! Only gamin'.

LILLA Gee, you fellas should treat your mother with more respect.

RONNIE Yeah yeah, I'm sorry, [sarcastically] now I may be home.

SALLY Look, just answer the phone and don't mess up!

LILLA Ahh, hello?

CARLA Well, you took your sweet time.

LILLA Oh hi, it's you . . . It's Carla! [loudly]

CARLA A house full of university graduates and youse are frightened of a little telephone!

LILLA Everything okay?

CARLA Do an assertiveness course, get an answering machine.

LILLA Or an agent. How's the acting business?

CARLA So so, I suppose if I wasn't so selective.

LILLA Well, it's not as if there are heaps of parts for a spirited ideologically politically correct Black feminist to play?

CARLA What do you mean? [aggressive]

LILLA Cecil Brown, it's Friday evening and my date hasn't showed.

CARLA Since when have you had a date?

LILLA Wouldn't you like to know, she's just under 182 centimetres, writes for a feminist journal, and best of all she's Koori.

CARLA Have you been drinking?

LILLA Don't tell me I need permission to fantasise?

CARLA Just be careful not to let it get out of control.

LILLA How can I? Sally keeps me in line, and Ronnie.

CARLA Speakin' of Ronnie ...

LILLA What about him, and sorry, he's not home right now.

CARLA Not home?

LILLA Na, just little old me, all by my lonesome, waiting, waiting, waiting, fightin' back the tears of loneliness, of ...

CARLA Oh get a life, now when are you and Ronnie doing that poetry recital?

LILLA Which one?

CARLA Look, don't stuff me around ...

LILLA Hold on, I'll just grab my diary. [goes into lounge room] You bastard. [to Ronnie]

RONNIE What are sisters for?

LILLA Don't give me that bullshit, Carla loves you.

RONNIE I'll dedicate a poem to her.

LILLA You there?

CARLA What do you reckon?

LILLA It's at the Brunswick Hotel, the doors open at 3.00 p.m. We'll get there by 3.30 p.m., but the actual readings won't start until around 4.00 p.m.

CARLA [softly] You know how I feel about Ronnie.

LILLA Same way I feel about Paula. I'll save you a chair.

CARLA Catch you fellas tomorrow.

LILLA Carla, take care.

CARLA Yawoo.

LILLA Yawoo.

[Lilla returns to loungeroom.]

RONNIE Sshh, [to Lilla] it's a critical turning point in the movie.

LILLA Sure, Ronnie, it's not like you can't hire *Terminator II* on video.

RONNIE [sheepishly] Who was that?

LILLA Well, it wasn't your mother. You fellas know how I don't like lying, especially to ...

RONNIE Okay, I promise I will never place any of my sisters in a position of compromise.

LILLA And you call yourself a 'feminist'.

RONNIE Yeah, I was one of the first men, in fact the first Black man to enrol in Women's Studies, and that was back in the 1970s, so there. [smugly]

LILLA What exactly did you learn, internalise? It certainly doesn't give you licence to abuse women, and especially Koori women, and furthermore, involving me in your, your conniving, men's club schemes – I feel like ...

SALLY You two, cut the rhubarb, I'm trying to concentrate on the *Woman's Day* crossword.

LILLA Ronnie, it was Carla.

SALLY Give it a rest, I've been hard at work all day.

LILLA Sally, you know I wouldn't ask anything of you, well under normal circumstances but I'm not a well person.

SALLY Go on, always wanting to take something from a vulnerable, shy, frightened, oppressed, sad and lonely – now I'm startin' to sound like you two dopey nuff nuffs.

RONNIE Ha.

LILLA Ronnie, I'm saving a chair for Carla.

RONNIE You've always liked her.

LILLA True, but not in the sense you mean. Why can't you get serious with her? What I'd give to have someone, anyone in love with me.

RONNIE Anyone?

[The loungeroom conversation comes to an abrupt halt and hurried whispers are heard; someone is knocking on the front door. Initially a few quiet but firm paced knocks. Then more loudly and in rapid succession.]

SALLY [angrily] I'm not at home!

RONNIE Are we expecting anyone?

SALLY Sssh, some one check ... Or hit the lights and then hit the deck!

RONNIE Careful, Lilla, don't pull the curtains too ...

LILLA Quiet, I know what I'm doin'.

SALLY See ya's. [gets up]

RONNIE Where you runnin to?

SALLY I can't stand being terrorised in my own home.

RONNIE Our home, thank you, what are we, chopped liver?

SALLY I'll disappear down the back.

RONNIE But it's so cold in the laundry. [genuine concern]

SALLY I'm outa here.

RONNIE Can you see anything? [quietly to Lilla]

LILLA Na, it's too dark, ahh, I think I can just make out a car, Subaru, phew it's safe. I can unlock the door now. Coming. [out loud]

VICKI It's freezing out here.

LILLA Typical Melbourne summer. [laughs] Sorry about the delay, Ronnie mislaid the keys, again. I don't know how he manages to get through the day, hopeless, absolutely hopeless.

VICKI Is it okay, can I come inside now?

LILLA Yeah, err, I got a bit lost in thought then.

VICKI I tried calling earlier but the phone was engaged. [talks and is directed into loungeroom.]

RONNIE Hi Vicki, how's life?

VICKI Hello Ron, I'm feeling a bit worn out.

RONNIE Been a long day then?

VICKI I've just finished projecting films for the Gay and Lesbian Film Festival. [yawns]

RONNIE Sounds interesting.

VICKI Yes and no, where's Sally?

SALLY [rushing in] Here I am darling, oh you must be exhausted. Let me make you a percolated coffee.

VICKI I'll do it. [sighs]

RONNIE White, with one.

LILLA White hold the one, trade that for a piece of cheesecake.

SALLY What are you two doing home anyway? It's Friday night, you should be out on the …

RONNIE Lilla and me are participating in the Melbourne Poets Festival tomorrow, thank you very much. And so we will do our people proud, we are resting our spirits.

SALLY Oh, your date stood you up?

RONNIE That's below the belt. I am trying to improve my attitude and behaviour towards women.

SALLY Since when?

RONNIE Well ah um …

SALLY Since as recent as tonight, when Carla rang? Beats me how good, smart, strong women can find a man like you attractive.

RONNIE I've got the Black man's charm, and poisonality …

LILLA Ronnie's poetry is so moving.

SALLY You keep out of this Lilla, you are always sticking up for him, and while you do, then he doesn't have to own responsibility for any of his actions. And speaking of poetry, those words are meaningless if you can't live your own life by the words you write.

RONNIE Kooris cannot live by words alone.

VICKI Ronnie! [disapprovingly]

SALLY No, I'm not going to let you off that easy. I love you, you're my brother, and you are talented but you have to make a decision. Are you going to behave like a ratbag, an ignorant, no-good bum or what? You know how you should behave, and I don't just mean only to Koori women.

RONNIE I think the kettle's boiling.

LILLA I guess it's been a long day, for all of us.

SALLY There you go again, making excuses. You're just as bad as him.

LILLA That's not fair, you should know your brother by now. While you take the bait, he'll keep pullin' yer hairy legs, hey Ronnie. [laughs]

RONNIE I give up. In fact just to prove how ingenuous I am, I'll make the coffee.

LILLA I'll give you a hand dividing up the cheesecake.

SALLY [to Vicki] Can you see what time it is?

VICKI 12.40 a.m.

SALLY No wonder I feel tired, sorry I'm a bit snappy. With those two ham bones in the kitchen we can finally have some intimacy. Sometimes, I wish we could take off, to a place without racism, sexism and where you and me can be together, without some white or Black person passing judgement about our friendship. Life can be so depressing.

VICKI Come here, darling.

[Vicki and Sally embrace. In walk Ronnie and Lilla with coffee and cheesecake.]

LILLA Don't they make a beautiful couple?

RONNIE So loving.

LILLA I wish I could find someone as caring and thoughtful as Vicki.

RONNIE And it wouldn't matter if they didn't have a car.

LILLA Well, having access to a car certainly improves our standard of living.

RONNIE I hate being dependent on taxis. Which reminds me – what's that joke about Kooris, optimism and taxis?

LILLA What is the definition of optimism?

RONNIE I dunno, what is the definition of optimism?

LILLA A Koori trying to flag a taxi down ...

RONNIE And hoping that the taxi will stop. There's supposed to be laws against that type of discrimination.

VICKI Are you two alright? That coffee smells divine.

RONNIE Sorry, Vicki, we got a bit carried away.

SALLY I'll say you did. You know how embarrassed Vicki gets when you carry on like that.

RONNIE Oh, Vicki gets embarrassed?

LILLA But it's so true, I look at Vicki, and I look . . . have you ever thought about marriage?

VICKI That seems a rather misguided comment coming from a feminist . . . doesn't sound very ideological.

LILLA Since when has love, and being in love been ideologically sound and/or . . .

RONNIE . . . politically correct. Four years together . . .

LILLA And you tolerate me and Ronnie.

RONNIE Plus the rest of our mob. As well, you understand our needs for Land Rights and justice. There aren't too many non-Koori feminists who are capable of that type of depth and sensitivity, especially in relation to us mob.

SALLY Vicki?

VICKI Look, I don't believe in the institution of marriage.

LILLA Not even if it's between two women?

VICKI What is this caper? You lot never raise this subject of relationships and marriage, not unless it's really late in the evening. I'm always exhausted, and have to draw on some bottomless reserve of sensibility to counteract your airy-fairy antiquated notions of love. Pure fantasy land.

SALLY Fantasy, is that what you call our love?

VICKI Can you hear yourselves? Too silly for words.

RONNIE Sounds a bit heartless.

VICKI Ronnie, with respect, I'd be careful when it comes to handing out advice on relationships and treatment of women.

RONNIE I'm not a complete lost cause ... ye of little faith.

VICKI [doubtful] If actions didn't speak louder than words. Can I drink my coffee, before it gets cold?

SALLY You do love me don't you? I am offering my hand in marriage. I absolutely adore you.

LILLA I'd even be prepared to be a bridesmaid.

RONNIE And I bet you would even wear a dress. We hardly ever have any weddings in our community any more.

SALLY Vicki, I love you.

RONNIE/LILLA Vicki, we love you too.

VICKI [embarrassed] Thank you, I love the three of you very dearly, especially you, Sally.

SALLY Then marry me!

VICKI Hasn't the circus gone home yet? I'm starting to flag. It's been an awful long day.

SALLY Mum asked me if your intentions were honourable. I had to tell her 'I don't think so ...'

RONNIE Don't break another Black woman's heart.

LILLA And mine, you two are a match made in heaven.

VICKI What has me marrying Sally got ...

SALLY [gleeful] Oh, Vicki says she'll marry me; Vicki says she'll marry me. I'm so happy.

RONNIE/LILLA Don't forget about us!

SALLY Of course not, there will always be room for you two, wherever Vicki and me end up.

RONNIE I suppose we should let youse go on your honeymoon without a chaperone?

LILLA On that loving note, I'm going off to bed.

RONNIE Me too, and don't forget the poetry reading's tomorrow.

SALLY I was hoping you two will forget!

VICKI Pleasant dreams, Lilla, Ronnie.

[In the Brunswick Hotel, it's after 5.00 p.m, and Carla hasn't arrived. Ronnie reads his final poem for the session. Applause, then Ronnie joins the 'gang'.]

LILLA Well done, Ronnie, I'm so proud of you.
RONNIE I'm worried about Carla.
SALLY Since when?
RONNIE She's always punctual.
LILLA Give or take a couple of hours.
RONNIE Come on, Vicki, it's not like Carla to stand me up.
LILLA Maybe she had an accident.
VICKI Don't be so morbid, Ron, that was a very inspirational reading.
SALLY What do you expect? You won't even talk to Carla on the phone.
RONNIE Point taken, I still reckon Carla's special.
SALLY Then start behaving better. Every night of the week, you're out and about on the ran tan. It's no wonder your skin looks grey. Do you want to end up like your Uncle Pat. While he was young and popular and had pennies in his pocket, life was one big merry-go-round. And in the end . . .
RONNIE Yeah, yeah, it killed him, he died a broken lonely old man.
SALLY I wouldn't call 47 old. For two days, may God bless his dear soul, he lay slumped over, his head immersed in blood and vomit. Is that what you want? Look at me!!
VICKI Come on, you two, settle down.
RONNIE Sorry, sis.
SALLY Don't apologise to me. When and if Carla arrives, you know what to do. Now go shout a drink, pale ale will do nicely.
RONNIE Anyone else for a charge, aye Lilla?

SALLY She's pickled enough, how many bottles of chablis did you smuggle in?

LILLA Huh?

SALLY Vicki, sweet love of my life, more soda ... how about some potato crisps? Ronnie's shoutin'.

[Ronnie goes to bar.]

VICKI Don't be too hard on Ron. I understand that he's not the most responsible person/man around, but he has intimated a willingness to change.

SALLY Mmmm, I'm not convinced. Anyway, he needs someone to keep him in line, and it might as well be me.

VICKI Okay, I'll mind my own business.

SALLY That's not what I'm saying. Oh, maybe I do push him ...

LILLA [quietly] Just a little.

SALLY It speaks. Lilla, would you like a big jug of soda?

LILLA Ugg!! Keep me out of this. I want no trouble. I'm nervous enough without your bullying.

SALLY You ungrateful ...

VICKI Come on Sal, sounds like the MC wants Lilla to go on stage soon.

SALLY Where's that bastard, better bring me my drink, what's keeping him? He's probably chatting up some young, naive, white girl. It's so pathetic at his age ...

VICKI You're in full flight.

SALLY Na, I haven't started yet, and you Lilla [shaking fist] ...

LILLA Yeah?

SALLY No embarrassment! No mentioning Vicki, or me, when you do your reading or else!

LILLA From the bottom of my Black little heart, I want to sincerely thank you for all this unconditional support.

SALLY Get stuffed!
LILLA Hey, there's Carla, and Ronnie.

[Carla comes over to the table.]

CARLA Any room for me?
LILLA Your chair's getting cold.
CARLA Sorry about the late arrival, but my agent rang just as I was leaving.
LILLA We wuz all worried about you, especially Ronnie.
CARLA True?
VICKI I know it's hard to fathom what sincerity lies beneath that boisterous exterior.
SALLY Lovely to see you again, Carla.
CARLA You too, I miss hanging around with you fellas.
SALLY Imagine you and Ronnie, and me and Vicki all walking down the aisle together. A double wedding.
LILLA Dream on . . .
VICKI Do I sense some bitterness?
LILLA Changed your mind on the marriage fantasy, have we?
VICKI Oh, give it a rest. What's the news, Carla?
CARLA [excited] Like I said, my agent rang, there's going to be a big playwrights conference in South Australia next year and your friend [looks at Lilla] Susan has insisted I play the lead role – all Black women's cast.
LILLA Have you agreed, I mean surely there's no room for doubt?
CARLA I've got a few days to think it over. Susan is personally coming over from Darwin to deliver the script.
LILLA [envious] Gee, I wish I could act.
SALLY Ha, suffer, you know Susan doesn't give a rat's arse about you, you're the wrong sex and colour.
VICKI Sal, be gentle.

SALLY Reality and fantasy – the two can be a deadly combo. I don't want Lilla acting like a fool. It reflects badly on all of us.

VICKI Have a heart.

SALLY Well don't come crying to me when you get rejected again. You should be so lucky to have a friend like me.

CARLA Cecil Brown, it's a wonderful opportunity. With an international audience, I could possibly get the break I've only ever dreamed about. And Susan is such a fantastic writer, I've admired her work for years.

SALLY Don't forget your friends.

CARLA Never, you lot have given me strength.

MC Now if we can invite Lilla up on stage to read a piece which will take us to the break …

CARLA Go for it, sister.

SALLY And no swearing, and don't you dare shame me or Vicki.

RONNIE Can I slip you another chablis?

VICKI All the best.

LILLA I would like to dedicate this poem 'Chops n' things' to Carla – hi sis, who is a beautiful, courageous Koori woman, and someone whom I love very much.

Although I wrote this poem for another special Black woman, I guess this piece is also dedicated to all women who have been kicked in the guts, and told never have dreams, never have visions.

To all of you here, and beyond this room, I say don't give up, always maintain your dreams and a belief in yourself. And remember dreams can come true.

[*Reads poem*]

Chops n' things
I can't wait to curl around
a lemon scented gum tree
light a fire and
watch it burn down to
the embers as the sun
floats away, far away
our ancestors are
yarning and laughing
at this Koori woman
and through the
flames, the embers
and the burnt chops
and charcoaled
potatoes wrapped in foil
they're saying, tidda girl
you're okay,
keep on dreaming
keep on believing

LILLA Thank you.

[Lilla goes back to table]

CARLA Oh Lilla, you are such a sensitive soul.
SALLY Aye, don't encourage her too much.
VICKI I admire your ability to be so personal and upfront to an audience you barely know.
SALLY Once a ham, always ...
RONNIE The organisers wanted Aunty Maureen Watson and Mudrooroo and instead ...
SALLY They got lumbered with you two, at least there wasn't a cover charge. [laughs]
VICKI Sally, sometimes you cross the line.
SALLY Don't want their egos getting in the way of their responsibilities towards the Koori community.

RONNIE Ah sis, you know we love you. Believe what you will, I do listen to you, although at times it hurts. I mean who wants to acknowledge that they might have hurt someone, especially someone they purport to love ... Carla?

CARLA You've got no argument there, Ronnie.

RONNIE I'm going to work on being more understanding of and towards others, especially women.

LILLA And go on, say it and mean it.

RONNIE Yeah, more specifically, Koori and Torres Strait Islander women. How can we as a community ever be united and equal, if people like me don't treat Black women with the dignity and respect that is the basic right of all humans, irrespective of race, class, religion or sexuality.

SALLY [sceptical] You've changed all of a sudden!

RONNIE Come on, Sally, it's called being honest. Look around. I'd have to be one hell of an ignorant fool not to be influenced by Koori women. Sure I talk tough, but that's within the security of our home and only to my sisters ... and Vicki ...

VICKI Careful, Ronnie.

SALLY [warmly] You are such a gifted poet, Ronnie, and the bonus is you're my brother.

VICKI And Lilla ...

SALLY Well, she's got something to offer, and one day when I figure it out, you lot will be the first to know. And Carla, sister girl, how are you now?

CARLA Ronnie and I, we've come to a mutual understanding ... to be friends.

LILLA Lovers come and go, but friendships are forever, Sally taught me that.

CARLA So true.

SALLY Before we blow this joint I propose a toast: To friendship, with marriage being optional but not totally ruled out, to sisters, lovers and family, may we live love and learn.

LILLA And never forget or lose sight of our culture, heritage and spirituality.

SALLY Cheers, and Yawoo.

ALL Cheers, and Yawoo.

KERRY GREENWOOD

Marrying the Bookie's Daughter

A Phryne Fisher mystery

Rendering good for ill,
Smiling at every frown,
Yielding your own self-will,
Laughing the tear-drops down:
Never a selfish whim,
Trouble, or pain to stir;
Everything for him,
Nothing at all for her!
Love that will aye endure,
Though the rewards be few,
That is the love that's pure,
That is the love that's true!

W.S. Gilbert, *Patience, or Bunthorne's Bride*

'Phryne', said Lindsay Herbert, 'Will you marry me?'

Phryne Fisher had been drowsing, lying naked on her moss-green sheets with the young man's head on her shoulder. Now she was shocked awake. She released Lindsay and slid down so that she could look into his face, and a highly inappropriate laugh was smothered at birth.

A golden boy, slim and beautiful, rising on one elbow to look earnestly into her green eyes; light hair curling away from a high forehead, round blue eyes, a sweet red mouth now drawn tight over white teeth. Lightly-tanned skin lay smoothly over the slender musculature of a runner. Her gaze left the face and slid down over the body. Squared chest, flat belly, long legs.

'Why, Lindsay, I ... I don't know what to say ...' Phryne groped for a response, mightily puzzled. What had brought this on? 'I ... am very honoured, of course ...'

'Well, what do you say?' he demanded roughly. 'Yes or no?' She did not reply. He sat up abruptly. 'It's time we got married,' he stated.

'Why?' asked Phryne, reaching for her long dressing-gown and pulling it on. It was patterned with green and scarlet macaws and suddenly seemed gaudy.

'Well, because ... because ... we get on so well. I know I'm not very clever at law and things, but I've got excellent prospects ... Dad will give me a job in the firm ... we could be very happy, Phryne.'

'I thought that we were happy,' Phryne was finding it hard to keep her countenance. 'Get up, Lindsay, and we shall discuss it and have some tea. Look, it's five o'clock – perhaps a cocktail as well.'

'Yes or no?' demanded Lindsay, not moving.

'You can't expect an instant answer to such an important question, Mr. Herbert.' Phryne said coldly. 'I have said that we will talk about it.' And she vanished into her dressing-room to assume the usual habiliment of a lady going down to tea in her own house in 1928. Lindsay was left alone. He swore explosively and scrabbled for his clothes.

Half an hour later Phryne found herself entangled in an argument which even Mr. Butler's cocktails did not mitigate or unravel.

'But why, Lindsay dear? We are perfectly all right as we are,' she protested.

'Damnation, old thing, we don't need a reason for getting married! Everyone does it!' the young man spluttered into his ginger beer, 'I don't know why you won't say yes!'

'I don't know either,' said Phryne slowly.

'It's because I'm not clever, isn't it?' he demanded suddenly, with a broad generous gesture which distributed his drink over a considerable portion of the room. 'You only like clever chaps, that's what it is.'

'No, no, Lindsay dear, that isn't it,' protested Phryne, 'not at all. I think you're lovely just as you are. And you are quite bright, sometimes, though not at the moment.'

'It can't be my prospects,' he mused, as Mr. Butler refilled the glass, and began unobtrusively to mop ginger beer off the couch. 'It must be ... it must be ...' he stared piteously up into Phryne's eyes and whispered, 'another man.'

'Lindsay, dear ...'

'No, that's it, I see it all now,' he said feverishly. 'Another man, of course, a clever chap with lots of money ... he's the one you want.'

Phryne leaned over and took the glass firmly out of his hand. She was unable to account for this strange fervour, and was beginning to apprehend a scene. And she liked Lindsay, who was usually delightful, a good lover and an excellent and socially acceptable escort. Who was rapidly rendering himself unfit for female company.

'Now listen,' Phryne planted herself on his knees to keep the young man still and took a fistful of the soft, light hair, 'you listen to me, Lindsay. I am what I am and I behave as I wish and I will not be dictated to by anyone. If I want lovers, I take them. If I do not want to be married, I will not be married and there's nothing you can do to make me! Do you hear?'

The flushed face turned up to hers had tears in the eyes. She did not release her grip.

'Then the answer's no?'

'If it is?'

'Then I'll go away, Phryne, I'll walk out that door and you'll never see me again. I can't go on like this. I'm never sure of you.'

'And you'd be sure of me if I was married to you?' She could not stop her eyebrows from rising. The young man drew a long breath and said earnestly, 'Yes. If we were married then . . .'

Phryne judged him calm enough for her to resume her seat. She did so, loosing a few flax-pale strands of hair from between her fingers as she listened.

'Then?'

'If we were married, then you'd belong to me. I'd belong to you.'

'And?'

'Then we'd be happy.'

'Because I belonged to you?'

'Yes. You could sell this house and come and live with me. We could buy a big house in Toorak and have a country estate and a place near the sea and we'd have such larks, Phryne, just you and me, without a lot of people bothering us. I could finish law and go into dad's office. In the winter we could go skiing and sailing in the summer and . . .'

'And we could have a little cottage with roses around the door and Old Mister Moon peeping in through the window?'

'Yes. You don't have to say it in that tone of voice. It could be fun. Please, Phryne. I don't want to lose you. You could give up all this detective work and go to parties with me, and the opera, and all sorts of jolly things. And we could have children? Two, perhaps, eh, Lindsay Junior and a pretty little girl like you must have been? Please say yes, Phryne. It came into my head because the pater is going on about being settled and the mater keeps introducing me to nice girls and . . .'

'Well, what's wrong with the nice girls?' Phryne lit a cigarette. She didn't want to break Lindsay's ingenuous heart, so she was listening. Lindsay reached out and ran a skilled hand down her breast and heard her gasp.

'That's what's wrong with the nice girls,' he said simply. 'They're nice.'

'Of course they are. That's how they are trained to appear. You may be agreeably surprised at what they are really like. Lindsay, I can't decide something as important as this immediately. I have to think about it. Can you wait for an answer?'

'If I have to.'

'You have to.'

'Then I can wait,' he said miserably. He was not, however, altogether cast down. Phryne had not rejected his honourable proposal out of hand. There might still be a chance of securing her for his own.

'And in the meantime,' she said, taking another cocktail and returning his glass to the young man, 'I am going to a wedding on Saturday. The Sackville girl. Will you be my escort?'

'Of course. The Sackville wedding, eh? I didn't know you moved in those circles, Phryne.'

'Which circles?'

'Racing ones.'

'I don't, but the wretched girl is one of that pest Celia's protégés, so I really haven't a choice. You know how she takes up the *petit bourgeoisies'* ghastly daughters and launches them on what she fondly thinks is Society. Well, she launched Amelia Sackville, doubtless on the strength of her Papa's fortune. All got from doing down the working punter, Bert says.'

'Stout fella, Bert,' commented Lindsay.

'I see, so you propose to allow me to continue my friendship with the working class if we are married?' Phryne asked teasingly. Lindsay took her seriously and pondered his reply. He said solemnly, 'Well, no, Phryne, you won't need them if you aren't detecting any more.'

'Of course.' Lindsay wondered what he had said to bring that metallic ring into her voice. 'Yes. So, poor Amelia is to be sacrificed at the altar.'

'Who is she marrying?'

'You know him, Lindsay dear. Fletcher. Tom Fletcher.'

'Good Lord, old Fletch getting shackled for life? Well, well. How are the mighty fallen. He was my house prefect at Grammar, you know, a fiend at rowing, captain of the football team. But not just a rowdy, bit of a ladies' man. Nothing in skirts was safe from him. Cost his father a bit in breach of promise payments, buying them off, I gather. Imagine him marrying the bookie's daughter,' Lindsay laughed. 'Well, and that's what one would expect, too.'

'Why?'

'Terrible gambling bug he had, old Fletch. Used to run a book himself, at school. On the Melbourne Cup, you know, not as a business or anything.'

'And what's he like?'

'Fletch? Good chap, you know. Still plays for the Old Melburnians football team, does a bit of coaching of the fours.'

'Yes, but what is he like?'

Lindsay gaped. 'I've told you,' he said lamely. Phryne gave it up.

'Never mind, dear boy. I'll pick you up at two; full soup and fish, we have to go to a very swish reception afterwards.'

'St Peter's, Eastern Hill, I assume?' he asked, accepting his coat from Mr. Butler.

'St Peter's, Eastern Hill,' Phryne agreed.

'Marriage,' said Phryne, unaware that she had spoken aloud.

'Marriage, Miss Phryne?' echoed Dot. 'Are you thinking of getting married, Miss?'

Phryne looped a long necklace of amber beads around her neck, and said to Dot's reflection in the mirror, 'I've been asked.'

'Oh, Miss, how exciting! Who is it?'

'Lindsay Herbert. What do you think?'

'Oh, Miss, they say he's ever so rich, and he's very well-connected.'

'So you believe I should marry him?'

Dot was Phryne's maid and companion. She had always disapproved of detection as an occupation for a lady. Mirrored Dot clasped her hands.

'Well, Miss, you like him,' she said slowly. 'You ... er ... know him.' Phryne grinned, and Dot blushed. 'Er ... and well, Miss, getting married, you'd have to give up all this dangerous detective work. You know how I worry about you.'

'Why would I?'

Dot stared. Some things, she felt, were self-evident.

'Mr. Herbert wouldn't like his wife to be doing something so . . . so . . .'

'Unladylike?' Phryne's smile now showed quite an array of teeth. 'What else would Mr. Herbert not like his wife to do?'

'Well, Miss, it's to be expected. Gentlemen will have their house ordered the way they want. Perhaps you could do some charity work. But married ladies don't work, everyone knows that.'

'No? What about you, Dot? Aren't you a lady?'

'That's different. I'm not married, and I've got myself to keep. But my husband won't like me to work. He'll keep me.'

'How sweet,' said Phryne, without any inflection. 'The straw coloured dress, please, Dot.'

A caller was announced at three on the next afternoon. Mr. Butler came into the drawing room, where Phryne and Dot were examining the library catalogue.

'No, I don't think so, Dot dear, I really can't bear romances. One more heaving bosom, thunderstorm and white frilly nightgown and I'll scream. Get me some thrillers. That new one, Charteris, he sounds good. Yes, Mr. Butler?'

'Mr. Aloysius Fletcher to see you, Miss.'

'Never heard of him. What does he want?'

Mr. Butler came a little closer and said quietly, 'It's the racing gentleman, Miss Phryne, the one whose son is marrying the bookmaker's daughter.'

'Oh, yes. Well, I've finished with the catalogue, Dot dear, send it off, and you might stay, if you don't mind. I don't know how racing gentlemen behave. Wheel him in, Mr. Butler.'

Mr. Aloysius Fletcher was not alone. He strode into the room, large and magnificent, if a trifle past his prime, a big, stout fleshy man in a quiet charcoal suit evidently chosen by his wife. His own taste announced itself in the shape of a violently patterned cravat and a horse-shaped gold stickpin with a diamond glaring from the middle. He had another diamond on his left hand, big enough to choke a parrot. Scurrying behind him was a small, thin, plain woman of perhaps thirty. She was so self-effacing that she was hard to see. Her long blonde hair was scraped back into a migraine-inducing bun. She looked modestly down at the carpet. She was clutching a large black-bound diary in her arms, and had a pencil behind her ear.

'Miss Fisher?' he bellowed. Phryne offered him her hand, and he shook it hard, then let it go as though he had found himself holding a fish. Phryne judged him to be a hard man on china and invited him to sit down, hoping that he was reliable with chairs.

'I'm Aloysius Fletcher,' he said. 'Perhaps you have heard of me.'

'Yes,' said Phryne, 'I've heard of you.'

'You know my son's marrying the bookie's daughter on Saturday?'

'Yes, I'm coming to the wedding. And who is your companion?'

'Companion?' he started, and looked around. 'Oh, that's just Smithy. My secretary. Sit down, Smithy. She's a fool,' he confided in a ponderous undertone, 'but she'll do, if I watch her like a hawk. Yes, well, Tom's managed to snare the bookie's daughter. Stout fellow, Tom. The family might get back all the money the scoundrels have taken off me all these years!' He laughed. Phryne watched politely. Mr. Butler offered a drink, and was sent for whisky and soda, 'and don't drown the whisky!'

Phryne waited until Miss Smith had found a perch on the extreme edge of the sofa, and then said, 'To what do I owe the honour of your acquaintance, Mr. Fletcher?'

'Meaning, what do I want, eh?' he laughed again. 'Well, I want you to do something for me. Smithy! Show Miss Fisher the drawings!'

Smithy jumped, dropped the diary, and scrabbled for three spilt sheets of paper. She handed them to Phryne. They were watercolour drawings of jewellery done by an expert hand, showing a bridal set comprising High Victorian brooch, zone, necklace, earrings, and tiara. They were heavy, solid and respectably opulent.

'Yes?'

'They're the family heirlooms. The gift of the bridegroom, you know. Not that I expect that a girl with pots of money, like the bookie's daughter, will care for them. But it's a tradition, y'know.'

'Yes?' Phryne was beginning to dislike her unwanted guest so much that she was hoping he would choke on his whisky, even though it was not the good whiskey. Mr. Butler had his own system of class determination.

'They're missing.'

'I see.'

'I went to the safe this morning – it's in Smithy's room, so that there is always someone in the way if burglars break in. The safe was open and the room had been torn apart, eh, Smithy?'

Miss Smith nodded.

'And the jewels were gone.'

'Have you called the police?'

'Of course, but they won't get quick results. I told my son about it, and his friend Herbert – you know him, apparently – said that you could find things faster than Sherlock Holmes. So here I am, Miss Fisher, asking you to help.'

'I'm afraid that I'm rather busy, Mr Fletcher.'

'Come along, girl!' barked Mr. Fletcher. 'I came to get you, and get you I shall. M'wife's upset. And Herbert said you were a genius. Should have known better than to trust the little twerp.'

Phryne considered this. She detested Mr. Fletcher, but Lindsay's good opinion of her was flattering and should be supported. She nodded, got up, and found her handbag.

'Very well. My fees, Mr. Fletcher, are high. Can you pay them?'

'Fees?'

'Yes. This is my profession, you know.'

Mr. Fletcher appeared to have been struck dumb. Smithy said in a soft, deep voice 'There won't be any trouble with the fees, Miss Fisher. Can you come now?'

'Yes.'

Mr. Fletcher was assisted to his feet and they left the house.

Phryne examined the room. It was a small, crowded bedchamber, where all the things in the house which were not immediately needed were stored. Smithy's bed stood in front of a collection of walking-sticks, golf clubs and tennis rackets. Her clothes hung in a cupboard which also contained a vacuum cleaner and several boxes of illustrated racing papers. The only sign of her occupancy were hundreds of exquisite pen drawings pinned up all over the walls.

Phryne exclaimed, 'They're beautiful! Who did them?'

'Smithy. She's always scribbling,' grunted Mr. Fletcher. 'See, there's the safe, and it was open. They must have got in through the window.'

Smithy's only window was small, but unbarred, and a smashed pane announced that the lock had been rendered useless.

'Hmm, yes. What was in the safe?'

'Nothing else of value. Papers, mainly, deeds and so on.'

'Was the jewellery in a box?'

'Yes, about ten by ten inches square. Why?'

'Nothing.' Phryne noticed that a tin trunk had also been forced. From the female underclothes and drawing materials, she judged it to be Smithy's. A bottle of green ink had been smashed, and the contents appeared to have been tipped out, and then roughly piled back inside.

'Hmm.'

'Well? Can you find them?' demanded Mr. Fletcher. Phryne smiled up into the beefy face.

'I'll try.'

'Good. Come up and see m'wife, will you? She's upset.'

It was possible to gauge the level of upset by the sobbing and wailing, which was apparent from the hall. Mr. Fletcher muttered something about an appointment in the stables and fled. Smithy, unexpectedly, gave Phryne a sympathetic look, revealing that she had beautiful, large, expressive eyes the colour of forget-me-nots. She led Phryne into a large room, which contained a tall young man, a well-dressed young woman and an older woman in the throes of what appeared to be inconsolable grief.

'Mama, please!' the young man begged. 'Smithy, can't you do something with her? Oh, I beg your pardon,' he added when he caught sight of Phryne. 'Hello! Are you Miss Fisher? Herbert's told me all about you. I'm delighted to meet you.'

He was a very good-looking young man, Phryne thought, with chestnut hair and brown eyes and a red, full mouth. He held her hand a little longer than was necessary and the quality of the contact suggested that Lindsay had indeed told him all about Phryne. She smiled wickedly and released herself.

'This is Miss Sackville, my fiancée. Amelia, this is Miss Fisher. She's going to find the family jewels.' He grinned down at her and she shook her neat head.

'I told you, Tommy, I don't care about the family jewels. I've got jewels enough of my own.' The girl was taller than Phryne, offhandedly elegant, in a lapis lazuli suit with sapphires in her ears. Her dark hair was bobbed, her cosmetics reticent, and her manner unaffected. She was holding Tom Fletcher's hand to her breast as though she was cradling it. 'I just want you, old thing,' she said, and Tom Fletcher smiled and replied, 'And on Saturday, you will be mine.'

Phryne caught her breath. This was the exclusive love which she had been thinking about; one creature claiming another, in complete indifference to the rest of humanity. For a moment, her heart ached. She wondered how it would feel, to love like that, or trust like that, so perfectly and forever. Phryne had never before considered that there might be someone so close to her always, in whom she could have such single-minded faith.

Mrs. Fletcher stopped sobbing. Smithy was fussing around her with salts and brandy, and a large gulp of spirit had temporarily taken her mistress's breath away. Smithy introduced Phryne. There was little that she could say.

'I'll do my best, but the wedding is on Saturday, Mrs.

Fletcher. I think you'd be better leaving it to the police. It is their business, you know.'

'That's what I say,' agreed Tom vehemently. 'Leave it to the cops. That's what we pay taxes for, isn't it?'

But Mrs. Fletcher looked as though she was about to start wailing again, and Phryne, to keep the peace, agreed to continue her investigation.

Another inspection of Smithy's room revealed nothing positive, except Phryne noticed that folios of drawings had been emptied and rifled, the contents replaced carelessly. She sat on the floor with Smithy to smooth the paper and stack it again.

'These are very fine,' said Phryne admiringly, leafing through life drawings of a nude young man, done with loving care. The muscles were shaded with red chalk. The face was turned away. Smithy snatched them from Phryne's hand and crumpled them into a ball.

'I'm not good on the figure,' she said hastily. 'I'm better at still lives.'

Phryne admired flowers and fruit and asked, as she was leaving, 'Did you go to art school? You're very good.'

A painful blush burned Miss Smith's face. 'No. I couldn't afford it. I've been working here since my mother died, when I was sixteen. She was Mr. Fletcher's cousin. He gave me a job and a place to live. It was ... very kind of him.'

'Was it?' asked Phryne, dryly. One gleam of passionate emotion was allowed to escape from Smithy's blue eyes, and then it was veiled.

'Of course,' she muttered.

By the afternoon of the next day, which was Friday, the day before the wedding, Phryne had the solution to the mystery of the missing jewels and was at a loss as to what to do. She took a long walk, and returned out of breath and with the problem still unresolved. She was also considering Lindsay's proposal. After all, Phryne was twenty-eight. She might never get another proposal so fitting. Yesterday's glimpse of the lovers, perfectly and passionately devoted to each other, had planted a splinter in her bosom. Tom and Amelia, smiling at each other with that embracing, exclusive smile, that forced all of the world out past the boundaries of their magic circle, and declared 'Mine,' but Phryne and Lindsay, the sweet boy with the soft mouth, forsaking all others, alone with each other for the foreseeable future? She had never experienced perfect love; was it possible that it had never come because she had never tried hard enough? It could probably be accomplished, she thought, if she put her mind to it. She reached her own door still wondering and found the front hall full of flowers.

'What are these?' she asked, looking for a florist's label. Australian flowers, strange and spiky; waratahs, banksia, and sheaves of gum leaves. She inhaled the bush scent with delight.

'They're from Mr. Herbert, Miss,' said Dot from behind a shrubbery of everlastings. 'He wants you to marry him.'

'Yes, I know.'

'Have you decided, Miss? 'Cos Mrs. Butler was asking.'

'Mrs. Butler? Why?'

'Because of the arrangements, Miss, they'll have to find another place.'

'Oh, Lord!' Phryne dragged herself out of the scented haze. 'Tell Mrs. B that I haven't made up my mind, but in any case I shall be keeping them on and this house, too. A fig for all this perfect love,' she snarled, 'I don't think I'm strong enough for marriage, Dot.'

Suppressing a private delight in muslin wedding veils and orange blossom, Dot handed Phryne an armload of wax-flowers and went off to the kitchen, leaving her mistress in possession of a magnificent fit of bad temper.

Phryne dressed for the wedding in a state of bemusement. She did not know what to do for the best, or even what to avoid for the worst. The state of the window, the folios, the reputation of Tom Fletcher and Miss Smith's position in the house seemed to point to one conclusion, but the research which Dot had undertaken had not confirmed it. Phryne got out of the bath, scented with 'Jicky', and allowed herself to be dressed in champagne-coloured stockings and underwear, and then sat in front of the mirror while Dot brushed her hair.

'Glass on the outside,' she said aloud.

'Miss?'

'Glass on the outside of the window,' she said, 'means that the window was broken from the inside. And no one would search flat cardboard folios for a box ten inches by ten inches. The burglar wasn't looking for jewels. There's only one solution, Dot, and I don't know what to do. Tom Fletcher and his Amelia, they really seem to love each other, Dot. At least, she loves him. Whatever that means. Oh, these society scandals are too, too enervating. One will have nothing to talk about for months and months but the disruption of the Fletcher boy's wedding. And it will not aid the lady.

'I have it. Stop brushing, Dot, run down and get Lindsay on the telephone. He'll be at the Fletchers' if he's not at home – Tom Fletcher is an old friend of his.'

Phryne allowed Dot to drop her apricot and silver dress over her head and then found her bag and her cloche as Dot ran for the telephone.

'Lindsay dear, it's Phryne. Can you give Tom Fletcher a message? It's important.'

'Yes, I'm going there now to see the poor fish into his garments and help old Jack to keep custody of the ring. What's the message? Don't tell me you've fallen for Tom, like all those other swooning females?'

'Lindsay, have you ever known me to swoon? Well, then. Tell him to bring the jewels to the ceremony with him. You can carry them. They're in a little box, ten by ten.'

'But I thought that they were stolen!'

'They were. But Tom has them now, or my name's not Phryne Fisher. Then scurry home again and I'll pick you up in an hour. Will you do it?'

'Oh, of course, Phryne. If you say so,' he replied stiffly.

'It is offended – see, it stalks away,' quoted Phryne, hanging up the phone. 'Mr. Butler! A cocktail, if you please. I am in need of strengthening. And I wonder,' she added to herself, 'now that Tom Fletcher knows that I know his secret, what he will do. This should be an interesting afternoon.'

Mr. Butler supplied the cocktail, made with special care and to a secret recipe, and forebore to comment.

St Peter's Eastern Hill was crowded, and Phryne had some difficulty in manoeuvring herself through the press of Melbourne's shrillest and most fashionable in order to sit next to Smithy. The secretary was unbecomingly attired in a charcoal suit evidently cut out with some agricultural implement and a dark cloche was dragged brutally down over her high forehead. Outside, Tom Fletcher was hopping from foot to foot, smoking like a chimney, and taking little nips when unobserved from a flask kept by his best man. Lindsay Herbert, in full elegant evening dress, sat next to Phryne, nursing a small box on his knee and looking bewildered.

'What did Tom say when he gave you the jewels, Lindsay?'

'He said he had to go through with it, whatever happened. He said he was sorry, to tell you that he was very sorry.'

'I see.'

'What is going to happen, Phryne?' begged Lindsay. She kissed him on the cheek.

'I haven't the faintest. Look, here comes the bride.'

There was a stir at the door. The groom threw away his cigarette, paled and was escorted into the church. A carriage drew up and out of it stepped the bride, supported by a rubicund father bursting with pride. Amelia was draped in a Valenciennes veil so generous that it flowed over her and in careless folds to the ground. Her gown was of ice-pale silk, dipping down towards her heels, embroidered in silver with lilies and garlands. She carried a trailing bouquet of gardenias, and their sweet indecent scent reached Phryne and Smithy in their pew, stirring both of them in different ways. Smithy clutched her hands together and shut her mouth hard. Phryne breathed in the scent and remembered a certain hot night and the taste of salt on a young man's skin.

The organ pealed, a voluntary which slid into the full

triumphal wedding march, and the bride was led toward the altar, leaning on her father's arm, to be given away to her husband. Smithy began to shiver. Phryne took her arm.

'Are you feeling faint?' she asked. 'Why don't we go out? Very close in here.' Smithy turned on Phryne eyes which reminded her of a mortally injured dog, and nodded. They reached the church wall, which was low, and sat down. Phryne lit a gasper and said quietly, 'It wasn't like that at the registry office, was it?'

'No.'

'But Dot couldn't find the certificate.'

Smithy groped in her bag and thrust a folded paper into Phryne's hand. She read it.

'That's why,' she commented. 'I didn't ask her to go back far enough. How old were you, for God's sake?'

'Sixteen,' muttered Smithy. Phryne realised that she was a lot younger than she looked. Life could not have been easy in Mr. Fletcher's house, in possession of such a secret, and despised by her employers, used like a pet and mercilessly overworked.

'That's what Tom was looking for, when he staged that break-in and searched your room.'

'Yes. I loved him,' she said through clenched teeth, 'I loved him so much! There was I, small and insignificant and plain and worthless, and he paid attention to me. He liked me – no one liked me – and . . . and . . . '

'And you slept with him?'

'Not until we were married. I held out for that. I was brought up well. If I'd wanted to be a whore I wouldn't have put up with old Fletcher all these years. Then he got tired of me. Years ago he got tired of me. And I stayed because . . . I still love him, I suppose. And I had nowhere else to go.'

'And what are you going to do?' asked Phryne gently.

'There's a bit in the service – I looked it up. Where they ask if anyone has just cause or impediment . . . I was going to . . . '

'Stand up and object? Well, you have just cause, all right, just cause indeed! You have been treated monstrously, Smithy.

Smithy, what's your name?' Smithy shook her head, as though she could hardly remember.

'Chlöe. My mother ... liked ... novels ...' She started to cry helplessly. Phryne cupped a hand under the small chin and forced Chlöe to look at her.

'Listen, Chlöe, I think I can deal more advantageously for you than just disrupting the wedding. I know that it will make you feel better for the moment but what are you going to do after that? You can hardly expect to stay with the Fletchers. And I doubt if they'll give you a good character. And Tom ... Tom is not likely to be much use to you, is he?' The bowed shoulders shuddered, and Chlöe Smith whispered, 'No.'

'Right. Give me that marriage certificate, and have you got old Fletcher's diary with you, as always? Has it got a chequebook in it? Good. Ah, Lindsay,' she added as the young man came up to them, 'Miss Smith is a bit overcome. Can you stay with her? Give her some brandy if you've got some. I'll be back in a moment, Chlöe.'

Chlöe stared at Phryne as she stalked back into the church. Lindsay sat down beside her and patted her gently. Emotional women did not worry or embarrass Lindsay.

'Mr. Herbert – can I trust her?'

'Who, Miss Fisher? Of course. Have a little taste of this, now, just a sip. You can trust Phryne. If she says she'll fix it, then it will be fixed. I would trust her with my life,' said Lindsay, and Chlöe Smith leaned against his tailored shoulder and sipped at the brandy and closed her eyes.

By the exercise of bare-faced intimidation, Phryne managed to insert herself into the seat next to old Mr. Fletcher as he opened a hymn book with which he was evidently unfamiliar. Phryne laid the fatal certificate over the words of 'O Perfect Love' and watched his eyes bulge as he read it. He turned on her, about to demand an explanation, and she put a finger to his lips.

'Calm, Mr. Fletcher,' she said. 'We don't want to cause a fuss, do we?'

'What do you want?' he choked. 'Where is Smithy? I'll tear her limb from ...'

'No you won't. If you want Tom's marriage to go ahead, then you'll have to pay up. Your son abandoned the poor little thing and you don't value her. She needs an independence or . . .'

'Or?'

Phryne was interested in the colour of his face – a glowing purple – but reflected that it clashed lamentably with her gown. She opened the order of service and laid a finger on one line. He read it. There was a smothered silence.

'Dearly beloved, we are gathered together here . . .' began the bishop in a high, nasal, parsonical tone. Mrs. Fletcher took out a lace handkerchief and began to cry decorously.

'Well? How much?'

'Five thousand. Invested, that should be enough.'

'Five thou!' he began, then hushed as several people turned to look at him.

'It is a state which should be entered into reverently, discreetly, advisedly, soberly, and in the fear of God; duly considering the causes for which Matrimony was ordained,' said the bishop, with a reproving glance at the groom's father.

'All right. Later.'

'Now,' said Phryne, laying his own chequebook on the marriage service, and unscrewing his own fountain pen which she had somehow abstracted from his top pocket. For a moment she was worried that he would die of apoplexy before he could sign, but he filled in the cheque, and she took the book out of his grasp, waving it a little to dry the ink. 'I'll keep the certificate, in case you try to stop the cheque,' she said coolly.

Then she stood up, as though her movement was part of the service, and walked down the side aisle and out of the church.

Smithy had cried out years of suppressed humiliation and pain onto Lindsay's shoulder, and was feeling a little better. Lindsay's closeness was comforting, and his perfect faith in Miss Fisher's effectiveness was infectious. She had also told him the whole story, and he had been considerably and gratifyingly shocked.

'Phryne?' he asked, 'I never would have thought it of old Fletch. How did it go?'

'I've stung Papa Fletcher for five thousand of the best and brightest,' she said. 'Do you want to come back inside, Chlöe?'

Chlöe clung to Lindsay's arm in a way which he found touching, and Phryne led them inside, along the side aisle to where Tom Fletcher could see them. He stood straighter when he saw Chlöe Smith. Ever since Phryne's message about the jewels had arrived, he had been waiting for this.

'Therefore if any man can show any just cause or impediment why they may not lawfully be joined together, let him now speak, or else hereafter forever hold his peace.'

Tom Fletcher stiffened, his gaze on Smithy – the familiar and ill-used Smithy, who was in a position to ruin his life, and did not beg for mercy. He blinked once and Amelia's hand stole out to take his, divining that something was wrong. There was a silence thick enough to slash with a sabre. Leaning on Lindsay, Chlöe Smith smiled slightly, and in that smile released herself from Tom Fletcher. She nodded to him.

'I require and charge you both,' the bishop continued, wondering what these three were doing standing in the side aisle and hoping that something socially unfortunate was not going to happen, 'as ye will answer at the dreadful day of judgment, when the secrets of all hearts shall be disclosed, that if either of you know any impediment why ye may not be lawfully joined together in matrimony, ye do now confess it.'

Amelia looked up at her soon-to-be-husband. He looked at Chlöe, who nodded again. Tom Fletcher gusted out a sigh of relief which caused the altar candles to flicker, and said nothing.

Phryne saw Chlöe Smith into and out of Mr. Fletcher's house and into the car, with the trunk full of drawings. She drove her to a suitable boarding house, paying the first week's rent and seeing the young woman settled.

'I really couldn't do anything else, could I?' Chlöe asked, sitting down on the bed and bouncing. 'This is a nice bed. It's got springs.'

'My dear girl, revenge is always sweet but it is not generally profitable. Now make sure that you bank that cheque first thing Monday morning. You can post the certificate back to Mr. Fletcher as soon as you have the money.'

'I've got nothing to do. I've worked for them all my life. I kept the household accounts and minded the dog and looked after Ma Fletcher when she threw conniptions and dealt with the servants and paid the bills and they never appreciated me or noticed me and now I've got nothing to do.' Miss Smith seemed to have grown younger. She tore off the ugly hat and pulled her hair out of its bonds. Hairpins flew like fireflies. A cascade of corn coloured hair tumbled down over the charcoal suit. 'What shall I do? What shall I do now?'

'Why, anything you like. Why not go to Art School? Buy some nice clothes. And you may find another young man,' suggested Phryne.

Chlöe thought about it, running her ink-stained fingers through the silky strands. 'No. I don't know any young men. And I'm not a virgin. No one will marry me now. Oh, but what about Tom? What if he has … children? Won't they be …'

'No, that was not a legal marriage, Chlöe. Both of you were under age. Neither of you had parental permission. You could have caused a massive scandal, though. So you can marry again, if you want. You're in the same position as a widow.'

'I'll never forget him, Tom, I mean. Yes, I am a widow. It's like he's dead.' She wept for a few minutes, then tossed back her hair and wiped her red eyes. 'I think I'll have a cat. A house, first, then a cat. I can afford a house, can't I? Oh, dear, I'm going to cry again. Don't stay with me. I like being alone. I have to think. I haven't been able to think, not since Tom brought Miss Amelia home. But you must go back to the wedding, Miss Fisher. Tell Tom to be happy. And don't worry about me. I'm free,' said Chlöe Smith, and laughed a little as she realised that it was true. 'I'm free of them all. At last.'

Phryne drove away, humming. After a while she found that she was singing Patience's song. 'Rendering good for ill, Smiling at every frown …' Mr Gilbert had a satirical humour, but it was hard to tell from the song whether he was exercising it or not. 'Everything for him, nothing at all for her!' Phryne bit her tongue and found that she was unable to avoid the conclusion which had been forming in her mind since she had seen Tom Fletcher and Amelia together. Lindsay and Phryne were not like that. They could never be. Striving to place Lindsay in the position of Tom had forced her into the position of Amelia, and Phryne would not fit into the frame. She could not do it. She could not marry Lindsay Herbert.

She pulled the big car over and stopped, to press both hands to her breast, sick with sudden loss. Beautiful Lindsay, so smooth and deft and loving. A hallucinogenic flash showed her the long body lying beside her, the red mouth which would never again open under hers. Never. If she did not marry Lindsay he would go away, to find his own Amelia, and she would never touch him again, never see that turn of the head as the hair fell just so over his eyes, never kiss the nape of his neck again.

Even so, she thought, putting the Hispano-Suiza into gear and resuming her journey. Even so, she could not marry Lindsay Herbert.

Phryne found a chair, after dancing with a succession of rowers who had no use for tempo and no regard for her feet, and Lindsay brought her a glass of champagne and a water-ice. The moment could not be delayed any longer. She drew a deep breath. 'Thank you, Lindsay dear, and I won't marry you,' she said, gulping down the drink and beginning thirstily on the ice. Lindsay gasped. 'I'm sorry, my dear, and I love you very much, Lindsay, but I have thought about it and I can't do it.'

'But . . .' protested Lindsay. Phryne put down the dish and took his hand.

'You are lovely,' she said softly, 'don't think that I don't love you.'

'I love you too. Phryne, old girl, listen . . .'

'I'll miss you,' she added, with tears springing to her eyes, as she realised how much she would miss him, 'but I can't, Lindsay dear, I really can't.'

'Phryne, please . . .'

'This has been a hard decision to make, Lindsay, so don't argue with me. Please don't make this more difficult than it is.' He had come closer and now kissed her cheek. The caress, so familiar and delightful, went through Phryne like a knife. He was saying something, which she did not hear. Then he pulled away from her and dashed across the room to the wedding presents. Returning, he solemnly handed her a silver fish-slice. 'What's this for?' she asked, wondering if he had taken leave of his senses. He sat down next to her, seeming rather jaunty for a man whose matrimonial plans had just been dashed.

'I had to get a word in edgewise somehow. I know you won't marry me. That's all right, Phryne, if we can go on as we have been. Seeing that poor Smith girl has rather turned me off matrimony, don't you know.'

'Oh? Get me another glass of champagne, will you?' Phryne felt rather faint with relief.

'Yes.' He collected two glasses from a passing waiter. 'Anyway, I told the Pater that if I married I could only marry you, because I loved you like billy-ho, and he turned red and choked and went off the idea completely. Not such a good idea, marriage, eh? What do you think?'

Phryne looked at the bride and groom, enthroned at the high table. Amelia, glittering in Victorian garnets, was laughing as her spouse kissed her hand. Whatever explanation Tom had produced about that strange pause in the ceremony, he had clearly been believed, accepted, and forgiven. The lace was thrown back to reveal the pure line of the bride's head and the groom's profile, dark against the white wall behind. They were engrossed in each other, elevated with relief and wine, and as beautiful as they would ever be.

'Not for me, thank you,' said Phryne, and kissed Lindsay Herbert hard on the mouth.

SARAH NEAL

Daughters – and Dilemmas

Weddings and wifedom – anathema or salvation? Does being a wife mean anything any more? Is it irrelevant? This film explores the meanings of weddings and wives across three generations. There are three characters.

CATHY has never believed that being a wife is an option worth considering: she equates it with the suburban conventions she rebelled against in her youth. But now, in her late thirties and with an adult daughter, she is having second thoughts about weddings and wives ...

RITA (Cathy's mother) blames the loss of her husband and her status as wife for her later social and mental demise. The only control she has in her life is over her lap dogs. To her, being a wife means protection against isolation and loneliness.

JESS (Cathy's daughter) has grown up to be independent. Marriage isn't part of her vocabulary ...

SCENE 1

Brisbane: present day . . .

Cathy is deep in thought. She is standing in the middle of the living room of her old Queenslander house, surrounded by clutter. The room is in a state of chaos with sewing paraphernalia. Shafts of light stream through large uncurtained windows. A long wooden bookshelf expands along one of the walls and is filled to capacity with an eclectic mix of titles and subjects – from gardening to politics. Above the sewing machine, pinned haphazardly to the wall, are coloured sketches of a 1930s-style wedding dress which Cathy is making, and a photograph of Cathy as a young girl with her mother, Rita. The photograph shows Cathy dressed in a twin-set identical to that worn by Rita. Neither of them look particularly happy.

Something about the familiarity of the hot day has triggered her memory and thoughts of the past flood into the present as Cathy handsews a button onto the back of the almost completed garment. She moves in front of a full length mirror, and holds the dress up against herself. As she gazes at her reflection, her eyes are shown in extreme close-up, and contrasted by a quick cut to a close-up of Cathy's eyes as a young girl in the photograph. Both expressions show a determination which has not been lost over the years.

As Cathy adjusts the dress against her body, her attention is again drawn to the mirror. A small crack has appeared in the corner. Dogs begin to bark.

SCENE 2

Brisbane: 1972, Cathy's flashback

Amongst a bleak, inner-city street of derelict houses is a block of three terraces, peculiarly out of place with the other architecture. From the last terrace on the row an argument can be heard from the street. The voices of two women shout in competition with the shrill barking of two small dogs. A close shot of the front of the house shows the name of the property – *URBANA* – in wrought iron on the stucco. The shutters on the balcony are flung open by Rita. She is a huge woman in her fifties with a severe face contorted by pancake make-up and her fury. Rita is partly hidden by a mountain of girls' clothing, which she flings down into the street.

A scraggy boy riding his bike along the gutter is suddenly swamped. He pulls a t-shirt off his head and yells up to the huge woman above him, before speeding off.

BOY: Freak!!!

Rita has returned to the balcony with the mirror from a dressing-table. The action becomes slow and fragmented as she hurls it to the street. It sails through the air, reflecting the sky, before smashing into smithereens on the bitumen. The action returns to normal speed.
Cathy, aged sixteen and wearing a school uniform, runs out of the house, to where her belongings lie scattered. She hurriedly stuffs them into her bag. As she grabs for the last pathetic item, Cathy's face is seen reflected in a large splinter of glass. Her usually impassive espression is scarred by fear, and the urgent need to flee. Shocked by this, she picks the glass up to look closer, but cuts herself in the process. Cathy yells out to her mother, and whoever else can hear.

CATHY: I don't need you!!!

As Cathy runs away, Rita appears at the front door, with two lap dogs at her feet. Her feet are crammed into strappy cork sandals, and fat bulges over the edges. Her image is distorted in monstrous reflection in the shattered mirror on the pavement.

RITA: Just take a good look at yourself, girl!!!

SCENE 3

Brisbane: 1972, Cathy's flashback

All that is seen is Cathy's point of view of the footpath blurring beneath her pounding feet; and the sound of her muffled quickening breath. She chants to herself in rhythm with her pace.

CATHY: Freak. Freak . . Freak . . .

SCENE 4A

Brisbane: 1973, Cathy's memory leaps ahead . . .

Cathy, now aged seventeen, is nursing her baby Jess in the front seat of a Holden stationwagon. It's a Saturday morning, and a day at the beach has been planned. Music is blaring from the radio, and Anna, Cathy's girlfriend, is singing along loudly as she drives out of town. The view from the passenger window is colourful, the sky is bright and trees line the road. For the moment, Jess is content on her mother's breast and Cathy is able to enjoy the company of her friend uninterrupted. She feels her freedom and her youth and closes her eyes.

SCENE 4B

Brisbane: 1973, later that night . . .

Cut to a black screen and the sound of a telephone ringing. It's late at night in the house Cathy shares with Anna. The hall light is switched on and Anna stumbles out.

ANNA: Hello? . . . I think she's asleep, just a minute . . .

The noise has woken Jess, who starts to cry. Seconds later Cathy walks into the hallway carrying Jess and a bottle of milk. Anna covers the receiver and whispers.

ANNA: It's your mother.

Cathy is wide-awake now, shocked by the intrusion. She shakes her head vigorously, being unable to play the role of daughter and turns abruptly to leave the room. Her sudden movement jolts the bottle from her grasp and it falls to the floor, the glass smashing on the wood. The broken glass is seen from Cathy's point of view. She bends to pick up the pieces and cuts herself. The cycle of her memory has been broken.

SCENE 5

Brisbane: present day . . .

Cathy and her boyfriend Martin are seated at the kitchen table of Cathy's house. Between them is an engagement ring in a box. Martin's face is intent as he gazes at Cathy. Cathy is distracted and lights a cigarette as Martin pushes the box closer to her. She glances at the ring, flicks the ash off the end of her cigarette into a pot plant on the windowsill, and looks Martin in the face.

CATHY: Jess isn't going to like this.

MARTIN: I thought we got along well.

CATHY: It's not that. It's the idea of marriage she won't like.

MARTIN: Well you haven't spoken to her yet, so stop anticipating a drama.

SCENE 6

Brisbane: 1978, Jess recalls . . .

Rita is busy cutting up meat for her lap dogs in the kitchen of *URBANA*. The decor exhibits decades of bad taste and decay. As she drops titbits of fat to the animals, her movements and expression show a barely contained sense of anticipation. A dry-looking fruitcake with luminous pink icing is plonked on the laminex bench in preparation for visitors. A rare occurrence. Rita hums snatches of a song to herself as she finishes her tasks. The action is accompanied by a voice-over of Jess, aged 20.

> JESS: I remember visiting my grandmother once when I was five. Cathy, my mother, hadn't seen her for a few years so we were both a bit scared. When we got there, I was sent out the back to play. I remember there was a cake that was meant for us, but we never got to eat it. Rita fed it to the dogs in front of us, so we left. Mum hated those dogs. She reckoned they were treated better than her. It's true.

SCENE 7

Brisbane: 1971, Jess imagines her mother's past . . .

Cathy, who is fifteen, is tending to her mother who is sick in bed. Rita's bedroom is small and cramped. The windows are closed to keep the flies out, but the heat is oppressive, and Cathy wrings out a wet washer to dampen her mother's forehead. The pomeranians lie across a patchwork quilt at the foot of the bed, their tongues hanging out and dripping saliva.

Women's Weeklys, a tray of dirty dishes and a box of tissues covered in pink fun fur are scattered on the huge bed, which fills most of the space. A fuzzy black and white television drones in the corner as Cathy pours Rita a cup of tea.

> RITA: You can take all the wire coathangers out of the cupboards and throw them away, and then I want you to take the babies for a good long run. They've been in here all day, so they'll need a good, long, run.

Cathy feigns a smile at her mother and strokes one of the dogs. As Rita reclines further into the pillows and lowers the washer over her eyes with her pudgy fingers, Cathy pulls the dogs off the bed by the scruffs of their necks and hurls them to the floor. They yelp.

> CATHY: Oops, sorry!

SCENE 8

Brisbane: 1971, a few moments later . . .

On the corner of Cathy's street the sound of a pile of wire being dumped into an industrial bin is followed by the snarling and yapping of the pomeranians. From the side of the terraces, Cathy emerges dragging the animals on leads. Both dogs have tartan jackets strapped on despite the heat.

> CATHY: (to the dogs) I hope you both feel embarrassed.

Cathy storms down the street to the local shops, where she ties the dogs to a mail box in front of an old cake shop. A long thin mirror borders the window display, which features a huge tiered wedding cake. The cake catches her eye. Everything about it reminds her of her mother; its size, its artificiality and its representation of safety. This angers her. Cathy glances away and is confronted by her own reflection. She registers the look of disdain and arrogance which colours her expression and accepts it. Snarling at herself, she moves closer to the mirror until her nose is pressed against it. Then pushing her face and palms against the coolness of the glass, she obliterates her image.

SCENE 9

Brisbane: present day . . .

Cathy has her face and palms pressed against the window of her semi-enclosed verandah. Her reverie has been disturbed and she is characteristically taking a moment to compose her thoughts. She has her back to Jess who raps her fingernails on the table defensively. The tide of the conversation has inevitably turned towards the subject of her current relationship. Cathy inhales in frustration and turns towards Jess, prepared to launch into a tirade, to gain control of the situation. For a split second Cathy's train of thought falters as she looks at her daughter. Jess has her mother's eyes, but is tall and lean. She sits composed and dignified. She is an adult. Cathy is startled by the recognition of this obvious fact, and feels proud despite herself and the situation.

CATHY: (almost pleading) I'm thirty-six years old. Your grandmother had been widowed for five years at my age.

JESS: (incredulously) I don't believe this. Mum, why are you trying to justify this to me? I'm not going to buy it. You might be able to convince your friends that marrying Martin is a good idea, but I'm not going to let you get away with it that easily. I know you too well.

CATHY: I'm sick of defending myself, Jess.

Jess stands up and takes her mother by the shoulders, looking her straight in the eye, with her full twenty years of life experience.

JESS: Not good enough.

Cathy recognises her own wilful nature in her daughter and it divides her between anger and understanding.

CATHY: Shit Jess, why can't you be on my side about this!

JESS: (infuriatingly calmly) I'm on your side, but you're not in your right mind.

SCENE 10

Brisbane: some time in the future . . .

In an unguarded moment, the fears which have been simmering in Cathy's subconscious cascade into reality via a technicoloured vision.

Cathy and Martin are about to be pronounced husband and wife at a small gathering in Cathy's garden. A Buddhist monk stands before them. Cathy turns to look at Jess who was standing beside her, but she has vanished. In the distance, Cathy can see Jess running away, her bunch of stralitzias scattered in her wake. In Jess's place stands Rita nursing her two dogs. They have pink bows in their hair and wear tuxedos. Rita is grinning madly and feeding them iced fruitcake, but it is old and dry, so they cough it up. Cathy looks down at her wrists and finds them handcuffed to Martin, who smiles sweetly and swallows the key. The monk is juggling religious icons. Cathy panics and struggles to flee. Her wedding has become a grotesque circus.

CATHY: Jess!!!!!!

SCENE 11

Brisbane: present day . . .

Cathy and Martin are seated at the kitchen table in Cathy's kitchen. An engagement ring sits in the space between them. It is an extremely hot day, and everything in the room is limp and listless including the cranky lovers. A cactus in a small pot on the windowsill frames the desert-like exterior. Harsh sunlight has burnt Cathy's plants, and the garden looks barren and neglected. Martin distances himself further from Cathy by rolling a cigarette. His movements are precise, but his anxiety causes his hands to shake slightly. Cathy lethargically grinds the flint off a match and flicks the tiny pieces out of the window. She looks at the ring and gently shifts it towards Martin with the match, fastening her eyes on him as she does. His response is immediate.

MARTIN: Look, Cathy . . . I think you're over-reacting.

CATHY: I'm not. I'm not, Martin. There's just no point.

MARTIN: Well, you're turning something quite normal and natural into some . . . some political agenda.

CATHY: (in control of the situation) See what I mean?

Cathy leaves the room. Martin remains uncomfortably alone.

SCENE 12A

Brisbane: present day ...

Eventide Rest Home for the Aged is seen from the street. It's a small establishment with a spartan, manicured garden. The lawn is being mown by an ancient gardener. Mirages form along the path to the entrance – a result of the intense heat. Cicadas drone. The sound of Cathy's wheezy Renault drowns out the lawnmower, as the car pulls up outside the home. Cathy is driving, and Jess occupies the passenger seat, holding a bunch of flowers. Cathy turns the engine off.

JESS: (sarcastically) Nice garden.

CATHY: Mm. Look, you can wait in the car if you want, or go for a walk. You don't have to come in.

JESS: I know.

CATHY: I'm glad you came with me, Jess. Couldn't have done it on my own.

JESS: I'm a fantastic person.

Cathy grabs her wallet and keys and gets out of the car. Jess gets out with the flowers and hands them to her mother on the footpath.

JESS: Whatever happens, don't let the old dragon upset you, okay? Just remember, her values are irrelevant now. They mean nothing.

CATHY: Easy for you to say.

Cathy brushes the creases out of her trousers, all movement being an effort in the heat, and squeezes Jess's arm as she heads towards the entrance. Jess watches the gardener watching her mother.

SCENE 12B

Brisbane: present day . . .

Inside the Rest Home, a nurse briskly leads Cathy down the corridor. It's her first visit to Eventide and she is shocked by the sterility and desperation of the place. She glimpses the elderly in their rooms. Some of them smile at her, others dribble. The kaleidoscope of faces, senility and hope, touches her core. Finally they come to a closed door at the end of the corridor.

> NURSE: This is it, number 66. Clickety click. Likes her privacy, your mother.

Cathy doesn't move. She is rooted to the spot. The nurse looks her up and down tactlessly.

> NURSE: You can go in if you like.

The nurse turns and leaves abruptly. Cathy remains in front of the door, noticing the quickening pace of her heart. She opens the door. Inside, the room has four beds. Three of them are unmade, and there's no one else in the room except her mother. Photographs strike her first. One of Rita's wedding. One of Cathy as a baby. One of the bloody pomeranians.
Rita is asleep on a commode chair by the window. She is elderly, but there is a strength about her. Cathy has no desire to wake her, so she places the flowers in a vase on the bedside table. Picking up the photograph of Rita and Charlie, husband and wife, she lies down on her mother's bed, the photo to her chest. She contemplates Rita's life; her shortlived marriage,

her loneliness and neurosis, wondering how Rita feels about it all. If her mother felt fulfilled, or just cheated of a life.

Thoughts circulate in her head.

SCENE 13

Brisbane: present day, Eventide. Cathy's dream ...

Lying in the quiet of Rita's room, Cathy's mind drifts. She visualises her parents' wedding in the 1940s. The images are black and white, like an old newsreel. Rita as a young, robust woman, full of vitality, grabs her new husband Charlie on the steps of the church and kisses him passionately. Rice is thrown by guests.

The next image to appear is of Rita, still a young woman, standing in front of a modest headstone in a cemetery. She holds a bunch of stralitzias. The image cuts.

SCENE 14A

Brisbane: present day, Eventide ...

Rita has woken and is standing above Cathy. She moves closer, slowly, shuffling in her slippers. She sees her photo in Cathy's hands and grabs for it. Cathy stirs, but doesn't wake. Rita uses the moment to evaluate her daughter. She notices the early signs of age on her daughter's face. Time has advanced, and her daughter is a mother too. She places the photo back on the table. Cathy wakes up with a jolt.

CATHY: Mum! Mum, are you okay?
Aren't you glad to see me?

RITA: I suppose.

Cathy gets up off the bed, and turns towards her mother.

CATHY: I haven't changed much.

RITA: Still on your own?

CATHY: (laughing) You haven't changed much either. Yes, I live by myself.

RITA: Where's that child of yours?

CATHY: She's outside. She thought we'd want some time alone.

RITA: Couldn't face her grandmother, you mean.

CATHY: Can you blame her?

RITA: No.

CATHY: Look, I don't want to fight anymore. I'm sick to death of fighting.

PAUSE

SCENE 14B

Brisbane: present day, Eventide . . .

RITA: Are you happy?

CATHY: I'm content. I'm not afraid of being alone.

RITA: Don't you talk to me about being alone! You could save yourself a lot of pain, and find someone who'll marry you. That's if they don't mind a kid into the bargain.

CATHY: Jess isn't a child anymore, Mum, and neither am I, so you're not hurting me by saying that.

RITA: You don't want to end up like me, do you? I bet that's your worst fear, isn't it.

CATHY: Not anymore. Actually, I want you to come and stay with me for a while.

RITA: Don't push it.

CATHY: Just think about it. All right?

SCENE 14C

Brisbane: present day.

Cathy opens the door of her car at the front of Eventide. Jess is seated in the front, with the radio on. Cathy turns it off.

JESS: Well, how'd it go?

CATHY: I stayed calm, and she's thinking about it.

JESS: Guess that means progress.

Cathy starts the engine and they drive off. The gardener has finished mowing.

SCENE 15

Brisbane: present day . . .

Cathy's old house is seen from the street. It is set high and has leadlight windows along the front. One of the windows is open. The following is seen as though through the eyes of a fly which zooms in through the open window. Inside Cathy's kitchen, Rita, Cathy and Jess are seated around the table. 1930s music is playing and this drowns out the actual conversation, although it is obviously animated. A huge fruitcake that Rita has made is in the centre of the table. The three generations of women are icing the cake with pink frosting. Cathy is laughing loudly as Rita pushes Jess's face into the bowl of icing. The moment is frozen like a photograph.

DOROTHY PORTER

Wives

There's a darkness in women's warmth
there's a trapdoor in women's talk

I married for warmth
I married for talk

forever, we said
exchanging vows over cigarettes and cappuccinos

forever, we said
toasting ourselves in an empty house

And who did we marry?

I married the moon
I married my silver remotest self

she married the mirror
she married an echo of ravishing kisses

lightning strikes/melting skin
we lived in an electrical storm

we didn't care who paid the bills
we didn't care who swept the floor

we had the moon, we had the mirror
we smelted silver in echoing kisses

forever, we said
holding hands on the street

forever, we said
giving up our friends

each other's fantastic familiar
like flying black cats

each other's eyes and ears
like spies in a black-wise thriller

we muffled our clocks
we blurred our faces

we tick. tick. ticked. like silky bombs
under each other's breasts

day and night ran together
like whirling dyes in a wild wash

And what was the world
without our joined pulse?

it trashed and trafficked
monotonously beyond our walls

she was wine
I was delicious insomnia

awake and intoxicated
we talked up shimmering lives

where we were the crackling streets
where we were the diamond constellations

fire and smoke gusted us about
we floated in the air like torched cities

forever, we said
over New Year valley sunsets

forever, we said
wearing each other's caressing clothes

the lawn grew to our necks
the vacuum cleaner choked

our house closed its threadbare fist
around our dancing ankles

we tripped
we fell on each other

it's her fault
it's her fault

our echoing thoughts resentful
our echoing thoughts finding each other

you're not me
you're not me

in bed there's always present tense
zipped in each other we ignore the phone

It was the world calling

girls, it called through the dustmotes
girls, it called through our mouths.

I unmarry you
I unmarry you

we're wives, we replied
our hair tangled like blackberry vines

we're wives, we screamed
tearing roots and scalp

we're free, we groaned
touching the air where our other had breathed.

HELEN HODGMAN

Blue Skies

When my novel *Blue Skies* was published in London in 1976, there was immediate interest in turning it into a film. An Australian producer bought the rights and, on my return to this country in 1983, the lengthy, dogged, delicate process required to make a film here began. Now, in July 1993, it is about to go into pre-production (despite being $200 000 short of the budget of $2 million – a mere bagatelle, we can always mortgage the house) and by the time this anthology is published it will have been made.

In those intervening years *Blue Skies* has ceased to be a contemporary novel and has turned into a 1960s film, a period piece. It has also undergone three changes of producer and two of director.

My first adaptation, begun under the auspices of the now defunct Women's Film Fund and completed with the support of the Australian Film Commission, was considerably different to this one. Tony Buckley was to produce the film and Di Drew was to direct it. The story of why it did not go ahead at that time is complicated; a series of public and personal events and for me, a basic dissatisfaction with the script, led to the shelving of the project with the sense of relief on my part. Because the AFC had invested money in the above process I would occasionally receive an enquiry from them concerning what they called the 'status' of BLUE SKIES: P2195. Since I had no producer and no director, the answer was always that unfortunately P2195 had no status whatsoever. Meanwhile, other scripts were written for other people and I completed my novel *Broken Words*.

In 1991 I was approached by Nadia Tass (*Malcolm, Stark*) who was keen to make a film with Roger Hodgman. Roger had long been a supporter of the '*Blue Skies* would make a terrific movie' idea and nominated it as something he would like to do. I was sufficiently intrigued (and amused) by this idea to agree. So it was back to the AFC to work out a deal, and then we sat down and took out anything useful in the original script and threw the rest away and the writing process began. A crucial decision was made to set the film back where it belonged, in the 1960s when shotgun weddings were rife. Indeed, in Tasmania (where the novel is set), a better word would be endemic. I was particularly interested in this. *Blue Skies* has often been referred to as a feminist book but this girl (and she is a girl, 19 years old at most) was marooned on a flat sea with the 1970s feminist wave no more than a dot on the horizon if it was visible at all – and she cannot name her discontent. This, perhaps, makes her more individual and entertaining than she might have been if someone had handed her a good book on the subject. Who knows, if *Weddings and Wives* had been around at the time, my heroine may have resisted her fate, her next-door neighbour would have lived and ... but then there would have been no novel, and no film either.

This is a selection of early scenes from the screenplay of *Blue Skies*. The first 24 scenes are in their narrative order. The others are taken from the text at different stages. The length of the finished film is estimated at 100 minutes. The shooting schedule is 8 weeks and 3 days. It will be shot in several locations, including Tasmania.

THE PLACE: Taroona, Hobart and Orielton via Richmond, Tasmania.

THE YEAR: 1968

THE PEOPLE:
POSSUM, 19 years old
JAMES, 21, Possum's husband
MIL, late 40s. Possum's mother-in-law
DIDGIE, 16 or 17. Possum's brother-in-law
GLORIA, Possum's best friend, a young woman in her mid to late 20s
BEN, lives with Gloria
BANJO, Gloria and Ben's son
PICKUP, mid to late 30s. Possum's friend
OLLIE, Possum's neighbour, an energetic woman of late middle age

AND ALSO: A mermaid Two aunts A teenage friend and her disapproving mother A greasy English bus driver A team of lady bowlers A surveyor A workman Four garbage men One man with a dog A paperboy Bruce the barman An Avon lady A doctor Some small drab Tasmanians A whispy, hippie waitress Some dogs and Two rubbish removalists

EXT. A BEACH SUNSET

An ocean beach, wild and deserted as though this were the world's first sunset but it isn't – it is in fact a Saturday night in Tasmania sometime in the 1960s, and in the midst of all this primal splendour a small car parked on the sand is a very stranded, incongruous dot on the landscape.
TWO FIGURES (JAMES and POSSUM) walk hand in hand. They stop. They kiss – the camera swoops down and in on them. This is high romance with gothic tinges, reflecting POSSUM'S natural frame of mind. JAMES and POSSUM walk to the car (his mother's car, as it happens). JAMES opens the back door. POSSUM gets in. JAMES follows. The door closes.

INT. CAR NIGHT

A very intense squash of limbs as JAMES and POSSUM engage in amorous activity on the back seat. All the windows are steamed up. POSSUM'S bent leg is crushed against the front seat, the other raised and squeezed against the back window. JAMES lies between. We clearly see the look of dazed dismay on his face as he tries to withdraw, can't in the confined space, and comes.

EXT. CAR DAY

Tight on steamed-up back window of car. From inside, a finger draws a pierced heart in the condensation.

EXT. CAR DAY

Close on back door so no sense of where the car might be parked can intrude. The door opens. A white satin shoe appears. Instead of the tousled girl we might expect, POSSUM fills the screen, hatching before us like a great bridal butterfly. She wears a dress cut from a designer pattern which has been wittily and stylishly adapted for bridal purposes by her best friend GLORIA. She carries a bridal bouquet. Being newly hatched, POSSUM must be still for a moment to look round at her new world.

EXT. BEACH FADING SUNSET

But what she has emerged to is not the splendid beach above but the pretty domesticated crescent of Taroona Beach: suburban, safe, equipped for family outings, boat launching, barbecues and the usual squat and ugly 'amenities block'.

EXT. THE SUBURBAN BEACH SAME

The car, having served its purpose as chrysalis, is never in the shot as POSSUM sets off along Taroona Beach. The light subtly changes to the end of a long afternoon full of water colour tones. Follow her progress until she stops to look out to sea. Despite the cheerful paraphernalia of the beach – the children's swings and so on – the fact remains that out to sea all there is, and all there ever is, is …

EXT. SEA SAME

… the bleak sweep of the Derwent Estuary to the horizon. There is nothing out there, no matter how hard she wishes for something to break the monotony. Then a gleaming, black shape breaks the surface of the steely water. A whale, a seal, what?

EXT. THE BEACH SAME

POSSUM steps out of her shoes and walks a short way into the water. She watches hopefully for something interesting to emerge.

EXT. SEA SAME

A baroque and beautiful mermaid on a windswept, wave-washed rock smiles down on us. She smiles, she stretches out an arm …

EXT. THE BEACH SAME

POSSUM, thrilled at her vision, throws the bridal bouquet out over the sea to where she imagines the mermaid to be waiting to catch it …

EXT. SEA SAME

The flowers spiral out over the water and fall with a disintegrating splat in the flat, cold sea.

EXT. MOTHER-IN-LAW'S GARDEN (FRONT) SAME

JAMES, now very much the bridegroom in his wide floral tie and pretty brown suit with slightly flared trousers, walks through the garden with an ELDERLY AUNT on each arm. JAMES is observed smiling and chatting as he escorts them to their car and endures gracefully their hugs and kisses before settling them in their car and waving them off.

Meanwhile, other car doors are heard slamming, and engines starting. James's MOTHER (now Possum's mother-in-law and thus hereinafter known as MIL) stands smiling and waving in the direction of these fading sounds of departure. JAMES and MIL turn and begin walking toward each other across the lawn in front of the house. It seems like quite a distance they have to cover.

EXT. SUBURBAN STREET SAME

POSSUM flits along the road, a faded moth in the twilight. THE AUNTS' car roars past, fixing her momentarily in its headlights.

INT. AUNTS' CAR SAME

The YOUNGER AUNT (though not by much) turns in her seat to look back at POSSUM.

YOUNGER AUNT: Well, I think she's sweet. And she and James look very sweet together, too. I do hope she likes that tea set. D'you remember how mother used to dote on it?

OTHER AUNT: It's my belief she'll break every last bit of it by Christmas. And a good thing too.

EXT. MIL'S GARDEN SAME

JAMES and MIL make their way round one side of a marquee. Inside the marquee the party's over though a FEW PEOPLE remain, talking and laughing together.

MIL: Where is she, darling?

JAMES: She's gone for a walk.

MIL: I think we can congratulate ourselves, don't you?

JAMES: Yes.

MIL holds his arm as they step round guy ropes.

MIL: Watch your step.

MIL can stuff the simplest instruction with meanings and pitfalls when she wants. They reach the area of the rose bushes. MIL picks up a hose, holding her finger over one end to make a fine spray. She hoses roses absentmindedly. JAMES is uncomfortable, expecting a scene.

MIL: It went off rather well I thought. Considering.

JAMES: Yes.

MIL slowly turns the hose on her son and proceeds to spray him lightly but thoroughly. She does this with panache. Her bright tight smile never wavers. If it did, she might cry.

MIL: Considering the rush.

JAMES: Yes.

JAMES stands and takes it. His eyes don't leave her face. JAMES loves his mother.

INT. MARQUEE DAY

GLORIA cuts a large slice from what remains of a wedding cake. The party's over.

GLORIA: For Ben. Hope you don't mind.

POSSUM: Course not.

POSSUM finds a clean table napkin to wrap it in. GLORIA looks over to where JONATHAN PICKUP is talking earnestly to a ROMAN CATHOLIC PRIEST. As she watches, PICKUP and the PRIEST shake hands. This PRIEST is particularly emphatic and sincere about this, gripping PICKUP'S proffered hand with both of his. The PRIEST goes.

GLORIA: What was that all about?

POSSUM: God knows.

PICKUP: They're always the last to leave.

GLORIA: Are they? I don't know. Weddings are my least favourite kind of party.

PICKUP: Ah. That's why you've never had one, I suppose.

GLORIA picks up this snide comment.

GLORIA: Perhaps.

POSSUM: Never mind.

What follows is a sort of minor vaudeville routine which amuses GLORIA and POSSUM. They have known each other for a long time.

GLORIA: We may be all too bourgeois

and boring for him – but he does like a bit of cake.

POSSUM: And some champagne to go with it.

POSSUM fishes out a bottle from a full case, looks at it and puts it back.

POSSUM (cont.): Oh here ... take the case.

She lifts it and puts it in GLORIA'S arms. Then she picks up the slice of cake, looks at it, puts it down and picks up what's left of the cake.

POSSUM (cont.): And take the cake. You might as well. And a fondue set. No home's complete without one. And an iron or two. Or a toaster or three. Or a ... a ...

POSSUM picks up an impossible-to-identify knitted thing and waves it about. A ... (she flings it away)

POSSUM: What am I supposed to do with all these things anyway? I've never had so many things in my life!

PICKUP has wandered over to a table with wedding presents on it.

PICKUP: My my. What a lot of fondue sets ... isn't she a lucky girl?

EXT. BACK OF MIL'S HOUSE SAME

DIDGIE, a handsome teenage boy all dressed up for his brother's wedding, is looking round the paved area between the glassed-in back of the house and the garden.

He spots a half-full champagne bottle, picks up an empty glass and pours himself a drink. POSSUM enters frame and watches him. DIDGIE senses her presence, turns and offers her the glass. POSSUM takes it gratefully. She drinks. DIDGIE drinks too, from the bottle.

POSSUM: I'll have to change.

DIDGIE: I think you should've before. I think they were expecting you to. You were supposed to put something different on to go away in.

POSSUM: I'm not going anywhere.

A SMALL BOY hurtles round corner of house and flings his arms round POSSUM, pressing his ear to her stomach. He is Gloria's son and his name is Banjo.

BANJO: Is it in there? I can't hear it. When's it coming out?

DIDGIE: Big mouth.

EXT. GARDEN/STREET NIGHT

POSSUM and GLORIA are loading champagne and cake and a toaster and an iron and a casserole dish and finally the BANJO, who's half asleep, into the car. When this is done GLORIA hugs POSSUM.

GLORIA: You will come up and see us, won't you? Soon? It's so hard for me to get to town now I'm back teaching full-time. And Ben's so busy getting this mainland show together.

PICKUP is leaving the house by the front door. He's a bit drunk. DIDGIE holds his arm briefly, laughing as they negotiate the steps down from the front door. They walk across the garden to the street.

PICKUP: Lovely party.

GLORIA'S getting into her car, starting it and driving off. PICKUP'S doing the same while talking half to DIDGIE and half to himself.

PICKUP (cont.): There's no great virtue in work, my boy. And don't let anyone persuade you otherwise. Means to an end, that's all it is. Means to money I mean.

DIDGIE can relate to this, it seems.

DIDGIE: Yeah.

POSSUM waves after GLORIA'S car.

PICKUP (to Possum): No chance of you coming back to work I suppose? Not very attractive I know, catering to the public stomach.

PICKUP roars off.

DIDGIE: Streuth.

DIDGIE shoves his hands in his pockets and starts to walk away.

POSSUM: Where are you going?

DIDGIE: Geoff's place. Got a couple of

girls coming over. Play a few records and ... (suddenly embarrassed) ... you know.

POSSUM: Oh well ... goodnight then.

DIDGIE turns away.

DIDGIE (over his shoulder): 'night.

POSSUM watches him go. POSSUM feels a little lost.

EXT. BACK OF MIL'S HOUSE NIGHT

It's all in darkness. Clink as bottle is kicked over. A quick flitting shadow inside the house as MIL switches on the outside light which floods the area revealing JAMES sprawled on a two-seater swing chair with a tasselled canopy.

MIL (V/O from inside): It that you?

JAMES and POSSUM look warily at each other. Finally:

JAMES: Your feet are filthy.

POSSUM goes to JAMES who's still looking damp.

POSSUM: And you're all wet.

POSSUM gives the swing a push with her filthy foot. POSSUM sits herself on top of him and spreads her dress so it covers him completely.

JAMES (muffled): So are you.

The chair swings more. POSSUM giggles.

MIL (V/O): Is it?

EXT. MIL'S HOUSE/FRONT NIGHT

JAMES is backing MIL'S car out of carport. POSSUM and MIL stand on front porch. POSSUM is piled high with presents.

POSSUM: We could walk.

MIL: Nonsense. You've got too much to carry.

POSSUM (hopefully): We could leave it all here.

MIL: Whatever would you want to do that for?

MIL takes some of POSSUM'S load and sets off purposefully across lawn to the waiting car.

POSSUM trails after. POSSUM sees that the car is covered with shaving foam and confetti, with tin cans tied on behind. POSSUM drops her bundle. JAMES gets out. They stand looking at the car while MIL struggles to load the presents into the back seat.

POSSUM: Who did that?

JAMES: Didge, I bet. Looks like a very Didgie touch to me.

POSSUM: Well, I'm not getting in it.

JAMES: Don't be silly.

POSSUM: I'm not.

JAMES exasperated.

JAMES: Well don't then. Shit! See if I bloody well care.

POSSUM sets off down the road (not up the road which leads to the highway to Hobart but down it, deeper into the suburb and towards the beach). JAMES and MIL stare after her. MIL'S tight, bright smile again.

EXT. SUBURBAN STREET NIGHT

POSSUM turns into the street where she and James will live. The car roars past her at speed and stops with a squeal of brakes. POSSUM stops. JAMES leans over and opens passenger door. POSSUM watches the door swing open. POSSUM hesitates then walks slowly to the car and gets in. Car pulls slowly off. It's not going far. It passes a vacant bush block and then the blinker goes on and the car turns into a short driveway and pulls up outside a dilapidated, wooden garage with double doors.

INT. CAR NIGHT

JAMES: Feeling better?

POSSUM: No.

POSSUM marches toward her new home.

An impression of this house: it is reasonably old – it has the faded air of a once much-loved but recently neglected beachside house which has slowly been crowded about by brick veneers as the suburbs spread. It is weatherboard, paint cracked and peeling but it has an appeal the soulless numbers all round it lack. Most importantly it has a vacant lot next door where trees and scrub survive.

POSSUM *opens flywire door which squeaks loudly on its hinges – a sharp shriek as it opens and a slow whine as it closes.*

NB: *This ghastly shriek persists throughout film every time anyone uses this door.*

Now, lights come on inside, strips of yellow between the slats of venetian blinds. JAMES gets out of the car and opens back door. He's searching through stuff on back seat. He finds what he wants which is the box where his aunt's tea set is wrapped up in tissue. JAMES goes to house but the screen door has barely completed its noisesome sequence when it hurtles open again. POSSUM emerges. She wears a large shirt that must be JAMES' and a determined expression. POSSUM proceeds to take all the wedding presents from the back seat and throw them into the garage.

INT. KITCHEN NIGHT

POSSUM enters triumphant. JAMES is sitting at the breakfast bar – a flecked formica and chrome creation that divides the kitchen. He's unwrapping the tea set and arranging it in a neat line. The kettle's on the stove, about to boil.

JAMES (putting a cup gently on a saucer): Feeling better now?

POSSUM: Much.

POSSUM seizes tea-pot shaped package, sheds the paper round it and finds tea and puts some in pot. JAMES amuses himself by turning over tea cups and trying to decipher the marks on the bottom. POSSUM examines the tea pot.

POSSUM: I like this. It's pretty.

JAMES: Be careful.

POSSUM pours water into tea pot. She sees a cobweb clinging to the shirt and brushes it off.

JAMES: I was planning to wear that tomorrow. Mum ironed it for me especially.

POSSUM: Oh, did she?

POSSUM goes and sits on JAMES' lap. She kisses him. He responds. As their kiss gets more involved, his elbow slips and sends tea cup over the edge. A sharp tinkle of breaking china. The kiss continues.

INT. LIVING ROOM DAY

POSSUM snaps open blinds. They are very dusty because they haven't been opened for a long time. There's a house next door, a real horror surrounded by the raw mess that follows building. The large moving van judders to a halt. POSSUM watches as a WOMAN OF LATE MIDDLE AGE, and possessed of a relentless energy, jumps down from cabin followed by the REMOVALISTS. The WOMAN, whose name will prove to be OLLIE, rushes happily across the devastated earth to her new front door. OLLIE spots POSSUM watching. She stops, looks, gives a cheery wave. POSSUM snaps the blinds closed. Somewhere, a tiny baby starts to cry, it is a tinny sound, scarcely human but it builds . . .

INT. HOSPITAL NURSERY DAY

Possum's newborn BABY GIRL lies in a crib crying furiously. Pulling back we see the rows of peaceful babies on either side. Pull back further to plate glass of viewing room. Pass through it and out into . . .

INT. HOSPITAL CORRIDOR SAME

Silence, though the BABY continues to cry behind the glass. MIL is thrilled. POSSUM stands apart from them at the far end of the corridor. JAMES and MIL do not know that she is there, watching them watching the baby.

INT. KITCHEN MORNING

Transistor radio, tuned to morning talk-show aimed at housewives, plays as POSSUM takes BABY from her plastic bath on top of breakfast bar. She wraps her in a towel and walks past window, glancing out as she does so. OLLIE is out doing what looks like a slow dance on the ground in front of her house. POSSUM, curious, stops and watches.

EXT. OLLIE'S SAME

OLLIE has planted the area in front of her house with grass seed. Now she is gently pressing the loosely scattered seeds into the soil with her feet. The effect is rather bizarre and comic although the procedure is commonplace enough.

INT. BEDROOM AFTERNOON

POSSUM prostrate on bed, pillow over her face. The blinds are shut, the room is grey. POSSUM sits up. Looks at alarm clock perched on top of pile of books. It reads 3 p.m. With a great groan POSSUM grabs the pillow, rolls across the bed and smothers the alarm clock in dramatic fashion. POSSUM flops back on bed, covers her eyes with her hand.

BEACH sounds heard over. POSSUM'S fingers slowly part. POSSUM'S POV: bright sunlight shining through her fingers into her eyes.

MIL: You should get out into the fresh
air more . . .

EXT. BEACH DAY

POSSUM lies on sand peering up through her fingers at MIL who stands over her. MIL is dripping wet, having just emerged from the water. She wears an exotically-petalled, rubber bathing cap. The BABY lies on a blanket, next to MIL'S handbag. MIL peels off cap and grabs her bag and fossicks through it, dislodging quantities of tissues and lifesavers to find a packet of cigarettes, talking to POSSUM at the same time.

MIL: It's not good for you to sit in that house all day.

POSSUM sits up. MIL settles herself, next to BABY, takes out a cigarette, waves packet at POSSUM, who takes one.

MIL (lighting cigarettes): It's rather a shame, don't you think, when you have such a beautiful beach at the end of the road, not to use it?

MIL inhales deeply, exhales with a sigh of contentment.

MIL (cont.): Best one of the lot. After a swim.

POSSUM considers the beach. It is dotted with girls of POSSUM'S age with babies. Some LITTLE KIDS are playing.

POSSUM: I do come down here.

POSSUM keeps watching the beach as MIL talks. The YOUNG MOTHERS. The BABIES.

MIL: I only want to see you happy, you know. And James too. It worries me to see you brooding by yourself all the time.

One by one the BABIES start to cry. It's getting noisy, though MIL doesn't seem to notice.

MIL: Such nice girls.

To POSSUM'S horror and disbelief one by one all the YOUNG MOTHERS start to cry too: big, lusty infant cries, not choked grown-up tears.

MIL: And they all have tiny babies, bless them. So you would have such a lot in common. You have to make an effort to cultivate people. If only you'd get out and meet them.

POSSUM: Like lawns.

POSSUM can't stand all this crying going on. She jumps up and goes to water's edge. MIL watches her, irritated with herself for having said the wrong thing and with POSSUM for being so difficult. The crying fades and dies as POSSUM gazes out at the Tasmanian horizon which is so dauntingly beautiful and achingly empty.

MIL (V/O) (shouting): What do you want?

POSSUM hesitates, struggling to find an answer to so complex a question but when she turns, it turns out to be nothing more than an ice-cream van which has appeared on the grass slope above the beach. EVERYONE is flocking to it. MIL stands clutching her purse.

MIL (cheerful): My shout!

ANNA MARIA DELL'OSO

A Toast to All You Brides of Fortune (A homage scrawled in the margins of life.)

Marriage is many things to many people but it is rarely a place for solitude.

So when I'm unexpectedly alone at 1 a.m. – the kids are asleep, my husband reading in bed and my computer and fax have been shut down for the night – I have an urge to make notes in the margins of the day to ... it's hard to say ... maybe to the wind in the trees, the lights in far windows, the blades of grass under cat's feet in the park beyond ... It's as though I'm hearing, against the ticking of my life, a howl of something old and wild outside, out there. On nights like this I feel emboldened to whistle a few strange songs that have nothing to do with the work of the day, the husband-and-wife talk, the children or 'the thousand and one things'.

In this mood, I get out my diaries, my notes to my notes: the oldest things of myself I can find. I look at them as a kind of inner carbon-dating, a musing over the bones.

Photographs come tumbling out of old shoe-boxes. They are pictures mostly of the women of my family, *contadini* women, the Abruzzese mountain brides, mothers of large

My grandmother, Nonna Anna

families, and black old crones. They are followed by colour snapshots of my generation, their Australian grand-daughters and grand-nieces. I have photos of us holding our newborns in hospital maternity wards or receiving our degrees at university ceremonies or smiling at café tables in Chapel Street, South Yarra. There are photos of us as single Italian Princesses living unwillingly at home, running around in the zippy cars and imported clothes that were our pay-off for staying put.

Being of Italian blood doesn't mean I have privileged access to the past or a notion of 'close extended family' or a predilection for marriage. On the contrary, emigration as well as industrialisation has broken many cultural threads. The matrilineal heritage is not consciously strong in me; I don't know much about my grandmothers, I don't know their full names or what kind of people they were or whether they married for love or money or land or to avoid scandal. But what little I do have of them comes through marriage.

The tradition of the wedding dowry means that at least I have the beautiful rough linen nightgowns the Abruzzese women made by hand (and I mean *by hand*, from harvesting the raw flax to weaving the cloth, to stitching the garment; the work of years and years). My mother made more than a dozen of these embroidered nightgowns for her dowry. She received some from her mother, and in a visit I made to Italy in 1988 my old Zia Fiorina gave me a dowry nightgown that belonged to her grandmother.

In my drawers now I have three generations of these peasant bridal nightgowns, yellowing, virginal, cool and tough, their tissue paper still pinned under the *broderie anglais*. When I touch them, I know how useful they would have been for a young bride-wife in the middle of the night – to protect against post-coital chill, to soak up lovemaking sweat or wet or to firmly regain one's modesty before sunlight. The rough, thick linen is absorbent and practical, able to be bleached for a hundred years or more without losing its strength; perfect for handling menstrual blood, childbirth blood, hot flushes and no doubt, *rigor mortis*. You can't buy weaving like this, it's almost sacred. I can't forget that in an Abruzzese woman's life, this dowry linen started off as a veil in the night and then became cut up as swaddling, rag, sheet, bandage and shroud.

Marriage and the maternal line: I don't have much except my genes, garments from several women's dowries, paper roses, linen, photographs, baby health centre books and notes of notes of an opera libretto I wrote, *Bride of Fortune*, a piece that attempts to stitch together a tribute to the women in my culture for whom marriage was fate. It's not much but still, let me unpin the tissue, see the threads. Let me hold the words, the songs and the photos to the desk light. Let me see what I've been given and sort out a little of what I've been hoarding, to pass on to my daughters and their daughters.

Here is an invitation to my wedding to David in 1986. It's a Rodinesque black-and-white photo of our two hands held together; inside are the details of the ceremony.

I've always wanted to get married and have children.

It's not cool to admit that in an age of drop-dead sophistication, exhausted feminist freedom fighters and the cynical non-commitment of the Me, Me and Only Me Generation, but it's true. Let me be frank; I could never see why being married with children was a crime against feminism or incompatible with being a writer. (Let me add that I didn't realise it would be so *hard* but I don't see it as inevitably the fault of an individual marriage. Rather it's due to outside pressures upon the relational life and the family – whether traditional and non-traditional, extended and nuclear. Family – by which I mean the earthy art of living with others in a committed way – has been both derided and exalted at various times but rarely fed and nurtured in our technological society unless it suits the economy to do so.)

As a girl, I saw that marriage was about love, food and spectacle. It was about feasts in big public halls, dancing to imported piano accordians, eating *antipasto*, roast chickens, *cassata* and *tirami su*. At Italian weddings, I'd fall asleep on my mother's coat under the table, watching my father ash his cigarette into an empty wineglass and my mother pass strong black coffees down the table to perspiring relatives back from dancing to *La Cumparsita*. Weddings smelled of sweat-seeped silk, cheap perfume, aftershave, *bomboniere*, *sambucca* and *prosciutto*, all liberally salted with gossip and Abruzzese village stories I didn't understand.

At the centre of it all was The Bride, the Girl With The Raven Hair at the centre table. All of this joy of the feast was for her and her beloved. Getting married meant being The Bride, wearing The Bride's spectacular gown and dancing at a sumptuous feast with The Bridegroom, the man whose heart beat closest to her own wild heart.

So I decided to get married myself. But not to the wrong person – that would have been the False Bridegroom, the tyrant who would 'make a fool out of me' as my mother warned. I thought I would marry. But not because my parents told me to – not the Social Contract marriage, the What Will People Think – Good Italian Boy meets Good Italian Girl marriage.

I was inspired in this by the Juliet-like bravery of my 'cousin' Grazietta Vaccari, the love-struck 17-year-old daughter of *paesan* (family friends). Grazietta was forbidden from seeing Ray, her Aussie-Irish boyfriend. Ray was not considered marriage material by the patriarch because he was a mechanic's apprentice, had sideburns and was not Italian. Grazietta cried for a week to no avail. When she began to refuse food, however, her mother went white. There were whispers, negotiations, slammed doors and temper tantrums. At around the third untouched plate of *lasagne al forno*, Grazietta's mother cracked. Signora Vaccari leaned on the old man, sense prevailed and the dreaded multicultural match was struck. Happily ever after as it's turned out. Grazietta and Ray are still married, have three grown kids and a grandchild on the way, and live a relaxed forty-something life around the barbecue on a leafy double block in Ringwood.

(I'm actually amazed that more Good Italian Girls don't resort to hunger striking and anorexia when the acceptance and preparation of food is so often crucial to our mothers and their marriages. But strangely, that never seemed to occur to us. It's hard to knock back a plate of salted olive bread and chicken cacciatore under any circumstances. Maybe that's why angry and depressed Good Italian Girls got fat, while skinniness and anorexia was left to ambitious middle-class Anglo girls with polite and quiet-voiced parents who no doubt dominated them in more subtle ways.)

Most girls I knew at school and at the Irish-Catholic church I attended wanted to be brides, to one day wear 'princess ballgowns' (as my little daughters call them, with no prompting or teaching or romantic glorifying from me, I swear.) Because being a bride *is* magical, part of an old and all-too-human longing to find one's deepest Other/Self. And that is where all the (probably necessary and inevitable) confusion about marriage begins. For when little girls and young women say they want to *get married*, they generally mean they want to be The Bride. They are not generally talking about being a wife. Yet that is the snakepit – or the challenge – or the strengthening reality – or the maturational crisis – waiting for the bride after the guests have left.

As Mary Kay Blakely writes as a wry understatement in her amusing essay 'The Married State', 'Marriage is the process that transforms a "bride" into a "wife" and the changes can be dramatic.'

(You've got to hand it to a lot of bridegrooms though – they often instinctively seem to understand this fundamental process better than the bride. A lot of bridegrooms know that once the guests have left, they will become husbands. Maybe that's why so many men resist marriage, whether formal or de facto, to begin with. Later, it's a different question – ah yes, later men take to marriage like you'd take to a comfy country sofa ... but by then women are screaming and knocking them over in the rush to flee Bluebeard's dungeon.)

Ultimately it doesn't matter. Call it what you will, people will persist in marrying (and if it fails, they'll re-marry again and again) in one form or another – and ultimately the marriage will be tested by life, whether it's by dirty nappies and boisterous kids, a morgage at 11.5 per cent and a frantic life as a wage slave/mother/homemaker or, more commonly now, a wage slave/parenting duo ... or simply the shock of waking up next to a beloved who is often/sometimes/always different to the one you had imagined and married within.

That's life. Good choices, bad choices, naive choices, economic choices or calculated choices – a respectful marriage undertaken in good faith is about getting into the muck of life, getting hands-on experience of the world of surviving, living, loving – with the community and family gazing upon you, and without being able to flee the minute the dream collides with reality. Getting married in our society is a loaded choice like the bearing of children – you're damned if you do and you're damned if you don't. So you may as well if your heart is set on it. And though The Bride might suffer a shock to wake up to find herself a wife – as it can be a shock to wake up to find herself a mother – she is also bound to find it ... illuminating ... an initiation, one way or another.

All I know for sure from seven years of marriage so far – and before that, about the same time of unmarried questing and questioning through various dangerous liaisons – is this: a good marriage is worth more than rubies, flowers, flattery and French perfume; a true, loving husband or wife is a passionate gift from life. A bad marriage is hell on earth and more predatory and dangerous to a person's body and soul than the thing from *Alien*.

That's my only advice to my daughters and all I have of a theory of relationships.

Here are photographs of me as a sulky 15-year-old, a strained 17-year-old and an openly rebellious, about to be exiled 19-year-old patchouli-scented Melbourne University student. Each time, I'm glaring, glowering and smirking into the camera as my family are snapped by Roberto Bario Photography outside various wedding reception halls in Coburg, East Kew and Doncaster-Templestowe.

I never wanted to get married. Not like the girls around me were getting married – to flee home, to get their parents off their backs and to have as much sex as they liked without any hassle. To grow up finally, to be free, to get on with life. To have children, to rule their own roost, to snap up their gorgeous man before anyone else did. To leave their father's house and never have to listen to another word about marriage ever again.

In our teenage years, Italian mothers became obsessed with their daughters marrying and the younger the better. Those daughters who coped best were street-wise and materialistic. The Italian Princesses lived out their mothers' dreams of powerful wealth and thoroughly enjoyed their fathers' ability to indulge offspring as they had seen the upper classes, the *baroni* and *signori*, do in Italy. For immigrant parents, success from gut-breaking work in The Lucky Country meant their kids drove new cars, had their own semidetached apartments within the house. Many owned houses and blocks of land before they were 18, all ready to be converted into investments upon marriage. The Princesses were not averse to their mothers' match-making so long as it was done with style. They knew what they wanted – and it wasn't half-a-dozen of *nonna's* linen nightgowns, an apprentice electrician and a flat in Moonee Ponds.

Many of us who were not so worldly rebelled. We were repelled. Because suddenly we were no longer innocent children, free to dream and wander, but dangerous women to be chaperoned and quickly partnered before something went wrong. This offended our adolescent dignity. It made us feel shame when there should have been none. We felt the terrible pressure to conform to 'The Community' – I saw it then as an entity of watchful, spiteful eyes – to domesticate our sexuality by becoming wives and mothers as soon after our first periods as possible. This scandalised whispering and bullying was probably little different to what our mothers must have had from their own families.

This is how it was for me, as I tried to write about it.

... The streets seemed full of bridal shops, sugared almonds and white tulles stiff with the terrified hysteria of virginity, the last, sickly stubbornness before the blood and all the sorrow of the exhausted. On Saturday morning on S-- Street, walking with her mother, black and plump with fruit groaning from her shopping bag, Rosanna strained to ignore the white bride shop, the purveyor of veils for holy communion, the snowy plumage that seemed to her obscene, stinking of femininity.

It embarrassed her to pieces, shivers that splintered her body to shame. *Disgraziata*, the word of the curse that cut her for blood and weddings, the whispers of sending back to Villa Marino for husbanding, her adolescent breasts like barrels of hidden oil, ripe prosciutto, *carne*, carnal, obscene. *Disgraziata*, her increasingly morose mother stabbed at her – *disgraziata, disgraziata* – as though severing her into the white sanctity that preoccupied the gossips of S-- Street, murmuring of *la bella figura*. Rosanna tried never to look at these shops, never for her mother to see her looking.

She would never look that way.

So some of my generation (but not all that many) rebelled and left scandalously unmarried to study, travel or work interstate and abroad, weathering the damage to family relationships. Others stayed at home and rebelled inwardly, imploding for years, fighting to be themselves without losing their language, culture and family.

I've talked to many first generation Italo-Australian women caught in this dilemma and nearly all of us grieve for that wounding in adolescence when we discover that we must hasten into marriage and motherhood to be acceptable. For quite a few years after the first period, all the warmth and laughter seemed to disappear from our lives as we tried to handle this view of girlhood. The family and the community in my culture is so strong; not for nothing is The Mafia called The Family. The nurturing and loyalty you can expect from the family is absolute but so is exile if you transgress tradition. We were told again and again – there is no middle path; either you do things the traditional way, Our Way, or you take your chances out there with Them, the Australians. Marriage is the bloodline of Italian community and to cut oneself off from the nourishment of that would be fatal. Or so it seemed at the time.

This is why our mothers hit us with the same stick that had been used on them. To be a good mother was to browbeat daughters into marriage. They genuinely wanted us to be happy in marriage, to find the Prince Charming they maybe hadn't *quite* managed to score themselves – because they weren't educated enough, rich enough, pretty enough or because they made the mistake, as my mother says, of 'having too many children. Marry, Anna Maria – but don't have children.'

I now see it as a kind of ritualised wounding of young girls by our mothers because they want us to fit in: a 'we just want you to be happy' kind of cruelty. It was mothering by wounded mothers, mothers who had their souls bound and twisted like a woman's feet in old China. The alternatives were unthinkable

– although some of their Australianised daughters proceeded to educate them about that, at the cost of many terrible years of family turmoil, exile, ostracism.

In the end, time was on our side. Australian life was overwhelming and the older generation were unable to carry out their threats to the end. Conflicts were then patched up by our parents, they had to acquiesce. For the most part differences were eventually tolerated but hidden from the larger Italian community. Where they really couldn't be handled by the older generation – divorce, children out of wedlock, gay offspring and their gay lifestyles – these were ignored or left alone, to be wept over in private by mothers in searing late night phone calls. But even these eventually dwindled to almost nothing. New times – the spirit of the age – was on our side.

Here is a letter from David, studying violin in Germany in 1981, when we were both having similar love turmoil with different people. Here is a program from a Melbourne youth orchestra tour of 1973, with both our 16-year-old names in it. Here is a photo of a musician's party we went to in Melbourne in 1972; a picture of David at a moratorium march in the middle of Swanston Street, a note from David about Hamlet when we were in high school.

David and I were never going to get married. Especially not to each other. David had taken a public vow of non-commitment. At the age of 16, at his older sister's wedding – a 1970s hippy affair, the bride in a pink hand-crocheted dress, and children, beads and beards everywhere – he urged the guests to drink up and be merry because this would be the last marriage in his family.

I met David when we were 14 years old, at a camp for musical kids held over the holidays at the Methodist Ladies College in Melbourne – a strange meeting ground for two brooding, pre-Whitlam era, Little Red Book teenagers with a contempt for private education and the status quo. He was a long-haired, Jewish, middle-class radical with strong left political views, permissive ex-Communist Party parents and a wild style of violin playing. He went to a radical community school called Brinsley Road where kids smoked dope and made films and wrote poetry under trees. I was a terrified, intense, shy, daggy, working-class Italian girl at Kew High School and I'd never spoken more than a few sentences to a boy in my over-protected life.

Weirdly enough, we became fast friends. It was a loyal fringe friendship, part of a group of ever-shifting musical alliances – we were like two wolves running with a crowd of teenage musician rebels-with-a-cause.We were the wild and indulged 1970s baby-boomer generation – but our sub-group was dedicated and even obsessive. We got the best classical training in the best music high schools and spent nearly all our time playing and listening to music; we were competitive and lived to perform. We watched each other fall madly in love with others in the pack while remaining for each other confessional, philosophising, on-the-same-wavelength friends. We shared an adolescence, an HSC year, university, study at the Tasmanian Conservatorium, breaking away from home and puzzling out relationships with other people. Finally, we had a passionate two-week fling at 19 but threw it away as just one of those things, not realising what it meant. It took us till we were nearly 30 to fall in love and get married. Fortunately it was to each other.

I like to think it was Fate. There was a mysterious element to it, as in all emotionally charged relationships. But we're an example of how easy it can be to miss what's really going on with life. There we were, under each other's noses the whole time but unable to value the other person because of immaturity and all kinds of preconceptions, unable to see that *there* was love. It took so long to sort out illusion from reality, to listen to the instincts and separate true feeling from false obsession. So that is why I think that marriage – a true, good-faith marriage freely chosen – is about transformation. It's about cycles. It's about stripping away the false, about letting your fantasies about the other person lead you to a deeper understanding of what is real, of what is love.

Because you need to be stubborn, strong and wise to take

on marriage and children – and this wild headstrong wisdom is closer to true passion than the sexy-sexy, I-wanna-live-in-your-pants stuff (though naturally that's all part of the deal). You need a grit-real emotional strength because when culture and society starts to put pressure on individual marriages – to make its insidious contributions and definitions from both within you and without – you will need it to survive, to defy the odds of divorce, to get past sex-war bitterness (a territory as mined as Cambodia, as ravaged as Bosnia) and society's cynicism, the lack of support that an industrialised society gives to family and relationships in general.

Having such a long, shared pre-romance history with my husband is a gift in this marriage. I don't take it for granted. I appreciate it and take strength from it. Growing up with a basic liking and respect for the person you eventually marry – an instinctive but shrewd assessment made well before the unreliable madness of being in love – gives you faith that you can weather the ups and downs of marriage over the long haul. This way there are unlikely to be major nasty surprises, tragic disillusionment. Sure, there is no end to finding how different you are to another person; the closer you get, the more different you appear to be. Love can fade and partnerships disintegrate but a basic, natural, instinctive friendship is harder to destroy.

Here is a photograph of my mother and father in the Fitzroy Gardens in Melbourne shortly after my mother arrived in Australia. She is 23 years old, he is 34. Looking at them – to all appearances lovers resting languidly against each other – you can pick up small clues that show they actually don't know each other well. My mother had barely spoken to my father before she married him by proxy in Italy six weeks before. Now they are married strangers. They hardly know each other. Yet they are alone together in a foreign country.

They were a mail-order couple taking a risk on marriage.

Maybe it will be hard for their children's children's children to understand, but an arranged marriage like theirs could sometimes be as wildly romantic as it was practical and

My mother and father as newly-weds

deferential to morality. My parents' marriage was arranged by age-old propriety and tradition, no doubt about that – but, as it happens – and what the photo also shows – is a marriage of hope and escape, of parental defiance, of adventure in a new land, of growing up at last, of the thrill of being with someone as determined as you are that you will succeed in being happy and that you will not live again in poverty and in war.

Today you wouldn't give a marriage like theirs three weeks. Even in the early 1950s, before the Italian government had to discourage proxy marriages because of the problems they caused in Australia, America and Canada, there were many who rebelled against what fate and tradition brought them from the Old Country. There were many who couldn't stand the man waiting with flowers on the wharf or the woman disembarking with her suitcase from the big white ship.

Yet my parents' marriage has lasted nearly forty years, producing three children and, so far, three grandchildren. It wasn't easy, especially for my mother. Women of my generation, who were born from marriages like this, have respect for their parents' struggles and we constantly try to understand the accommodation and sacrifices our mothers made in their marriages to preserve family life, often at all costs.

Me, aged 2, with my parents

This may be an unfashionable view but for me not to pay tribute would be churlish, unfair. I, along with other Italians, have sometimes been accused of romanticising 'Mamma', of turning the Italian matriarch into a saint. But our mothers' and grandmothers' lives really were tough. They did amazing things. They coped in poverty and in war and in dislocation. But they didn't do it silently, like colourless drudges taking up little emotional space and not bothering anybody. No, our Mammas started off by screaming like banshees in childbirth and freaking out the medical staff in Australian labour wards. From there they continued to take everything to heart. Our mothers felt they had the right to be happy in this country and they certainly weren't quiet about what they felt they were owed by their husbands, children and others. Yes, they were manipulative and even downright aggressive about the debt owed to their motherhood – and so what? Their kids put them down at their peril!

Few of us are prepared to badmouth our mothers in public even though they might be driving us insane, even though their cultural perspectives might be destructive to our true selves in this society. Italian immigrant mothers of the 1950s were Suffering Mothers like the Virgin – and they were tough and ferocious too. I respect their attitude even while I personally had to fight it every inch of the way in order to become my own person. Because I have a sneaky respect for the Italian Mamma role model more than the traditional image of the passive Aussie mum with no self-esteem, the 'I'm nobody' style of suburban mother who's wishy-washy about what's owed to her and lets her husband and kids – and the academics and advertisers – run all over her, including a mother-scapegoat literature that whines 'Mum was a bitch and it's all her fault.' I find it hard to explain to many young Anglo-Australian feminists I meet, the appreciation I have of the strength of the Italian mother as the keeper of the stories, the gossip and the bloodlines of marriage.

It wasn't easy for the men either. It's not a simple question of patriarchal exploitation. That's not the model of marriage I grew up with, the Mother-Father force that nurtured us and passed down so much that was good about our culture.

I remember my father as optimistic, kindly, well-meaning, hard-working and solicitous of the health of his wife and kids. He just didn't know anything of women's business. For a man of his generation, that was proper. In the days before a husband and wife were supposed to be 'equal' and 'best friends', he did the best he could as a person limited by maturity and culture, as we all are. He did many things an Italian man would never do no matter what. My father crossed lines – he fed us, bathed us and tidied the house when he had to – but ultimately his job as the patriarch – the breadwinner working in a factory – meant that certain things could not change, even though what worked in the old village culture broke apart in his hands here in Australia. So often he saw things crack up helplessly, without knowing what to do. The pressures on the marriage came from lack of understanding of how loneliness can become a health hazard. Of how a young woman needs her mother and sisters to help her in labour and in raising three children under four. Of how losing a baby without properly mourning him can make you go mad.

But on this languid afternoon in the Fitzroy Gardens, those days of trial and misunderstanding were far away. The photo sings to me about the hope and dreams of a young couple who have just been through a world war. I am lucky to have this image of marriage as adventure and journey. In my culture – essentially a peasant culture, close to the basics – marriage is not always romantic; it is celebrated with red wine and white tulle and *bomboniere* but it's about survival, land, work and children, it's about bonding yourself to your community.

The husbands, the fathers, are nominally in charge but the women, the wives and mothers – *Mamma* and especially *Nonna* (Grandmother) – have the true power within marriage and family. Outside of marriage of course, you're dangerous, mad or bad. Unless you're a Catholic nun, the punishment for being an unmarried woman is still to be exiled from community. But within marriage, you're no pushover either.

To this day in the villages of southern Italy – and in the streets of Carlton, the brick veneers of Bulleen and Leichhardt and Fremantle – a piece of this domestic goddess power is still alive and celebrated in the processions of the Madonna at Easter and other holidays such as The Blessing of the Fleet. As a kid, I got the message loud and clear. If God the Father is supposed to be the Big Boss, then why are the dollar bills, the jewellery and supplications for favours still firmly pinned to the Madonna who rides supreme through the streets of my parents' generation of Italians? This is why I cannot follow – I can't swallow – a model of woman's subjugation in marriage.

Here is a program from an opera, *Bride of Fortune*. On the cover is a woman in a kerchief and heavy coat. She is the opera's heroine, Grazia, an Italian girl who arrives in Melbourne in 1952 married to Vito, the husband she has never met, a man she knows only through an exchange of letters. For months thin airmail letters have been carrying the words that change lives and make hopes flesh. From the ship, Grazia carries a suitcase and looks into the distance. Her idea of her husband is as light as the letters in her pocket. Like the ribbon tied round them, the rest of her life is bound tight in the commitment she has naively made.

I remember as a child rummaging through forbidden cupboards and drawers in my parents' bedroom and coming across a sheaf of letters that my father wrote to my mother before they arranged to marry. Because they were written in Italian in obscure and florid handwriting with a spiky fountain pen, I couldn't read them. I was locked out of poking around that primal relationship. That made the letters magic and fascinating, a mixture of spirituality and sexuality, a grave romanticism (because those words had led directly to me and my brother and sister) that confronted me with the shocking idea that my parents might have expressed dangerous ideas of being 'in love' with one another . . . or whatever . . . because who knew what those secret letters said?

By moonlight, at Port Said, on the voyage from Italy, Grazia writes a madly passionate letter which fuses (and con-fuses) her unknown husband with her sense of destiny and of the wild Bridegroom, the inner 'soul husband' that Grazia has willingly married, as well as her real-life partner. She doesn't address Vito by name in this letter because it's not entirely about or to him. Her 'real' husband, being unknown to her, becomes tinged with an almost spiritual quality – that of a woman's own will to imagine and create The Lover.

Husband, destiny, my Unknown,
You are the spirit who calls me.
Your ring burns fire on my flesh,
Willingly I am marked by you.
I am the bird who can never look homeward
But must fly straight into the face of the sun.
Day follows night on this water
As I whisper your name,
My Unknown, who are you?

So close to my flesh yet more distant
Than the earth's red rim,
I have felt your breath in the air as I fly,
As I fly towards you.
I have seen your eyes in the glint of waves.
Negroes in the bazaars all know of you,
Their eyes offer me oranges, silk and jewels.
Cigarettes and the mad music of radios
Point to your footsteps, forever ahead of me.

My Unknown, I've smelled your skin in the fields,
In the cool of evening you have lain beside me
Over the morning hills and in the night's snowfall
I have heard you calling.
My Unknown, I will make you a good wife,
Better than any fragile beauty.
Against wind and wave,
Through the cold light of stars,
Over the spinning angle of the earth,
I fly to you
I fly to you!

Grazia throws the letter into the waves, as if realising she's talking to the forces of nature within herself and so the words belong in the sea. Whether she's actually written that letter, or whether she is singing the true feelings that are behind a more prosaic letter, it is all too passionate; no two human beings can live in that burning place for too long.

That's the problem with passionate (in) love – some people naively try to live forever in that realm of zipless passion. The romance junkies and the multi-marriage addicts are not just happy to visit there, to pass through it and touch it with awe – they want to actually set up a permanent camp right next to Venus and Eros. But it's a mistake to eat, drink, quarrel and *be human* in the sacred grove – punishment is to be struck with bitterness when The Lover with the Raven Hair leaves the toilet seat up, forgets the groceries, watches the football and hates changing nappies!

No way can you live in the steamy rainforest of mad love all your life!

Yet it's essential, it's part of the natural world, to visit that place, to chase shadows, to follow the glimpses of The Lover. The inner marriage may be in another dimension, it may have another geography, yet its existence – its vigour and its fertile erotic wilderness – is essential to the success of the prosaic marriage, the working human marriage of every day life.

Performed at the Perth Festival in 1991, *Bride of Fortune* was unusual in that it was written by two women – a collaboration between myself and Gillian Whitehead, a New Zealander living in Sydney and acknowledged as one of Australia's finest composers.

Opera, as I soon discovered, is a conservative genre – mostly a Dead (Male) Composers' Society. There are few women composers; two women working as a dramatist-composer team was at times bordering on the bizarre. It's lucky I didn't know this when I naively set out to write an opera set in Australia in the 1950s, using an Italian heroine and not an elevated one at that but a working-class proxy bride who spoke no English and worked in a Collingwood shirt factory.

At the heart of the opera is the phenomenon of the '*Vedove*

Bianche', the White Widows: Italian women who married by proxy in their villages and then waited years – sometimes forever – for their husbands to bring them out to Fremantle, or Melbourne or Brisbane. In this opera we see a man and a woman who don't trust each other, who are disappointed in each other, who are hiding secrets from one another. We see a couple who want their marriage to succeed but don't know how to be frank with each other when times get tough. External forces – war, post-war economics, social pressure, racial prejudice, industrial exploitation – all conspire against Grazia and Vito's marriage.

When it was performed in 1991, *Bride of Fortune* was practically the first Australian opera to be set in our times, in the relatively recent past of the 1950s. The story of Grazia and Vito is *not* the story of my parents – on the contrary my parents' story fits like a mosaic into the larger picture of the kind of marriages that Italians made in coming to Australia with so many hopes and dreams one, two, three generations ago. Grazia and Vito's story is part of the street gossip, the stories – the 'aural history' if you like – you will get with a cappuccino in the cafés and homes of Carlton, Bulleen, Leichhardt, Fremantle, Rockhampton, Brisbane and anywhere the Italian community is strong.

Grazia and Vito's arranged marriage is part of who we are as Australians. It is not a phenomenon of the past only. From Phillipino 'mail order' brides to *The Piano* (fiercely adopted as Australian even though it is set in New Zealand), the arranged marriage is not only part of the history of settlement in the 'New World' – the 'America' of the southern Italians setting off from Naples and Messina – but it's still happening, it's still being contracted today in suburban streets, caravan parks, and outback shacks.

So I found it disquieting to see *Bride of Fortune* first publicised and then reviewed (no matter how enthusiastically) as an 'ethnic' opera by an 'ethnic' writer. No, I can't accept that: it's an Australian opera about Australian life by an Australian writer. (To put it another way, Richard Meale and David Malouf's *Mer de Glace* was not described as an 'ethnic' opera because it was about a group of British poets last century. Nor was their *Voss* dubbed an 'ethnic' opera despite the subject being the life of a German explorer in Australia.)

The subject of marriage also seemed to make *Bride of Fortune* a 'domestic' opera in the mind of at least one reviewer, who wrote disdainfully of 'mythologising the domestic.' This reminded me of Margaret Atwood's comments twenty years ago in 1973 about '... The (usually male) habit of concentrating on domestic themes in the work of a female writer, ignoring any other topic she might have dealt with, then patronising her for her 'interest in domestic themes.'

Which all proves that opera is a crazy genre to have chosen to work in. It's stacked with everything I hate – it's male-dominated, backward-looking, elitist, expensive and the soprano always dies. Yet despite everything, the Perth Festival and the Western Australian Opera supported what we wanted to do. By 1991, the time was finally right. Resplendent with funding, the Bride went to the altar and we got an excellent mainstream production of the opera in the Perth Festival that was, for all concerned a happy collaboration and a great success.

My rewards were to see the darker side of marriage – such as violence between a husband and wife escalating into a siege – become operatically tragic. Marriage is a gamble. For many people it's the scene of their greatest sense of failure as they struggle with a rage that's burning out of control on the debris of having tried so hard.

Of his failed marriage, Vito sings:

Where is honour, the hope in the suitcase?
For months I carried your picture in my wallet,
Waiting and working in the heat and dust
I saw you in a house built by these hands,
The little one home from school,
Bread on the table, wine in the glass,
The smell of basil, grapes on the vine.
It was too much to ask.

Yet for once it's not the woman who loses her life over the loss of the heroic dream. It's left to the nervous police, the administrators of society's values, who – culturally out of their depth – pull the trigger.

Here is a poem written by my mother, at the age of 62 when she took up writing partly because of insomnia and partly because she was sick of her daughter ripping off her stories and speaking for her – mostly wrongly, as it seems to her (including probably even now, sorry Mum).

Lidia Valerio Dell'oso had five years of formal education in pre-war Italy, followed by a lifetime of work in fields and in factories in Italy and Australia. This is an excerpt from a longer poem, 'Il Grande Passo della Mia Vita' – 'The Great Step of My Life.' These lines concern her marriage and the day she left her homeland as a young bride.

. . . in quel gelido mattino stellato
mi senti quel pentir
d'aver quelle carte firmate
e scesi per l'ultima volta, quei gradini
della mia casa . . .
La macchina arriva, un bacio, un abraccio,
E due lagrime mi scende
Come pure i miei amici e parenti
Mi sedetti, i pensieri mi si affollavano in tanti,
Mi feci coraggio di andare avanti . . .
Addio paese mio, addio, ma sperando ancora
Di rivederci a tempi migliori . . .
Dio Madre, non so dove andro
Ne che gente li incontrero . . .

. . . On this cold starry morning
I regretted having signed those papers.
For the last time, I climb down the steps of my house.
The car arrives, a kiss, a hug
And I shed a few tears, as do my friends and relatives.
I sit down, my thoughts in turmoil,
I can feel my courage leave me –

Farewell my village, my home, goodbye,
I can only hope I will return to you
In better times . . .
Mother of God, I don't know where I'm going
Nor what kind of people I will meet there . . .

On nights like this when I'm alone at 1 a.m., I look through these things of mine, rattling in my head like the bones of ancestors. It's like I'm hearing, against the ticking of my life, a howl of something old and wild outside, out there. On nights like this I feel emboldened to whistle a few strange songs . . . *'But in the garden-bower the bride and bride-maids singing are . . . Farewell! farewell! but this I tell/To thee, thou Wedding-guest! . . .'* At the back of the feast-laden hall, as a member of an eternal wedding, I stand up for a ballad to us all – wives and non-wives, mothers and daughters, Amazons and Athenas, old crones and exiles, unmarriageable witches and enchantresses, celibates and sexpots – and when the glasses are raised I'll give a toast – a toast to all you brides of fortune.

LYNNE SPENDER

Down the Aisle – and Up the Garden Path

You have to laugh. What other response is there to the discovery that you have been had – in all senses of that word? That you have been duped, deceived, taken for a ride – tricked. And this has not been effected against your will or even against your better judgment. When you finally recognise that you have been a willing accomplice in your own demise – you have to laugh ... or you would die crying.

If only you had known the significance of the traditional image of the caveman with club in one hand and the woman, as object, in the other. If it had even been suggested to you that this was not a symbol of male power and authority but visible evidence that no woman would ever voluntarily set up house with a man, you might have had a chance. You might have recognised the ploy, rather than playing the marriage game – blind woman's bluff.

For under many sounding compliments, words that have nothing in them, this is his true meaning; He wants one to manage his family, an housekeeper, one whose interest it will be not to wrong him, and in whom therefore he can put greater confidence than in any he can hire for money. One who may breed his children, taking all the care and trouble of their education, to preserve his name and family. One whose beauty, wit, or good humour and agreeable conversation will entertain him at home when he has been contradicted and disappointed abroad, who will do him the justice the ill-natured world denies him; that is, in anyone's language but his own, soothe his pride, flatter his vanity, by having always so much good sense as to be on his side, to conclude him right when others are so ignorant or rude as to deny him . . .

Mary Astell, 1694

Romance

You have to laugh – looking back on those all-night sessions discussing love and romance with girlfriends. You allowed yourself to believe – even if you didn't admit it openly – that the knight in shining armour would come along. If you could just find the right one. And, being a modern woman, you knew that there might be some sorting out to do, some feminist territory to establish but basically you would be the beginning of a family that would live happily ever after.

Famulus means domestic slave, and *familia* is the total number of slaves belonging to one man . . . The term was invented by the Romans to denote a new social organism, whose head ruled over wife and children and a number of slaves, and was invested under Roman paternal power with rights of life and death over them all.

Freidrich Engels, 1942

And you voraciously read *Cleo* and *Cosmo* – and believed that if you could just get him talking to you, he would immediately recognise your charms and accomplishments, your wit and vivacity. He would be inevitably and eternally smitten. Of course at nineteen, you had no idea of how dangerous these magazines could be. That they could make you deny your own experience and understandings (there must be something wrong with me) in favour of the *Cleo/Cosmo* world view (that's how I should be).

'Get him to talk about himself', they said. And you did. What they didn't tell you, of course, was how to stop him once he'd started. Nor did they give any hints on how you then made him move on to talking about something else – anything else. Even sport. Virginia Woolf knew what she was saying when she stated that for centuries, women have reflected men at twice their natural size. Not only do we play a part in constructing men as the centre of the universe, they come to believe their status is deserved. And, you, in spite of an awareness that this was a sort of game, played along. Your devotion convinced him that your main aim in life was to please him.

All men, except the most brutish, desire to have, in the woman most nearly connected with them, not a forced slave but a willing one, not a slave merely, but a favourite.

John Stuart Mill, 1869

And sex. The notion of sexual equality and compatibility. Those magazines convinced you it was modern (in terms of psychological theory) to check your sexual compatibility. To use sex to please him. That he should use sex to please you. All that information about the perfect orgasm. The one you searched for, for years, believing that if you didn't have multiple orgasms on the spot, the relationship was doomed. The strategy was meant to make men actually involved in pleasing women but what developed was yet another situation where women jumped, blindly, onto the bandwagon of pleasing men. How much easier it would have been to lie back and think of England – or plan the shopping list – than feel obliged to convince him that of course you experienced multiple orgasm and yes, of course it was good for you too. You, who had mocked Rousseau for his notion that women should be educated to please men. Still doing it in the 1990s. In spite of being a modern woman, you had fallen into the age old trap of believing that he was trying so hard to please you while all the time it was you performing, making the effort to please him.

The Courtship

You have to laugh – recalling the feeling that somehow your relationship was special, that you were special, that *he* was the Mr Right who would cherish you forever, protect you from being ordinary, from being unloved. Once 'spoken for', your life would change. You would be regarded by the rest of the world as an autonomous, adult person who could operate independently in the world.

... it has taken a lot of processing and 'psychological work' to make women eager accepters of the status of wife. The glorification of marriage has had to be built into our society. One way has been to profess great respect even reverence for the role of wife, to accord it high moral, if not legal status. Still, despite the high status professed for it, the wife has, since the 18th century, suffered a relative loss of status.

Jessie Bernard, 1977

You were safe in the knowledge that you would never be one of those bitter and twisted, unfulfilled women. Those self-centred women without emotional commitments, who live their selfish lives, pleasing themselves and others as they choose.

Single women ... report greater happiness, are more active in working through the problems they face and appear in most ways stronger in meeting the challenge of their positions than men ... contrary to the popular stereotypes of the frustrated old maid.

Jessie Bernard, 1972

You, on the other hand would live within a safe cocoon – cosseted by emotional generosity and perpetual good will. Not for you harsh words and hectoring but a harmonious place – an adult space in which to nurture and be nurtured.

It is still the case that over three quarters of the women murdered in NSW are murdered by their partners after a period of physical and emotional abuse. Family violence is said to occur in one in every three homes in Australia.

The Law Handbook (NSW), 1991

The Reluctant Bridegroom

Men have cursed it, aimed barbed witticisms at it, denigrated it, bemoaned it and have never ceased to want and need it or to profit from it.

Jessie Bernard, 1972

...Despite all the protestations of men to the contrary, married life makes them happy.

Jessie Bernard, 1972

You remember feeling flattered by the comments of his friends – his 'mates' – as they mocked him for 'getting caught', 'hitched', 'getting hooked' like an unsuspecting and gullible fish. But you were the one who fell for it – hook, line and sinker. You had succeeded, passed the test, got your man, in spite of his reluctance and resistance. Not that you had proposed. It wasn't *you* who went to *his* mother and asked for his hand in marriage. You should have seen the pattern then. It was he who took the running but you took the rap. As the scheming woman, the one who roped him in and tied him down.

You really did believe it was fate or at least some biological imperative that drew you together. If anyone had told you the impetus was based on his wellbeing at your expense, you'd have smiled wisely and said that it may be true for thousands of other couples, but you were different. So what if Jessie Bernard established that married men rate higher on the mental and physical health scale than any other social group? And that married women vied with single men for the honour of being the least healthy, mentally and physically? What had statistics and sociological patterns to do with you and your perceived future life, full of warmth, generosity and shared understandings?

Marriage

Marriage makes women sick
Jessie Bernard, 1972

You have to laugh – remembering the pre-wedding discussions with your already married women friends. 'Don't do it,' they said. 'It's not what it's cracked up to be.' And the hint of hysteria which you took to be a sign that they were protesting too much. It was only much later that you realised their reaction was one borne of disappointment and despair. And the ambiguity you detected was in part a desire to protect you and in part their need for you to experience it as well – to make sure it was not just some terrible thing happening to them. The same situation exactly as when you had your first child. Only afterwards did they share with you how humiliating, painful and horrendous it was. 'Now we can talk about what it was really like. Now you're a member of the club.'

You cringe, remembering your complacency. You, the informed and educated 20th-century woman who knew it all, who understood the politics of relationships and the power of the patriarchy. You, who were so sure that the institution of marriage was simply a framework which you could adapt to your needs – and his. That you would both have a vested interest in establishing an egalitarian union, based on mutual respect. Between you, you would be strong enough to resist the pressures to conform to the stereotypes. You really did believe that it would be different for you.

To judge from the torrent of words about marriage that regularly bombard us, one would think that marriage is some sort of *private* pact which takes place in a vacuum; as though the two people concerned were really free to work out whatever arrangement best suited them, without regard to social pressure and convention, legal requirements, tax laws, housing facilities and so on.

Lee Comer, 1974

The Wedding

The wedding is the chief ceremony of the middle class mythology (of love and marriage), and it functions as the official entree of the spouses to their middle class status. This is the real meaning of saving up to get married.

Germaine Greer, 1970

You have to laugh – vaguely recalling your romantic vision of the one day that would be your day. A sepia image, slow motion, of flowers and laughter. And the reality of it? The months of preparation, the enormous cost. (At least you lost weight.) The vague unease that this was far more to please the family and to keep the wheels of bridal commerce turning than anything to do with you. The occasional doubts fostered by his dismissal of the issues that you thought worth discussing. Remember? The bucks' night. It was more a heated debate than a discussion. You thought it anachronistic – ludicrous. He thought it essential. You knew that the fashion was either a stripper or a prostitute – and that both were demeaning. What answer a week before a wedding to the question that would be raised time and time again – 'Where's your sense of humour?' You should have registered. You actually dismissed it on the grounds that 'boys will be boys' and 'what you don't know won't hurt you'. You actually thought it was a 'one off' and not a blueprint for the future.

And the wedding. The people that you didn't even know who were just there to eat and drink. The outfit that was a compromise between what you wanted to wear and what was considered 'proper'. The tiny protest in the ball and chain flowers you carried. The insistence in the face of all evidence that this was not part of a pattern or a politics. That your father 'giving you away' – free – was simply a quaint custom. Remember how pleased you were with yourself for eliminating the promise 'to honour and obey' from the service? As if this would somehow make a difference.

> ... the vicar pronounces them not husband and wife, not man and woman, but man and wife. The ritualistic incantation of these words which define her inferior status not in the eyes of God but in the eyes of the world, must be accompanied by as much physical adornment as possible. This is the *real* purpose of the display – the long white cover-all dress, the face hidden by a veil and the bent head ... the more beautiful she looks in this disguise, the more profuse are the tears. We weep for joy. Will she ever again know such happiness as she has known on this, her greatest day? Probably not.
>
> Lee Comer, 1974

The arrogance of the uninitiated. In spite of the fact that you knew that 40 per cent of marriages ended in divorce and that your friend and 'matron of honour' was in tears because she and her husband of six months were separating, you traipsed down that aisle, convinced that your decision was the right one. What did it matter that your new husband's family didn't quite approve of you (you heard one of them say 'she's really up herself'), that one of the groomsmen got drunk, made an impromptu speech that was both sexist and racist and that he swore at your father? You clung firmly to the belief that you had it right, that between the two of you, you could take on the world. Looking back – realising that 'down the aisle' would have been better described as 'up the garden path'.

Being a Wife

> When a woman gets married, she increases her unpaid work by almost 60 per cent.
>
> Office of the Status of Women, 1991

> ... marriage introduced such profound discontinuities into the lives of women as to constitute genuine emotional health hazards.
>
> Jessie Bernard, 1972

You have to laugh . . . remembering the shock the first time it really occurred to you that you had made a terrible mistake – when you first had to acknowledge the great gulf between you. In the first month. He swanned in and complained about the dinner, just like something out of a second-rate sitcom. You'd been at work all day, shopped, washed, cleaned and he'd stopped on the way home to 'see a man about a dog'. He'd had a drink with the mates. 'What's this rabbit food?' when he saw the chicken salad you'd carefully prepared from the 'bits' left over from dinner the previous night. A proper little housewife, saving his money for him to spend on his new golf clubs.

The housewife is an unpaid worker in her husband's house in return for the security of being a permanent employee . . .

Germaine Greer, 1970

Being a wife – a housewife – a kitchen wife – a bed wife. You who had thought that marriage would give you more freedom, more status, more time to be an individual and autonomous person suddenly found that you had no time to yourself. On call twenty-four hours a day for some sort of wifely duty. And he, who had so feared losing his freedom, being 'tied down' and 'caught' was simply a husband – free to come and go as he pleased. Expecting dinner, clean clothes, sex, companionship, as well as a patient and enthralled listener to his interminable stories about himself.

. . . to some extent the husband returning to his home at night unconsciously feels the journey to be a return to his mother's womb. He will expect to receive in the home all the comfort, protection and solace he once enjoyed in the womb. Also, unconsciously, the same male sees the sex act as again going to his mother's breast to get food strength and comfort, in order to return to the battles of his job properly replenished on the following day.

Patrick Tennison, 1978

You started to listen more closely to your married friends. You found yourself telling unmarried women, 'Don't do it. It's not what it's cracked up to be. It's a hoax.' You wondered whether you were not going a bit mad.

. . . to be happy in a relationship which imposes so many impediments on her as traditional marriage does, a woman must be slightly ill mentally.

Jessie Bernard, 1970

Remember the moment you realised that he and the rest of the world had stopped treating you as a person in your own right. It was one of those early dinner parties – before you refused to have them any more. You'd cleaned, shopped, cooked, prepared the food. You had, as usual, initiated the table talk – got them talking about themselves – only to find that your opinions and ideas were dismissed. 'What would you know about the real world?', while he poured forth, with authority, all those observations about the world that you had so thoughtfully prepared and discussed with him during the previous week. And your jokes. He told your jokes as if they were his. Not only no acknowledgement, absolutely no awareness that he had appropriated your thoughts and ideas. You were aware that you were in danger of becoming the sitcom wife. The mostly invisible and slightly ridiculous creature who, try as she might, will never quite get it right. Just a few months into marriage and you were aware that you were no longer the beloved equal partner. He had become the stereotypical husband – and he expected you to be a conventional wife.

The click phenomenon. Just occasionally at first and then almost every day. Remember the fight one night before you went to a party. 'You can't wear that outfit. It's provocative.'

'But I've worn it before.'

'That was before we were married.' Click.

In most Western societies permission for women to exhibit a healthy and active sexuality is given only with a consenting male and in private. At all other times it is dangerous for women to show any signs of response to sexual stimulus.

Phyllis Chester, 1989

And the arguments over housework. Approaching it rationally at first, explaining the unevenness of the work load, the unfairness that one person was expected to be responsible for all the dirty work. The becoming resentful. Then angry, trying to be gracious. Just doing it, without speaking, but seething inside.

The refusal of the majority of Australian men to do their share of the housework and childcare is the overwhelming reason why women have still not achieved equality, according to a Federal parliamentary report.

Sydney Morning Herald, 1 May 1992

'Can you just run the mop over the kitchen floor before we go out?'

'That's women's work.' Click.

'I said I'd do the shopping. Stop nagging.' Click.

'Of course it's a good idea for you to do some extra study – but not if it means I have to get my own meals all the time.' Click.

'Sorry I'm late. Had a flat tyre.' Click.

Within less than a year, waking up each morning with the feeling that it was not working. That you had to try harder. Convinced that if you just put more time into him, he would appreciate you more. The alternative? Acknowledging your failure. You who had been so sure, so smart, so convinced you had it right. Having to admit to yourself – let alone the rest of the world – that you were wrong. Not personally wrong but tricked, duped. You were in fact the gullible one.

Children

Male humanity has wobbled between two convictions – the one that she [woman] exists for the entire benefit of contemporary manhood; the other, that she exists for the entire benefit of the next generation. The latter is at present the favourite.

Cicely Hamilton, 1909

And did you learn – did you generalise from your experience when the marriage myths were exploded before your very eyes? Did you at least question whether you really wanted children? Did you take time to envisage the changes that would have to be made? Did you ever stop to think that this might break rather than make your marriage? Of course you did. Your child was a wanted child, a loved child. You were both ready for it. You read every book. You smirked at the idea that you should not try to be Einstein during your pregnancy but contemplate the warmth of your inner womb. You worked until the week before he was born.

And then – even some of your family disapproved because you went back to work. From someone who slept seven hours a day, you gradually found that your sleeping time was closer to six hours and then – less. By the time you washed, shopped, worked, cleaned, cooked, dropped off the child, picked him up, played with him (to assuage that little bit of working mother guilt), taught him to read and then marked essays at night – there wasn't much time for being wifely in the romantic sense. And the feelings of injustice.

Women do about 70 per cent of unpaid work. On average, a new mother's hours of unpaid work increased by 91 per cent to nearly 56 hours per week.

Since 1974, women have on average lost one hour of leisure time.

Office of the Status of Women, 1991

Divorce

There are 2 marriages . . . in every marital union, his and hers. And his . . . is better than hers.

Jessie Bernard, 1972

You have to laugh. After all the times you tried to talk to him about how unhappy you were, tried to discuss the problems, to *communicate* as all the advice columns suggested, he was absolutely stunned when you said you were leaving. 'I didn't know you were unhappy. I'm not unhappy. I didn't know you were serious, I thought all women complained and nagged.'

75 per cent of divorces in the United States are initiated by women and three women divorce their husbands in Britain for every man who divorces his wife. Bettina Arndt, 1985

The same is true in Australia. Many more women than men file for divorce. In spite of the statistics that prove that women's standards of living drop dramatically after divorce, and that their husbands' increase, it is the women who leave. When a man says to a new lover, 'I am leaving my wife', don't believe him. When a woman says it, you'd better believe her. It is her sense of self – her sanity that is at stake.

You have to smile, ruefully, looking back on the time between announcing your departure and actually, physically leaving. He finally realised you *were* serious. You finally realised you had a lemon. After all that work you had put into him and he still couldn't see or understand what you were saying. He even offered to take over the ironing, get a cleaning lady in, to stay at home more. 'You're destroying my life,' he said, 'on the basis of a whim.'

Remember the mixed feelings? Because it was true that you were destroying *his* life. His comfortable world would indeed fall apart. He had neither the personal nor emotional resources to make it on his own. You weren't completely sure that you had them either. You agonised over it only to find that he had already replaced you – in bed at least.

Half of all divorced white men who remarry do so within three years after divorce. Indeed it might not be too far-fetched to conclude that the verbal assaults on marriage indulged in by men are a kind of compensatory reaction to their dependence on it.

Jessie Bernard, 1972

You gained support and determination from a friend's 82-year-old mother who divorced at 78 – just for few years of peace before she died; from a sister whose mental health improved miraculously from just making the decision to divorce; from the friend who left an unfulfilling marriage with an unfaithful husband to go on and become head of a corporation; from parents who, after their initial shock, supported you emotionally and financially.

And finally you could laugh – a bit hysterically at first but then richly, deeply, spontaneously. You have to laugh . . . or you would cry.

BIBLIOGRAPHY

Arndt, Bettina, the *Bulletin*, 16 April 1985.

Astell, Mary, in *Before Their Time: Six Women Writers of the Eighteenth Century*, Katharine Rogers (ed.) Frederick Ungar, New York, 1979, pp. 41–2.

Bernard, Jessie, in *Women into Wives*, Jane Roberts Chapman and Margaret Gates, Sage, 1977.

Bernard, Jessie, *The Future of Marriage*, World Publishing, New York, 1972.

Chester, Phyllis, private correspondence, 1989.

Comer, Lee, *Wedlocked Women*, Feminist Books, Leeds, England, 1974, p. 67.

Engels, Freidrich, in *The Feminist Papers*, Alice Rossi (ed.), Bantam, New York, 1973.

Greer, Germaine, *The Female Eunuch*, Paladin, 1970, p. 216.

Hamilton, Cicely, in *Marriage as a Trade*, The Women's Press, 1981, p. 24.

Law Handbook, The (NSW), 4th Edition, Lynne Spender (ed.) 1991, p. 134.

Mill, John Stuart, in *The Feminist Papers*, Alice Rossi, (ed.) Bantam, New York, 1973.

Selected findings from *Juggling Time: How Australian Families Use Time*, Office of the Status of Women, 1991.

Tennison, Patrick, *The Marriage Wilderness*, Visa, 1978.

MARION HALLIGAN

The Generations of Women

Readers are always asking writers whether their stories actually happened. Is it true, they say, as though this were important. It's a question I mostly don't want to answer, since I believe that fiction is truer than fact, and has much stricter rules as regards verisimilitude. Fact can afford to be unlikely, or incredible; you just say, sorry, that's how it was, don't blame me if you think it's got problems.

Like the following narrative. It's somebody's biography. I've been wanting to write it down for a while now. I had a go at turning it into fiction, but that didn't work. Mainly because it breaks all those rules; it's over the top. So I've decided the best thing is to give a plain unvarnished account, with a minimum of art (of course I can't resist a bit), much as I learnt it. All I've changed is the names.

Kath, I'm calling her, comes to my house once a week to clean it. It's a good arrangement, though not one I was brought up to. But then I do a lot of things I wasn't brought up to. Kath likes it. She needs the money. She lives on a pension. She'd like a proper job; she had one once, cleaning offices from 5 till 9 at night. She loved it; she used to tell me how she polished the metal lift doors till they shone and how she got rid of the dust on top of the cupboards that must've been there for years. But Social Security told her that the rent on her small government house would triple and she would lose various benefits now she was earning money, so she had to stop. She had to get her employer to sack her which upset both of them because the employer thought she was a terrific worker, but unless she was sacked she couldn't get back on Social Security.

But it's not just the money. She likes cleaning. She paints the rocks in her garden white. She does her own house even when it's not dirty just to have something to do. And she likes coming to my house because there's nearly always somebody at home, all of us work at home some of the time, and me most of the time. She likes the sense of the house being inhabited; she'll say, Aw, you're not going out are you, if she sees me so much as look at my handbag. Even if we aren't talking to her, we're company. And we are talking to her, a good bit of the time, that's where I got these stories. I have to spend at least ten minutes at the beginning of the three hours hearing the latest news, with further bulletins as she remembers them. I mostly type things up on Wednesdays, then interruptions don't matter too much. But she never has cups of tea, and when she was smoking she would go outside and sweep the terrace. She's just given up, because of having pneumonia.

This is the first of her tales. It happened five years ago, when she'd just started with us. She came in and said, my daughter's boyfriend died last night. She always plunges straight in like that. I said something like Oh dear, or Did he? because I wasn't absolutely certain I'd heard aright. Yes she said. Had an asthma attack and died, just like that. It was such a pity, he and Renee were getting on real well, they were hardly fighting at all any more, well, a lot less. He was even taking a bit of interest in the idea of the baby. Just last night he patted her on the tummy and said Hullo, you in there.

This was the first I knew of Renee being pregnant. She was sixteen. A week or so after this she lost the baby. I thought at first Kath meant she'd had a miscarriage but it turned out the baby was born alive, Renee saw it and nursed it and then after two hours it died. She was seven months. My daughter who was a student at the time used to get more details than I did; I think Kath used to clean up her stories for my benefit. So Lucy heard it wasn't just asthma that Troy died of, it was drugs. He'd left Renee late and gone to his flat alone and done the drugs and something went wrong.

Troy's grandmother offered to pay for the funeral, he was buried at Hay which was where the family came from. They decided the baby should be there too but then its ashes got lost. The crematorium said they'd given them to the priest and the priest said Renee had them and Renee reckoned they'd gone to the grandma but she said she'd never set eyes on them. Tempers were upset and there were accusations but by the next week the ashes had turned up and were safe in Hay. Like 19th-century serials, Kath's stories come in instalments, weekly.

She tried to get Renee to give up on drugs too, but the girl was – is – wilful. Barely into her teens she was getting into trouble with the police, until Kath said she wouldn't bail her out anymore. She grows her own marijuana in Kath's tidy backyard; one day she came home and found the plant missing. I know who done this! she shouted, and stormed down the road and made them give it back.

Kath's son Jason has had trouble with drink and drugs too. He's one of them Christians, Kath said. She went to see him at some place they had up the coast, I'm not clear about the details. (Since I didn't know I was going to write this down I didn't ask questions, I wasn't keen to use up more house-cleaning time than necessary on the narratives.) It seemed to be a place he couldn't get out of, except on leave sometimes. Or if he runs away. The Christians took him to Barcelona for the Olympic Games, he sent her postcards which she brought to show us. Also a t-shirt from Penang which she often wears, it's cyclamen and tropical green.

Jason is sometimes a good son, and mows her lawn. She doesn't like him staying with her because he spends all his dole money on booze and the other stuff, and she can't afford to feed him unless he pays board. He's immensely fat and very expensive to feed. As soon as he saves money when he's back with the Christians, he's liable to break out and blow the lot and then he's penniless and goes back in again.

Kath herself doesn't really drink, except socially. She got done for drink driving after a night at the club. She'd only had a few beers and a couple of Irish Creams, but she came out over on the breathalyser. She had to catch the bus for a few months. This was when she had the office cleaning job, so she went back to court and got the judge to let her drive to that, since there were no buses at that hour, and the city was empty and dark and she couldn't afford taxis. At least when she wasn't driving it the car didn't cost any money. Once a friend of Jason's drove her up to see him and the engine blew up on the way back though she'd kept telling him to put water in. The husband of a woman she sometimes cleans for got her a new engine; she had to work for weeks for nothing to pay for it which got her down a bit. Now she won't take the car for long drives, too risky.

Another day Kath came and said, When I got home last week there was this policeman came and knocked on the door. Aw. Talk about die, she said. But it turned out nobody had done anything wrong. He was just seeing if she wanted to know her daughter she'd had adopted out. Kath too had been pregnant at the age of sixteen, and had to go to one of those Dickensian homes where they made you work in the laundry and when the baby was born took it away without letting you see it. This baby, a daughter now in her thirties with children of her own, had searched her mother out, and the policeman was there to know was Kath willing to be found.

She was thrilled. Kath is very family-minded, you will see from her devotion to her parents. Far beyond what they deserve, you'd have to say.

Kath and I were born in the same year. 1940. Sometimes I think of her as a kind of *alter ego*, living the sort of life that might have been mine if I'd been born of raffish rather than respectable parents and not had the luck to attract the attention of a good education. Hello darl, she says when she arrives, full of smiles whatever the misfortunes she is about to relate. (She has a lot of relations who provide material when things are quiet in the immediate family, but there's no space for them here.) When she calls up the stairs she uses my name, but close-up it's darl. She doesn't treat me as quite an equal; I'm clearly incompetent in quite a lot of things, not much chop as a housewife and all this mess of papers that she indulges me in. If I tidy something she says, Aw, what have you been up to, aw look at that, what's gone wrong? and cackles with laughter. Also I think she sees me as an innocent, compared with her, and of course she's right, in some ways; she's more street-wise, but I'm probably more worldly-wise. She feels good about the help she gives me. I polished the brass, she says, looks lovely doesn't it? I cleaned the kitchen windows, see, you can see out of them now. She arranges things in tidy rows. In return my strange life entertains her. I bet I make good stories for her friends.

She asks me what it's like being a writer. She decided she'd be one too, write down the story of her life. A lot of interesting things have happened to me, she said. I think there was another reason. Tilly Devine was her aunt, or rather, her uncle was one of Tilly's husbands; everybody else seemed to be cashing in on her family's stories, why shouldn't she? A famous madam, gangsters' moll, possible murderess; a hard-spending whore with a social conscience, at least where her girls were concerned; stories like Tilly's are hard to come by. Kath was keen to get all the mileage she could out of her.

Just my luck, I thought. A cleaning woman who turns out to be the Albert Facey of the urban scene. Another and equally ironic *Fortunate Life*. She'll probably sell the thing for a million dollars.

Unfortunately (or do I with a writer's jealousy mean fortunately?) when she wrote the stories down they didn't have the rhythm and energy they have orally. She tidied up and cut back to the bare record of what happened, and without her voice the terrible syntax was just clumsy. But this is how I know her life story.

When she was a small girl her parents went north and her father got work on a farm. When he came home in the afternoon he'd sit her on his knee and ask her did mum have any visitors today and give her pennies when she told him yes. One morning he pretended to go and do the milking but after a bit he came back and found his wife having – you know – with one of the other men on the place. So mum and the other man took off for Sydney with Kath and her brother. That was the end of living with that father. In Sydney the mother found she couldn't cope with the kids so she put them into care. A Home, a kind of orphanage.

Kath mostly stayed there. Her mother had her brother quite often, and Kath occasionally, but she was mostly in the Home. I imagine her like the Home Girls who went to my school, with blunt basin haircuts and something in their faces I still can't put my finger on, that made them different from the rest of us. A bleak look, perhaps, wary eyes, the absence of expectation. Then she met this boy, and got pregnant and in those terrible days, the 1950s, ended up in that other kind of Home, for unmarried mothers. Homes are interesting, in this context. They're actually anything but. There she met the boyfriend of her best friend. Kath started up with him and when she'd had her baby she took off with this bloke. He had a motorbike.

I'm not sure whether it was this one she married or another one. Anyway, next thing she's living in a government flat in Canberra with a husband who drives trucks to Sydney. The trucks keep breaking down. He rings a neighbour and sends a message that he's held up. Then she found out that he was seeing another woman. This woman came to Canberra and he went with her there. Kath said he had to choose.

The husband turned out not to be paying the rent, or any electricity bills, though he said he was. The authorities said he'd have to pay or go to gaol. He'd spent all the money on drink and other women so he went to gaol in Goulburn.

Kath got jobs cleaning, the neighbour minded the kids, and she saved money and paid what was owing and the fines and he got out of gaol. He was really grateful and said he cared only for her, but next thing he was on with the other woman again. He said he didn't mean it and Kath was the one, but he didn't stick to it. Kath got sick of this, so she took the kids to where they were living and told the woman that if she wanted the bloke she could have the kids as well. The woman couldn't cope and the kids got put in care. Of course they're adults now. One of them won't speak to Kath, but the other is okay.

Now I'm a bit vague about the details – I had to read the handwritten manuscript very fast, Kath didn't want it out of her hands for long. I didn't want to ask to read it after it was typed up (the woman whose husband fixed the car lent her a typewriter) in case she thought I'd be able to get it published. But I know she went up north with or met there the love of her life, the man who was good to her, who was a companion, not just someone who went to bed with her and beat her up and gave her kids and opted out. Living in Cairns with him she was happy. Then he died. Actually, he got killed. An accident at work, something fell on him, he thought he was all right, and they were nervous about going to hospital if it wasn't necessary, and then when they realised they should it was too late. Kath still grieves for him. She remembers him, in her way she is constant. He's the father of Jason and Renee.

After Cairns she came back to Canberra. Her father was here too. Living in a government flat. He'd turned into a drunkard. She'd go and see him regularly and clean up. Kath is always cleaning up for people. He was in and out of hospital but that didn't stop him smoking and drinking. When he died she was the one who found him, lying on the floor in a heap of vomit, his chair tipped over, the whisky bottle on its side under the table. (This is the kind of detail she left out of her manuscript, out of respect, cleaning up the story too.) He left her his bit of money, in his will, not a lot, but the family said she'd cheated him out of it, that she ought to share it, though none of them had been near him in years. They don't do much for the mother, either, it's Kath who goes every day to the pensioner homes and undresses her and baths her and gets her into bed, because her arthritis is too bad for her to lift her arms up. She takes her shopping too, once a week, she's got a disabled sticker on her car so she can park close.

Kath has had various relationships but nothing's really come of them. There are sagas of beatings and leavings. Some bloke who kept going home to his mother, who'd come and abuse her. The latest lover she told Lucy about, much more than me, until one day she came and said I hear you met my darlin last night, and I discovered he was the natty man in the cream suit I was introduced to at a reception at the National Library; he said The writer? and I thought he might have read a book of mine but he turned out to be this lover of Kath's. I think she met him dancing at the club. She loves dancing. I don't know what she'd wear, I only see her in track suits and t-shirts, but she's got pretty, elfin, blondish grey hair and a pointed chin and I bet she smiles and looks as though she's having fun. She's got quite a lot of wrinkles but so what.

What's the bacteria, she asked first thing one morning. Is it catching?

I got the medical dictionary and showed her. Germs, really, I said. The bacteria was what the lover had. Round his ribs. Very painful. It took a few weeks to discover it was impetigo. She wouldn't have anything to do with him for a while. He's been posted overseas. He writes.

She misses him a lot. Partly because of the dancing. She likes bingo too. She often wins, which makes life a bit easier. Once she won a lot of money on the pokies and spent it having the lounge room done up. Painted, and new curtains and a coral pink leather lounge. No point in putting it in the bank, the family would have done their best to get it off her. Safely spent, was the best thing.

She lives on a tight budget. She puts money aside weekly against the electricity bill. She's been bankrupt, she got caught by that Walton's credit crash, when they'd got people to spend up big on their credit cards and then when it all went wrong sold the lot to some sharky firm to get the money back. Kath owed more than $8000, the Legal Aid lawyer said the best thing was to go bankrupt. She's also been caught for Social Security fraud, they found out she had a job as well (hid and watched her comings and goings) and took her to court and fined her and made her pay it back, $20 a fortnight out of her pension. She won't have the phone, too dangerous. But when Renee and her new boyfriend were living at home she let them put it in. In their name. He's a handy chap; fixed up their bedroom in two halves, hers pink and flowery, his black with shelves for the hi fi. Then they went off travelling and Kath was back on her own. That's when she wrote her biography, using their room as a study.

Not for long. Soon they're back again. Renee's pregnant. Kath's thrilled, though a bit nervous because of the baby who died. Tries to get Renee to give up smoking, and the other stuff. The father's very happy too, from the beginning, quite different from Troy. Clint's a nice boy, she tells me. Looks after Renee real well, and handy, always doing something about the house. Well, when they're not smooching.

Over the weeks it emerges that there's one small problem with Clint. He's on the run from the police. He's jumped bail. He was up for armed robbery. Aw, says Kath, he only does it on the other side of the lake. Wouldn't do it over here, she says, not where he lives.

It wasn't a very good robbery. It was a toy gun and he only got $350.

What does he live on, now? I ask.

He's on the dole, says Kath.

How can he be on the dole, I say, if he's jumped bail?

He's using a false name, isn't he.

Well, the police caught up with him. His brother dobbed him in. Renee has spent most of her pregnancy being driven out to the remand centre every day by Kath. Two hours she spends with him. Floods of tears. Until the last couple of months. At the trial he gets six years and is sent to Goulburn. Kath wrote to the judge saying he was a different man now he was going to be a father and being with the baby was more likely to keep him from being a criminal than putting him in jail. But what with previous convictions and breaking parole and jumping bail the judge couldn't do much.

Renee has been saving money so when he got to Goulburn he could buy a television set, you can't take them with you, you have to buy them there. But then they decided to buy an engagement ring so when she went to hospital to have the baby everybody would know she wasn't just a single mother. So the two women went and bought a nice diamond. I don't know what's happening about the television.

The baby's got a lovely trousseau, thanks to bingo. Every time Kath won she gave Renee half, and she often spent her half on things anyway. And they got a fabulous bassinet from Vinny's. The baby grew beautifully, Kath brought the photos of the ultra-scans to show us. You could see its long hair. They didn't want to know the sex. Just that it was healthy. She was born last week, induced, over 8 pounds. Renee was 21 two days later. They let her go out to celebrate. Her cousin, the rich one who's a drug dealer, came and got her in his fancy car. I told her to give it up, said Kath, you can't tell her anything.

The baby's not being breast-fed, they think bottles are better, healthier. I wonder if it's so Kath can do it. She gets up in the night. Renee stayed in hospital four days and the next day drove to Goulburn to show the baby to Clint.

Little Madalyn. She's gorgeous. I spent a goodly portion of the three hours hearing what a marvel she is. Renee's nose, Clint's chin. Hair slightly golden-red like her mother's. Beautiful windy smiles. The girl they so much wanted. I'm to see her next week, I haven't got her a present yet.

It was this baby that made me decide to write Kath's story. Such hope. Such fecklessness. To believe against these kinds of odds that this time they will get it right. All the muddles, the failures, the tragedies of previous generations simply annulled by its newest member. This baby, fourth that I know of in a line of women battling to rear their children while the men self-destruct. Of course, it's not quite so simple as that. The women had their feckless moments too. Were unfaithful. Betrayed their husbands and children. And from the sound of

Kath's unjudging remarks, Renee is still more of a spoilt brat than a good mother. (She's never had a job in her life, will this be it?)

Nevertheless, it seems to me an archetypal image. Or anyway an ancient one. A little house, neatly kept, a mother, a grandmother, and a beloved baby, cosseted and cared for, while the men are elsewhere.

JACKIE HUGGINS

Alone Again . . . Naturally

My Mother always wanted a traditional, white, western, wedding ceremony for me. Just like the one she and my three sisters had had. My *tiddas* (sisters) all looked so beautiful decked out in their white lace dresses, flowers in their hair, make-up to a tee . . . and pregnant bellies.

Being the youngest girl I have failed in the marriage stakes but have managed to produce an heir to the family, my beautiful 9-year-old son, John Henry Huggins the Fourth. In a tokenistic way I escaped the pressures of 'full blown marriage expectations'. Tokenistic because my older sisters had already been there, done that, their white weddings for little Black girls was one of the immense joys in my Mother's life.

Not that I haven't had a couple of close shaves in my life. Of course there was Bryan, the first real love of my life at 17, and like so many other women I actually believed that I would marry the first guy I ever kissed and you know whatted. Janice Ian's song 'I learnt the truth at 17 . . . love was meant for beauty queens' became my life's theme song.

Well, for three torrid, immature years, my relationship with Bryan endured. I treated him like shit but he didn't seem to mind and kept coming back for more. How much could a man take? I reckoned he deserved a VC for tolerating my mood swings, selfishness, possessiveness and jealousy.

Jealousy was the worst aspect of our relationship. Being absolutely besotted by this older man (he was five years older) who looked just like a Black Mark Spitz, after relentlessly pursuing him for almost a year, finally wearing him down and both of us falling hopelessly in puppy love, was all too much for a stunning, young, vivacious girl like me – *gammon* (only joking). If he even looked sideways at another woman I'd enter into a horrible rage and attempt to kick him out of my life.

My second close shave came with Bill, who loved himself more than life itself. Boy of boy was he, and still is. Vain with a capital V. We were about to become engaged on his sister's 21st birthday but my bold act of bravery as I reminded him that it was her party and not *his*, became my saving grace. Later we drifted apart when I fell in love with, horror of horrors, a married man who was all I ever hoped to meet in my life. He was some seventeen years older than me which confirmed my Mother's much held suspicions that 'I was indeed searching for a father figure'. My Father had died when I was two years old.

For ethical reasons he cannot be named, although his wife and half the Murries in Australia knew who he was. The full emotional intensity of my love for Reg lasted for thirteen years. To this day I remain firm friends with him, his wife Margie and family. In fact Margie and I became close allies. Polygamy rules and I will always be known as 'his other wife'.

Now all this has shaped my world view about marriage. My relationships and the family pressures have not helped, or been encouraging signs. Basically I'm scared of marriage as a commitment and don't give a damn anymore if I do or do not get married. It has never been an issue in my life even when I was younger. I have never wanted to get married for the sake of it.

Now how does this 20th-century, Black-woman thinking fit in with my culture? Aboriginal marriages in pre-European contact time were regulated by 'skin groups' which determined marriage partners and who it was permissible to marry. As every individual had a place in Aboriginal society, no one would miss out on the duty of marriage with an obvious motive to populate the race. In fact Aboriginal australians have the highest birthrate and regrettably one of the highest infant mortality rates in the world.

When the policies of segregation and assimilation forced Aboriginal people onto reserves away from their borne countries or traditional homelands, marriage laws were severely disrupted. These laws, along with ceremonies, dances, religious beliefs and languages, were regarded as 'heathen or primitive' and were strongly discouraged and condemned. Mission superintendents and Department of Native Affairs officials controlled marriages and stated who could marry who.

One of the duties in reserve life was that around 12 – 13 years of age boys and girls would be sent out to stations as stockmen and domestic servants. So many Aboriginal children were born during domestic service days to both Aboriginal and non-Aboriginal fathers. The majority of white fathers comprised pastoralists, troopers and government officials, who never claimed paternity, usually after taking the women by force.

My mother bore two daughters to an Aboriginal man during her domestic service times. She never married him and suffered the stigma and scorn associated with single motherhood of all women of her generation. My eldest sister Mutoo, whose anglo name is Marion, was born in Cherbourg in 1941 and my late sister Gloria was born in Mackay in 1947. As a consequence of domestic service life Rita was not allowed to keep her baby with her and was therefore forced to leave Mutoo in the care of her parents, Albert and Rose Holt, at Cherbourg Aboriginal Settlement. Although Albert and Rose were loving grandparents Mutoo missed out on maternal bonding and became Motherless. Therefore domestic service denied Aboriginal women their maternity, while they were forced to look after white people's children.

My mother was exempted from the mission just before my

second sister Gloria was born. Some friends lived in Mackay and not telling anyone where she was going Rita took off to them. Now, being a 'free' woman with her exemption papers, Rita was able to keep Gloria with her.

Gloria was adopted by my father when he married my mother in 1951. Sadly, my father passed away seven years later at the young age of 38 leaving Rita with her four young children to raise alone. The trauma, isolation and loneliness that Rita had to endure as she cried all night in the train to Mackay leaves me chilled. I have often sadly reflected about my mother's story which she related to me only last year as part of a missing, eight-year gap in her biography. It continues to affect me so much that this is what I have to say to her:

My precious Mother, what can I say to you to ease the pain a little? I can just imagine what it must have been like in your time to be a single mother, not once but twice. Single motherhood is a hard and unrelenting job but the love for child and all the worthwhile outcomes far outweigh the stigma and courage of being alone. But I have never been 'alone' in the sense that you were. My anchor and the ability to do what I have to do, write, speak, travel etc. comes from the fact that primarily you and my wonderful sister Ngaire share the responsibility of being a mother, carer and nurturer to John Henry. It has been an unconditional act of love from both of you and I am so privileged to have been born into a culture and family who are so accepting of children and family.

You were like a child yourself when you ran away from your family to a strange town where you only had two friends. Luckily Aunty Lear and Uncle Teddie were family, who loved and cared for you as best they could and gave you a desperately needed home.

I saw not only the loving way you welcomed my child into this world when I was confused and so unsure myself what the responsibility of being a mother might mean, but I have seen the radiant way you welcome all young babies of strangers and the closest and distant friends and relatives, particularly your grandchildren and great-grandchildren into the world. I understand so much more now.

I'm sure Mutoo realised at some stage of your life that you had to go to work. You had no choice in domestic service life. You were bonded and on contract. If you could have taken her out on the stations you would have, but in working from daylight to dawn there would have been no room for a small baby. Today we have the right to take our children with us to work . . . no one would dare take them from us.

Personally, being a single mother today has meant independence, freedom, choice, acclamation, unreserved happiness, status and power among many things. All of which you were never afforded the luxury of. But the things we shared in common were love, strength, stubbornness, struggle, shame in the beginning, relationships with selfish, *yunjilbay* (rude), absent fathers, and most importantly being broke! Financial independence has to be worked at all the time but I have a far greater capacity to achieve this than you ever could have dreamed of.

All I want to say to you is it's okay, all your children and grandchildren love you, understand and forgive you because being a single, Black, penniless, oppressed, pregnant woman in your time was your greatest test and punishment.

So weddings and wives, I have never been there. To me it's irrelevant but I face the same pressures any single woman does, especially from my darling mother who regularly tells me and has reversed the situation somewhat, 'I wish you'd find a decent man and get married', or 'Johnny needs a father'. Well, I know some kids who've turned out finely without one and I've done pretty well without a husband to date too, so why spoil it?

SUE INGLETON

The Marriage Tree

Three visions of weddings and wives with tasty bits in between. Recommended background music: *The Girl That I Marry* by Rodgers & Hammerstein.

'I decided to put a little bit of magic into my marriage – I made my husband disappear!'

Seed

Hands clasped over the heart – the lady in white robes leans into the young man, her hands fasted over his heart. He looks away, he doesn't see her. She opens her robe, her flesh is bare, it carries a great wound, a vertical split, the purple edges flower and curl, there is a white light, gem-like, flame, from a diamond in her chest. She takes it out and admires it in the sun. She smiles a secret smile. She tosses it into the air, catches it with juggler's skill and hands it over to me.

Crystal or diamond, I wonder? Diamond, she says, inside my head.

HARDCUTTING, the light blinds me, hits me between the eyes. Its rays pierce my mind – my knowing – my non-knowing.

I want to write about marriage.

I want to write so folks will know at least a little history, at least a little journey to the Back Ground . . . out of the matrimonial home . . . down past the Hills hoist, the McEwans shed, over the fence, over the creek, under the electricity pylons pumping out invisible death, away past the illegal rubbish tip, to the edge – the edge, no trams here – the grass is untended, the grass is tough, its toughness allows tiny stars to grow beneath, little purple stars with white centres – my feet crush the stars, they bounce back – moving to the forest, to the trees, the great trees, the whispering dark, in there the Silence, the Gnowing . . . a small church in a glade, all white and cute, slate roof, arched door, a procession, a bride in white, a groom in a dinner suit – what's he planning to eat? Guests amongst the trees, they go in they come out, something's changed, they've done something in there, in the little white room. She's unveiled. He holds her tight. Before that her father held her tight. No one held him tight. No one gave him away. He's got her now. She is his, he's taller, older, it makes sense.

The women cry. The men laugh. Why do they laugh? They laugh hard – it's a good joke, he's done for now they say. Their mouths are hard and cruel they want a drink, spirits they want to drink spirits, they do, they drag him away as if last night wasn't enough they drag him away. She stares. She can keep him in her sights. They are only at the table under the pine tree but they need to pour spirits into him. Why?

Her friends still cry, they hold and squeeze and kiss her and touch her dress now they can touch her whiteness before she was untouchable before she couldn't speak now she's spoken for.

She's happy, so happy. He's on the edge of her vision, she's the apple of his eye. He breaks away, old ladies want to kiss him now they squeeze his young flesh and cast knowing glances at each other and bend towards the girl in white. She drinks champagne just sips, her teeth are white her lips are red the red begins to bleed from her mouth down the side of her lips to her chin her lipstick has melted, too much lipstick but now it drips on her white shoulder turning the lace into crimson spider webs her bodice is straining against some terrible flow it cannot contain it the flow bursts free and the blood envelops her – the white dress the green grass the champagne's pink now red she drinks it smiling always smiling her feet now bare are sunken into the bloodied muddied turf she loves the feel of it her toes part and flex the squelching sound makes her think of him her body thrums her legs tingle she feels a swelling there at the top just below just in there could the blood be coming from there why yes great bubbles warm and sticky how exciting she's vibrating oh tingling so fast now she seizes him with her black eyes he's torn by the look he comes in a daze his skin is white the hair on his chest is golden and new his loins glisten the sweat is trickling in the curve of thigh and hip bone his golden manhood slowly rising the shadows of vines and pines dance across the tumescent flesh everyone breathes and sighs – aaaah aaaah – they sip the spirits. She bursts upon him the white of the dress the red of the blood the black of her hair the light in her eyes his golden glory races to the darkness to the redness to be planted in there. She envelops him draws him up he seizes her hair flowers fall from the trees late blossoms of gold and green descend in the dappled light. A strange bird calls from a great tree, a bell, the bird has the voice of a bell.

The guests shudder and withdraw their gaze – the noises are rather disgusting, the roaring and sucking, the twisting sound of flesh in flesh Oh lord how long will they go on for? Honestly, there's a time and a place . . . but singing comes and the birds increase and the rain falls, the golden rain falls and falls and seems to rise so it can fall again and the earth shudders and weeps and sighs and stirs with new life.

You married me on the night my body was bleeding into the earth – that was the marriage. You filled me with seed, I bled and I bled. It was magic – the white and the red – the hotel maid would disagree so I stripped the bed next morning and put the sheets in the bath and ran the water onto them ran the water through them and saved it all saved it. I sat on the edge and put my feet into it – how extraordinary. The water, the blood and the seed – that's all it is really, the packets of soap strewn all over the bathroom I didn't open one of them – I put them all into my washbag along with sewing kits, shower caps that I never wear and a lovely big soft white towel and matching facewasher – I took the lot. Didn't touch the mini bar except for the vodka and the gin which I replaced with water – carefully opened carefully closed.

We fucked so beautifully that night so drunk we were, we were God and Goddess on the inner spring the well spring the well sprung spring – we didn't make babies then because of the blood – funny that. But we made them later oh later we made the most beautiful babies the boys, the girls became men and women, we did that we did that with the blood and the seed. I'm so glad you planted yourself in me. I devoured you devoured and ate up that tiny, infinitesimally tiny thing – we gave each other back to ourselves.

When Jeremy died you came back to me to hold me there where we'd created him – that night you came back to me there and everything melted, time dropped away even though it wasn't ours we took a moment extra and it was enough, cos by then I really didn't want you anymore.

Why?

What happened to it. What happened to the need, to the power of the blood and the seed? Perhaps after all it was a need created from way out there? Someone else's need? But the day, the days of madness they were ours, the day we fucked on the cliff at Johanna Beach the wind hurling abuse in our faces the ants biting my bum the VW Combi full of surfies that came and parked just behind us – us so well disguised, panting and tearing and wanting deeper and deeper touching – how deep we wanted we wanted the drowning place oh my head would buzz ring bells blow whistles my head would scream with despair when my trust was gone scream oh get out get out get out then the heart tearing tearing and Cleopatra's heart in my mouth 'let him forever go – oh let him not'.

I let you forever go – did we both want it? Did we not really try hard enough? Why did I release it? I pushed it away I finally didn't think I deserved it – was that the truth?

Truth has two faces, yours and mine. One person can never be enough, you can never have everything in one person said Annie so wisely to me – balance the good and the bad. But I'm hurting in here! snot dripping, whimping whine. I'm betrayed – medieval visions in my head – knights of betrayal.

One person's moment of truth is another person's place of lies. When did we ever tell everything to each other? Never. And after Rachel had been and gone Rachel Rachel the secret lover, after Rachel, you stood there and said 'but she wasn't the only one I ever loved before you …' Such a big black secret, a boy of secrets, a little boy with a little tin box full of secrets and dead insects – a little boy whose mummy didn't love him right. Why didn't I see that in the God who threw me down on the cliffs of Johanna?

I see a man wearing a three-cornered hat. He's dragging a woman in chains. Behind them walks a Spirit in White, neither the man nor the woman are aware of the Spirit. As she walks, babies fall from her body. The Spirit gathers them up.

She cries: 'What do you want me for, if you don't want to look at me and you won't let me have my children?'

'I want you behind me. I want to be in front.'

'Let me go and I won't bother you.'

'You do bother me. You bother me.'

'I don't want to be with you!'

'You'd miss me!'

'What would I miss?'

'You'd miss this,' and he takes his cock out.

'I don't need it!' She is on her knees. He thrusts his cock into her mouth.

'You do need it! you do need it! you do need it!'

She chokes, 'At least this way I don't get babies.'

The Spirit bends down to her and says, 'You are the strongest. I am behind you.'

Mask

The ladies gather their silken gowns, stiff heavy layers, and below them more layers of cotton muslin lace, stiffened with the bones of whales. How the whales howled when they took their bones, how the ladies howled when encased and wrapped up tight in the bones of dead whales. The hook and eye, hook and eye, a hook goes into the eye, jelly rolls. They are of a similar age. They are all married. They are all frigid. They are all burning with desire. They have all been cut off in their prime. They are all pregnant – again. The bones crush the foetus in each womb. They are all due on the same day but each in a different month – June, July, August – the fifteenth. That's when they have sex with their husbands. On that particular night each week – the rest of the time he's at the club, with a prostitute, with his mistress, with the musician's boy, with the actress, with the chambermaid – or her mother ... planting their flag in each little mound planting their seed oh willy-nilly really. Just a matter of luck for some if they don't connect, don't fall FALL. Fall. Fall pregnant. Fall in love. Fall from Grace.

Judith came into the drawing room. Her face was white, her hands were wet. She was absentmindedly drying them on her crinoline skirts, bits of flour stuck to her knuckles even egg white perhaps.

'James is coming home tonight! Tonight!'

He rose quickly – his gut gripped, the adrenalin pumped – 'God's teeth,' he murmured, his mind racing, how to get it all cleaned up? It must be 5 p.m. Judith pleaded with him in taut silence.

'I'll fix the bedroom,' he said.

'– and the bathroom! Don't forget your things in the bathroom. Oh God, Jack – this is just ridiculous ... a month early! A whole damned month early!'

'Don't, now – let's move!' He pushed past her and leapt the stairs two at a time, the brass rods glinted and winked up at him in the gaslight, 'naughty boy, naughty boy'. He panted at the top, the smell of lavender in her room, lavender and her sweet smell of cunt, the sheets crumpled and damp from them, from their mad thrashings, his cock began to tremble and activate. Oh Christ, not now not now. She came into the room behind him, her eyes were wide oh uh uh ... tears were swimming in there. He crushed his mouth to her sweet wetness. He was hard against her Christ Christ. She drives him to madness. His brain dances his hand seeks her darkness and heat. God she's hot, running already, juices running, slippery dip dip in, his cock is out, he lifts her onto it just lifts her, she clings, the wet hair on her cheek – he wraps his tongue in it. She's tight on him tight full blown raging down there another planet it's fast and furious and full of glory.

He can't stop laughing as he pulls the sheets down the stairs the whole bloody lot down to the laundry where He'll never go never go to the laundry will you James – could get yourself dirty in there old boy. His shaving brush his strop his blade all swept into the leather case – that's it that's all it's 6 o'clock. He's moving out of His house out of His blasted house.

James rides in on Chevalier, his huge grey stallion. His sword is drawn. His plumed hat casts a shadow over his right eye. His sideburns glisten with tiny drops of water.

'Goddam! You know it's bloody raining out there! Six months away and it's bloody raining when I left and bloody raining when I return! Well, m'dear, and how's the old gel eh?'

He slaps my bottom. I barely feel it through the layers, all I feel is the heat of Jack's hands between my legs like he's there crouched under the crinolines.

'My God! the Frogs are a stubborn bunch. Couldn't get them to shift an inch, not an inch m'dear ... pull these off for me would you . . .' He thrusts his great black boots into my face, his thighs bulge, he smells of sweat and snuff, disgusting bits cling to his nose hairs, the 'brown' stains his cuffs, his teeth are bad, his breath is bad, his tongue is white, I see the fur as he yawns.

'Miss me?' He pulls me down. From his stockinged feet rises the smell of stale cheese. 'Come on, you cold goose.' He's clumsy with me, rough and rude, his face is that close, his nose is covered with broken veins and smallpox scars – only his nose? He got smallpox on his nose? Perhaps I mean chicken pox. The main word is POX.

'James, let me clean your things first, your boots are wet, the carpet will be ruined.'

'Come here, woman,' his grip is like iron. 'D'y know how long it's been since I had my wife? My Wife! Six months! D'y hear! Got to plant the flag or you'll forget who you belong to! Eh what?'

His penis is out and he's masturbating himself. 'C'mon, m'dear, you can do this what?' his iron grip on my neck, his penis is pressed to my cheek I gag I want to vomit vomit the smell is of stale urine and rotten walnuts. 'There's a girl.'

'James, I can't, just like this, I can't.' His finger is in my mouth, blunt, tobacco stained, bitter tasting, 'like this, m'dear'. His penis is in there too then just his penis. It's getting hard and has a bend in it, it hurts the back of my throat, I can't breathe I can't stand this! I bite hard down on the bony thing – it collapses between my teeth, his hand pulls my hair nearly out of my head, my ear is nearly off from the blow, so nearly off, but he can't move for the pain . . . I taste blood on my lips . . . his or mine? My ear is ringing with awful silence, my jaw won't close, can't feel my teeth, more blood now, definitely mine – and he doesn't even know about Jack . . . he doesn't even know . . . I croon to myself to myself in the dark, in the laundry, buried in the damp sheets of my lust and my betrayal of the General.

Women have babies for themselves. Every baby a woman has she chooses. Man says, 'Where do I fit in?'

'You helped to create it! You share it with me.'
'I want to own it.'
'How can you do that?'
'By owning you.'
'How can you do that?'
'You see this hand? This hand makes a law (writing). My law!'
'*Your* law!'
'You see this hand? This hand makes a fist!' (threatens her)
' . . . and if I refuse?'
'Then you will suffer, both from *this* (writing) and from *this* (fist).

How did he get his power over her?

Woman's power is invisible it cannot be seen. Man has manifested his power (fist). Perhaps that is why male sexuality is so rampant – it operates on a visual level.

Safety

Had she persuaded her father behind her mother's back? The doctor's suggestion was rude but forthright.

The square lamp began to hurt her eyes. The darkness of the room increased, became redder. Around her she felt the walls begin to wheeze, the noise of her mother's breathing was coming out of the wood panelling. It clutched at her heart. She felt the iron pincers strike home, her mother's fingers pulling her away from the world, away from her life. How had her father borne it? How had he borne that woman, that ghastly creature that was her mother – Louisa May Alcott could never have written 'Marmee' if she'd had an inkling of Josephine's mother, how Josephine longed for that household, for those sisters, for that Mother – no father. He was always 'away', and in his absence all the men in the book were trying to break into the magic circle of 'Little Women'.

Her mother was little now. As a child she remembered her as tall and hard against her small face. The rings on her mother's left hand would scratch at her cheeks, the diamond would tear at her; a laughing, cruel stone set in sharp, smaller stones, an ugly ring.

Her mother's fingers were red and scaly in parts where the itchiness of eczema forced her to wear bandages a lot of the time. Only on her hands – she was forced to take off her rings. She tried using different soap powders in the laundry then she wore cotton gloves inside rubber gloves. She dyed her hair very black that year and the skin around the back of her neck was stained with black dye – the hairdresser had done it, on her pillow there appeared black smudges. Josephine hated the smell of the dye in her mother's hair – it was a cruel, hard smell. Her mother lost a lot of weight the year she dyed her greying hair black. She didn't look good thin. She wore a pale pink linen suit to the races at Flemington but her hair looked like it was dyed black and the suit hung a little loose, but her hat was beautiful. A wide, pink, softly-shaped straw thing, that made her mother softly-shaped and when Josephine smiled at her as she came out onto the verandah to get in her car, her little green Austin A40, she blushed and it almost seemed that a tear came into her eye, then she brusquely kissed the young girl and taking a deep breath she got into the car, carefully bending her laden head through the doorway.

Why is she going to the races, wondered Josephine. She never even knows the names of father's horses, she never remembers any of it. She doesn't understand how to place bets. Josephine understood. On her father's knee she would lie snuggled in as he went through the form guide with his fountain pen, underlining and ticking. She loved the names of the horses. Blue Fire, Archers Boy, Malaya Star. He named one of his racehorses after the four children. JOSATERO – Josephine, Sam, Terence and Rosemary. It started with her name and she knew why. She knew she was his favourite daughter, his favourite child – she loved him so closely, closer than her mother ever could – why her mother never sat on his knee like this, never held his hand, her mother was so cold to him and he looked at her with such sad eyes and sighed and patted Josephine – Joey he called her – and said things like, 'I don't know what's wrong with your mother . . .'

And the night Josephine followed her mother into the kitchen where she'd gone in a real huff after a strained silence between the two of them, husband and wife; the TV was on and suddenly her mother leapt up with a savage cry and thrust her way into the kitchen away from the warm feeling of the loungeroom. 'What's wrong with Mum?' she asked her father. He sighed and looked sadly at her. 'I don't know, I just don't know.' Her anger rose and she went out. Her mother was standing at the sink running her hands under cold water, cold water to ease the itchy pain.

'Why are you always so mean to Daddy?' Josephine hissed at her. She never forgot the look on her mother's face as she slowly turned to face her.

'I . . . I . . .' It was utter despair, utter despair – she had no answer.

Depression was something new in those days. The doctors put her mother onto tablets. The effect was extraordinary. She became another person, she was like a zombie. She couldn't remember simple things, she didn't want to remember. Her mind became locked away from herself and everyone – she took Mogadon at night to cope with trying to sleep, she took Valium in the day to cope with trying to be awake. She stopped going to the races. She stopped dressing up, she let the dye grow out and changed to chestnut which didn't cover the grey as well but it was a better match for her sallow complexion.

Josephine's father's car, the Chevrolet, would come up the drive late at night. He worked so late. For them. She never knew the time but it always woke her up. The lights would swerve across the flywire on her windows, splashing the underside of the verandah momentarily like day. The glow of the garage was just visible and then darkness. She knew he came in but she never heard that. She just felt safe.

He came in to the bedroom where his wife was a mound on the other side of the bed. He undressed, leaving on his singlet and his boxer shorts, he took a piss in the en suite toilet. She could hear him, like a horse she thought, a racehorse.

He pulled back the blankets and got into bed on his side. He was exhausted from fucking with his mistress who was also his secretary whom he took to the races every Saturday whom he'd been having an affair with for over six years now but she'd only found out this last twelve months because the other woman had been making anonymous phone calls to her, telling her the worst. Her sister advised her to buy some new clothes, get the grey out of her hair, confront them at the races. The eczema came quickly. The fear and the terror sat in her stomach and there was no room for any food, she dined on failure. She could stand it, for the children, she went on and on under humiliation; all her friends, who were really his friends, they all knew and felt relieved it wasn't their husband and felt secure and increased their power through her despair. And she coped with that and she went on and on until that terrible night, that terrible, terrible night when her daughter, her precious daughter, her wide-eyed girl turned on her and she saw the lie she had nurtured hanging above their heads like a great blade ready to cut them apart.

She turned in the dark. She lifted her head from her pillow. She sat up. 'Get out of this bed, Jake.' Her voice was iron grey, steel sharp. 'Get out of this house.'

He knew, he knew. The worm had turned. He read the danger in that voice, he read his path. He got out of bed. He dressed quietly and he left.

Josephine thought she heard a car again but deep in sleep she thought, 'Mm no, can't be, Dad's already come home.'

KATE GRENVILLE

Albion the Husband

Norah was a most appropriate wife for a man in the position of Albion Gidley Singer: there was a dimple in her cheek in just the spot where a dimple ought to appear on the cheek of a wife, she poured tea with much display of plump wrist, and she could keep up a tinkle of graceful chatter about the price of grosgrain and the sullenness of under-housemaids. A man of business needs to be a little careful in his choice of wife, but with Norah I seemed on safe ground.

I was a man who liked to come home to an embroidering wife. I formed the habit of pausing behind the plumbago before I entered my house, in order to watch my wife as she stitched at her petit point, and sighed, and crossed and re-crossed her little feet and glanced at the clock, a wife with every hair in place and every fold of skirt arranged for the delectation of a husband on his return from the shark-infested sea of business.

Before we were wed, I had thought I might grow to love Norah: once we were flesh of each other's flesh, I thought I might undergo some epiphany of emotion. It seemed to be the expected thing for a husband. I thought, too, that she might see inside me, and come to love what she saw there. Before we were wed, it seemed that a fresh start might be possible. But no epiphany took place for me:and frankly, the pert titties and bold ways of the various Valmais and Gertrudes I had sampled as a student made Norah a pretty pale proposition. For all the inflammation my wife could provide, a man might as well have been in bed with a roll of carpet.

As for Norah, she saw what there was to see within her husband, and turned away. 'No, Albion,' she began to say, 'no,' and took refuge behind headaches and indispositions, and she put away the petit point, and no longer watched the clock for the return of her husband.

These days, when I watched from behind the plumbago, I was more than likely to find her in the company of pale young men with hair in need of a good cut and big liquid eyes. It was like a roomful of spaniels. My wife would be radiant behind the teapot, her little red mouth shaping itself around smiles and exclamations, her little wet tongue flickering in and out, her head tossing and flirting so that her little earrings twitched and twinkled at them, and they hung on her every word, nodding and curving their long fingers further around their teacups.

When the dynamic figure of Albion Gidley Singer burst in on a gust of nor'-easter from the Harbour, their moonlike faces all swivelled towards me. A man could be made to feel an intruder in his own drawing room. 'Why Albion,' Norah would call from her position at the head of the tea table, 'you are just in time for a cup of tea, and Mr Reynolds here is just telling us of the fascinating paintings he saw in Paris. Please go on, Mr Reynolds,' and courtesy would force me to sit and accept a cup of stewed tea and listen to some lisping little pansy come out with a lot of poppycock about pictures.

They all fancied themselves as artists or writers. One of them wished to paint a portrait of my wife, while another had already written a poem which he had dedicated to her: to me it was just a page of piffle, but Norah spoke of having it framed.

It gave me a pang like the prick of something sharp to see

Norah's face light up in eagerness when she spoke to these charlatans. Her skin softened and warmed: she was like a wax figure coming to life. It made me realise how little she glowed and warmed with me these days, how cool and bland she was: she was politeness itself, but she never showed her eyeteeth to me in the sort of smile she squandered on her artists.

When they spoke to me, it was in an over-polite and over-clear way, as you might to a foreigner who was more to be pitied than blamed for being so stupid. They showed me paintings, and engravings of other more famous paintings, and I saw only bunches of flowers in vases, or women pouring milk out of jugs, or burning ships going down into the sea: I saw nothing in these but a representation, more or less accurate, of what I could see better with my own eyes.

It could make a man anxious. Was it possible that I was lacking some faculty, in the way that a deaf man cannot imagine sound, cannot even believe that sound exists? It was my student days all over again, with the circle of shoulders gently closing me out, the knot of people evaporating at my approach!

They were puffballs, but they were astute enough to flatter the provider of the admiring patroness with the elegant drawing room and the plentiful ham sandwiches. Reynolds was their leader, remarkable among them in being in paid employment: he had a sinecure with one of the papers to write about Art. He was a young man with a curl above his ear that he fingered, and a big floppy bow at his neck instead of a proper wing collar and tie, and dainty little feet in kid button boots.

'How I would love to do your head in bronze!' Reynolds cried out at me on one occasion. 'Mrs Singer, you must agree, your husband has a head that would suit bronze.' I flinched from his cry, like the call of a mad bird in my own drawing room, and stared everyone down as they all turned to observe my head. Indeed, it was a good head, and well-suited to bronze. But I did not like the way Mr Reynolds cocked his head on one side, considering me as an object in bronze, and the way he made little moulding gestures in the air beside my cheeks: even less did I like the way Norah stared and smiled, as if I were already nothing more than a bulb-eyed bust stuck on the top of a stand, to have its nose tweaked and the size of its ears remarked upon. There was a little ripple or gust of something very like laughter as they all stared at my head, which under so much scrutiny felt as hollow as a gong.

Enough was enough: after dinner that night, I came to Norah in her room where she was brushing out her hair and staring dreamily into the mirror at herself, with her hair electric around her. Whoever her dreams were for, they did not appear to be for her husband: when I appeared behind her in the mirror, she drew her wrapper up around her neck as if I was a cold draught.

'You have become quite the little patroness of the arts, my dear,' I began in my mildest way, 'Mr Reynolds and the others must be very grateful to you.' She was wary, but she could not resist. 'Oh yes,' she said, earnestly, 'you have no idea what a struggle it is for them, just to survive!' Now was the moment to speak frankly. 'Norah,' I said, 'I have to say that if Mr Reynolds cannot make a living from his art, then clearly he is in the wrong business. If the world does not wish to buy what he has to sell, he should stop producing it.'

I turned away, to indicate that, as far as I was concerned, that was the end of it. But to my astonishment, Norah answered me back, positively blurting, almost shouting at me, 'But, Albion, the arts are not just a business, they are what distinguishes us from the beasts!' I watched her blush, perhaps thinking of that other activity, the one that did not distinguish us from the beasts, but she ploughed on, 'The arts are the very soul of a people, Albion.' I had never before seen her argue a case for anything more significant than blue slip covers rather than green: her face was quite scowling with sincerity, so that her passion for the soul of a people looked very like bad temper.

'The fact is, Albion,' she announced ringingly, as though to a public meeting, 'that the arts are as fundamental to the health of a race as greens in the diet.'

A certain kind of silence fell after this announcement. Norah might appear guileless, but it seemed to me in this last declaration that I was hearing a pale parody of phrases of my own: I was a man who loved above all a fact delivered as an article of faith. She was not fiddling with her hair, or smoothing her collar, as she usually did when she spoke to me. She had not glanced away, or dropped her eyes: no! She was staring at me, bold and glassy-eyed, quite swollen with complacency: she actually thought she had the whip hand!

As with dogs and horses, so with women: a firm hand has to be taken early on, or things will go to the pack. I snorted, and pretended to pretend to turn it into a cough: my smile locked under my moustache, and I spoke in a way that conveyed both weariness and the tactful effort to disguise weariness. 'Norah, in spite of what Mr Reynolds has told you, the arts are a commodity like any other, no different from Argyll socks and gold-plated collar studs. They are of value because people are prepared to pay money for them, and they are prepared to do so because they bring them some pleasure, as Argyll socks do. You would do well to bear in mind, too, that what you dismiss as 'just business' is what keeps you in bone china and Broken Orange Pekoe. Dirty and soulless it may be, but it also supplies your friends with the ham sandwiches, at 7s 6d a pound, of which they seem so fond.'

She flinched, and her fingers began to worry at the neck of her wrapper. When she spoke, her voice had a strained quality to it, as if she were shouting from the bottom of a well. 'I cannot agree with you there, Albion: the value of the arts cannot be measured with mere money.' With that she lifted her chin and tried to stare me down, but thought better of it, and turned away: but she was determined to have the last word, and rang for Alma, who came immediately, so I was left with all my replies festering within me. *Mere* money, indeed!

I would have looked a terrible fool to have come the heavy husband: if I continued to oppose, I would become that stock character of farce, the philistine husband. How much Norah would relish carrying the torch for culture, and how well the pucker of her lips would suit martyrdom! I had no wish to come into my own drawing room to find them all falling silent, casting pitying glances at my wife: I had no wish to have them discuss me later, in my absence, and lisp disparagement of me.

No, there had to be another option available to the ingenious mind. I was confident that this problem, like any other, was susceptible to the operation of logic within a first-class mind.

Chance favours the prepared mind, some Frenchman said, and on this occasion a Frenchman was right. It was chance that took me past a gloomy little shop full of dusty moose antlers and elephants-foot waste paper baskets, with split bentwood chairs hanging up outside, and a window full of blackened briar-pipes, chipped china dolls, and paintings of horses. The pictures caught my eye: I had never wasted my time examining things in frames before, but I made it my business to do so now. In each of these pictures a horse stood side-on, every hair meticulously made to gleam in a way so true to life it looked false. The laborious over-precision of each part somehow made the whole all wrong: the head was too small, or the bottom was too big, or the spine had one curve too many; in straining after the natural, they had achieved only the grotesque.

I wondered what Norah and Mr Reynolds would make of them: to my unprejudiced eye these paintings were neither better nor worse than all those women pouring milk and all those burning ships. And it was in that moment of wondering that I laughed aloud at the idea that had just come to me, so simple and yet so scarifying was it.

It was no problem to accumulate a great many pictures of horses: in the course of a year I bought a couple of dozen in shabby little shops where they hung mercifully dimming beneath dust. I was not yet ready for the world to value them, so I treated them with the right degree of amused contempt, muttered about wanting them only for the frames, and never paid more than a few shillings.

How inexorable and cog-like, how wonderful to behold,

were the operations of the marketplace! The day came when I was asked to pay twenty pounds for one of these daubs, and instead of pocketing my money quickly, and speeding me on my way before I could think better of it, this ancient Mr Sampson stood before his pile of dusty canvases extolling their virtues at such length I knew that my time was ripe. Simply by buying enough of these pictures, I had caused them to become valuable: nothing about the pictures had changed, except that word had got around that someone had finally wanted them. Now I could make my move, and just in time: the presence of Reynolds and his twittering cronies in my house had become an irritant to me like a flea under the collar.

'That Mr Reynolds of yours,' I said casually to Norah, 'he seems an informed sort of fellow, I should like him to see over the collection with me some day.'

So Reynolds was invited to join us for lunch before the ceremonial inspection of the collection. Norah tried to take the initiative once or twice. 'Oh,' she exclaimed, 'the show at Bonnet's is quite astonishing, Mr Reynolds,' or 'Oh, Mr Reynolds, you will never guess who I ran into at Lipp's,' but poor old Norah was not going to get a look in today. With a flourish I filled and re-filled Reynold's glass with the second-best French wine, slapped him on the back so he choked on his fish, pressed delicacies upon him so he did not know which to put in his mouth first. And oh, how interested I was in Reynolds, his life, his difficulties, his dreams! How sympathetic I was to the limitations of his present situation, and how eager I was to be filled in on his own artistic ambitions! Reynolds grew warm with so much wine and sympathy, and perhaps the hope – I had not said anything precise, and Mr Reynolds could well have misheard – that Mr Singer might find it in his power to become a substantial patron of the individual artist.

After lunch he walked with me along the line of paintings, inspecting each one with an attention it could not possibly deserve. Norah paced behind us: she had never really warmed to the horse pictures, and had preserved a dignified silence on their artistic worth, but had encouraged me in my interest, had swollen with smugness on my conversion to Art. Now it was my turn.

How Reynolds flapped and yapped then, to assure Mr Singer of his wonderfully good taste and of the magnificence of his collection! He inspected the brushwork, and commented on the proportions, darted in to point with a slender finger, stepped back and cocked his head on one side like a puppy listening for a whistle, and generally could be seen to sit up and beg.

Of course, poor old Norah had to follow suit: now that her Mr Reynolds had approved, she found all manner of virtues in these daubs, and ventured several over-confident attempts at remarks involving the plasticity of the haunches.

'Yes yes,' Reynolds brushed her off as impatiently as politeness would allow, 'yes, and Mrs Singer, you will have noticed the quite remarkable depth to this segment here: my word, you have an eye, Mr Singer!'

I moved closer, I even put a hand on his arm while I pointed to a cowlick done on the horse's large globular bottom: and somehow my proximity to Mr Reynolds, and our close attention to the cowlick, caused Norah to fall somewhat behind us, where she remained. I saw her out of the corner of my eye clasping her hands as if praying, and fiddling with her collar as if it was tormenting her, and I heard her begin a sentence once or twice, but it was easy to obscure Norah's ladylike voice in the folds of a resonant comment of my own, and she did not persist.

In due course, Mr Reynolds proved a labourer worthy of his hire.

'Why, Albion,' Norah was flushed and flustered, 'you will never guess, Albion, just look, we are in the paper. James, Mr Reynolds I mean, has written such an excellent piece about your collection!' She held out the paper, already crumpled from her excited reading, and pointed at the article. I did not make undignified haste, but tweaked my trousers and sat carefully, and waited until Norah had poured me a cup of tea before shaking the pages back into alignment and then, finally, reading. There was a lot of fine meaningless wallpaper about the collection, and much flowery enthusiasm, and plenty of praise for the discerning eye of Mr Singer, who had spotted genius where others had not: Reynolds had earned his crust, as far as I was concerned.

The first dividend from my investment in Art was that I was again master in my own drawing room. There were no more polite silences when Mr Singer came in: no, Norah's little spaniels fell over themselves now, positively jostling to be the one to hand me my tea and sit next to me on the sofa. Their little voices grew shrill, outdoing each other in admiration of my taste: offers to do my portrait, or an oil of the house and garden, abounded: and would I care to come to their studio next week, so that I could admire their drypoints? Reynolds had not actually seen any cash, but lived in hope, and had taken to sketching my profile as I sat sipping my tea, and presenting me with them, just as the reps from Farquarsons and O'Brien's would press a few sample sock-suspenders or monogrammed handkerchiefs on me as they left: *Just for yourself, Mr Singer,* they would cry, *And no obligation whatever.*

Norah was still there, naturally: still there, sitting in her best silk from Mark Foy's, with her little finger crooked, and the bracelets tinkling along her arm as she poured, handing the sandwiches and making a to-do about mustard. But no-one remarked the charmingness of the tinkling bracelets, or the gracefulness of the hand holding the cup and saucer: there were no more odes to her eyes, and there was no more talk of portraits. Before our eyes her glow faded: it could be seen that even Norah's glow had not really belonged to her, being only the result of the blaze of flattery applied by Reynolds and his friends.

She had no choice now but to play the part of the proud wife, whose husband was a man of such fine feelings, and had been proved to have an open wallet where Art was concerned: and that was not such a bad role. Was it any fault of his that the young men now preferred to speak to the husband rather than the wife? Could it be the fault of her husband that she had now become nothing more than the dispenser of the tea and the ham sandwiches?

No, Norah had been, as always, wrong about nearly everything, but she had been right in one particular: she was right in thinking that the joys of Art were indeed infinite, and its uses manifold.

CAROLYN QUADRIO
AND LISA QUADRIO

Sta Thika Sou (And Here's to Yours)

Three Generations of Greek Brides in Western Australia 1900–1965

FORMAT: two acts: two monologues
ACT 1: Mother's monologue
ACT 2: Daughter's monologue

Set: Dark and dusty storeroom filled with boxes, trunks and an old full-length mirror.

ACT 1: Mother and daughter are centre stage opening boxes; mother settles down beside an orange picnic hamper, she begins sorting through photos. The daughter peers over her mother's shoulder, shakes her head with amusement, laughs softly – fade out smiling daughter. Spotlight mother, she commences her monologue with close-ups of the photographs. Closing scene: fade in daughter, laughing.

ACT 2: Spotlight the smiling daughter, she is returning the photos to the hamper, then she becomes serious and commences her monologue, fade out mother.

PREAMBLE:

'*Ke sta thika sou*' literally means: 'And here's to yours.' Implicitly, the reference is to 'your wedding', the word wedding is understood. Greek people employ this expression as a form of salutation in everyday life. It is addressed to a young girl from her early childhood and throughout her single life and a similar expression is used when addressing the parents or grandparents of a girl, literally meaning: 'Here's to your daughter's/grand daughter's.' Again, the word wedding is understood. This expression reflects the fact that marriage is highly prized and is regarded as the inevitable and major developmental milestone for a girl and for her family. The wish is expressed as a form of greeting, as a form of farewell, or it is expressed ritualistically at weddings and at all festive occasions.

ACT 1: Mother and daughter are centre stage opening boxes;

Looking through the various boxes and cases which are stored in our garage/storeroom, I am searching for travelling gear for my daughter, Lisa, who is about to embark on her first trip to Europe. I come across the large orange plastic picnic hamper which holds a collection of old family photographs. Finding them irresistible, as I always do, I open the hamper and begin to browse. Lisa peers over my shoulder, grinning, anticipating my 'oohs' and 'aahs' and 'look at Nanna when she was little!' We have been through this ritual many times before, but years slip by and then suddenly we will rediscover the photos and Lisa is always growing and changing and seeing them through different eyes so that for me too, each time is a different moment.

The box is filled with studio portraits, they are old and musty, some are torn and crumbling. Most of the photographs are of weddings – the era is early twentieth century, long before the advent of proficient personal photographic equipment, the days when a woman's first recorded appearance was usually in a long white christening frock. There might be no other record of her until her next public presentation – in her long white wedding gown. Sometimes that was it, the sum of a woman's life. Occasionally there was more detail – she might be pictured with her newborn on her lap or, later, she might appear as mother-of-the-bride in portraits of her own daughter's wedding.

Weddings and babies! These were the purpose of every woman's life. The details were continuously revised and updated in the various forms of unofficial oral history groups such as my mother's regular Saturday covens. She and three or four of her cronies met every week and sat outside on the front verandah of our small rented semi. As they talked, they watched and greeted passers-by, all of whom were known to us and were part of the inner city neighbourhood which was populated entirely by our kind – 'dings', 'dagos', 'yids'. The entire Greek and Italian community lived there, as well as Jewish families, a few Chinese, and some poorer Australian families.

Sitting and chatting on the verandah, Mother and her friends drank small thick black coffees (*kafethakia*), they 'read' each other's cups, they exchanged information, and they reviewed histories. The conversations followed a set form with which I was very familiar.

'The girl Panopolous' (they were all 'girls', regardless of age), 'who did she marry?' Immediately would come the reply, 'The Manolis boy.'

'Oh, the first boy, the one with the fish shop in town?'

'No, no, the youngest boy, the one who works in his father's shop. The eldest boy married Sophie's sister.'

'Oh yes, poor Sophie. She's had terrible problems carrying.'

'Yes, poor girl, one miscarriage after another. But she doesn't get a chance, day and night in the shop, poor thing. He's a mongrel you know, her husband, gambling every night, she's always by herself in the shop.'

'They're a bad lot that family. I don't know how Loula

agreed to that match. She knew what the boy's family was like. His grandfather was the same, old man Kitsoulis, he was a bad man that one.'

Knowing sighs, the clink of coffee cups, the click of knitting needles, the silent motion of a crochet hook through endless multi-coloured squares of left-over wool, creating those ubiquitous rugs which were tossed over ageing laps or which protected pristine sofas in rarely used *salonia*, or sitting rooms. We sat around kitchen tables or on verandahs or in gardens to talk in those days. There were no family rooms in our small houses – the sitting rooms, or *salonia*, were used only for very formal occasions. They would remain dark and clean and empty, crisp white doilies and lacy antimacassars adorning the tables and sofas, respectively.

The chequered rugs and the doilies were regular artefacts in all Mediterranean homes. Every young Greek girl learnt to crochet and to embroider and to tat, it was her preparation for becoming a *nifi*, a bride. From the time a Greek girl reached puberty she was regarded by her parents as a *nifi*, she was preparing for her life's work as wife and mother. This would begin as soon as she was ready and as soon as a match could be made – and the sooner the better, brides were all too vulnerable and best disposed of whilst unsullied. Grandmother had begun my *nifi* training as soon as I was old enough to hold a needle. I would sit at her feet and she would watch over my first stitches, chattering, encouraging, correcting . . . Grandmother!

I look for the photos of her – there are only a few and they cover a brief thirty years or so. The first is as a 17-year-old bride beside my 47-year-old grandfather. The photo is so old and of such poor quality that the detail is obscured. It is 1915.

Grandmother's wedding, 1915

These are the first images of grandmother Chrissie. Did she exist before that? She is a plain, plump young woman, her dress is even plainer. No finery for this poor young girl from the Greek islands. She has nothing to bring to the marriage except youth, fertility, strength, hope, her considerable skills as a seamstress and the standard (and extensive) linen collection. Other than this she has no *prika* or dowry of value to fortify her widowed mother's bargaining position. The best that she can do on the marriage market is to be chosen by a middle-aged widower with a young motherless brood. But there is passage to Australia, the land of opportunity, so the match seems to offer hope for her future. Indeed the next image of her is quite clear, it is a studio portrait, taken soon after arrival in Australia. Better dressed now, she stands besides her much older, seated husband, a hand on his shoulder in almost deferential pose.

Post-wedding portrait, 1916

Perhaps this portrait was sent back home to reassure grandmother's widowed mother, Akrivi, that the match had been a good one, that her daughter was now well provided for. It would have been with this hope that Akrivi had agreed to the match, surrendering her daughter that she might find a better life in that faraway land where, it was said, there were great riches. Indeed grandfather's small fruit shop was in the goldfields of Western Australia. What fantasies the word 'gold' would have conjured up for those poor Greek folk! How many Mediterraneans had already been lured to Australia after hearing stories of gold nuggets lying on the ground – just waiting to be found! How different the reality of Chrissie's life would be. She would wear a gold wedding ring of course, and acquire a small collection of other gold jewellery – earrings, chains, a bracelet or two – there would be little more. Gold is highly prized by Greek folk even now and must have seemed, back then, to be the ultimate possession.

Great-grandmother Akrivi was to send both her children, her two daughters, Chrissie and Kiriakoula, to husbands in Australia. Koula (Kiriakoula) followed Chrissie some four years later, once a betrothal had been arranged. Another middle-aged groom, Yianni had no previous marriage or children, and he owned a small fish and chip shop. Koula's wedding was a little finer than Chrissie's had been, her elder sister was already established in Australia and Chrissie was able to make the wedding arrangements and the gowns. The portrait of an unsmiling Koula shows her standing beside her groom who, as was usual then, is seated, just as grandfather is in the previous portrait.

Kiriakoula's wedding

If these depictions were intended to convey the sense of a handmaiden standing beside her master, then in Koula's case they were certainly appropriate. Marriage to her middle-aged husband was followed by a life of servitude. I wonder if any word of her misery was ever relayed home? Certainly Koula herself would never have spoken of it, proudly she would never have indicated that her lot was other than that which her mother had intended for her. *Theia* (aunty) Koula acquired a great reputation as a scavenger and hoarder. Whatever she could beg or appropriate or put aside, usually without her husband's knowledge, she would send 'home', to Greece. Usually these were parcels of clothing, hand-me-downs, probably there was money too, but she would have been very careful not to let this be known .

Alone and with no other kin, great-grandmother Akrivi must have grieved terribly for her daughters. She would never see them again. She remained on the barren island of Thaki, eking out a pitiful living making crocheted bedspreads, until her eyes failed her and she died at the age of 84.

Akrivi had been a *nifi* herself only long enough to bear her two children. At the age of 16 she was married to a local lad and three years later he had died of a fever. With two small daughters to provide for, and possessed of neither wealth nor beauty, Akrivi had no prospects of remarriage, nor of economic support. There is one tiny faded snapshot of her, it is hard to tell when it was taken – these women look old all of their lives.

Great-grandmother Akrivi, in Thaki

The background shows glimpses of the island, it is dry and barren. Great-grandmother Akrivi is tall and she looks strong, she is dressed neck to ankle in black. Greek widows wore black throughout their lives, marking their identity as non-wives, but signalling that they were not entirely without social identity, to the extent that they remained attached to a man, albeit a dead one.

It is a cultural given and was so especially in the past that Greek widows did not complete the work of mourning in the sense that Anglo women do. The Greek widow was not expected to surrender her attachment to her dead husband, except in the case of an especially rich or particularly beautiful widow who might be eligible for remarriage. Otherwise, widowed women had been in the possession of another man and were of no value on the marriage market. The absolute necessity for virginal brides in Greek culture gave rise to a particular para-medical profession which, for a price, would re-create virginity by sewing together a non-intact hymen beore the wedding ceremony. (Not only is it a wise man who knows his own child – it is a wise Greek man who recognises his bride's virginity!)

For a Greek girl, survival meant marriage and marriage was dependent upon both virginity and a dowry. Only those with exceptional beauty or important family connections could manage without a dowry. Survival outside of marriage was not possible except for a wealthy daughter (and women had no inheritance rights). The deflowered unmarried woman (if her condition became publicly known) would face almost impossible prospects – she might be wed to an elderly man with little money, or a sick or deformed or alcoholic man, or an impoverished widower with several children to raise. Female children in poor families constituted serious economic liabilities. Sometimes brides such as these were sent out from Greece, *logo* (the word or promise of marriage) having been given between families without the couple ever having met. Photos would have been exchanged but the prospective groom might have sent a photo which had been taken ten or twenty years earlier. A teenage girl might then be shipped out and arrive to find herself betrothed to a man of 40 or 50. These marriages were often the outcome for girls from particularly poor backgrounds, for those whose reputations back home had been compromised in some way, perhaps by some scandal in the family, or the hint of 'bad blood', that is, bad heredity of some sort. Greek people were very wary of mental or serious illness or bad behaviour of any sort, which was usually regarded as due to 'bad blood' and these families would have to trade their daughters off as best they could. Worse still, of course, was the hint of lack of purity in the girl herself.

The Greek widow wore black for the rest of her life but a compensation for this was a certain rise in social status, although poverty was also usual. Because of the incomplete work of mourning, the dead husband was much idealised and this idealised image was a potent force in the household. I well remember *theia* Koula's response to her husband's death. He had been a particularly tyrannical man, and had maintained her in a state of semi-slavery; she began work at six in the morning and finished at midnight. I spent many school holidays peeling and chipping the daily supply of potatoes which we kept in cleaned kerosene cans filled with water. After her husband's death, Koula donned her black and devoted herself to his memory. Every night, before retiring to bed, she would go through a ritual of kissing his every photo – and there were numerous portraits of the old man adorning every mantelpiece and side table. Remembering well the misery of her married life, I marvelled at this display. It was then that I first began to suspect that Greek widows might be motivated to maintain an idealisation of their dead spouses as an unconscious expression of gratitude that they had departed this life.

Greek immigrants maintained these attitudes in the new country and the welfare system in Australia strongly reinforced their social mores. Only widowed women were entitled to social security benefits. If a woman was without a husband (as my mother was to find herself eventually), she might receive some government assistance if she could be classified as a 'deserted wife', with the implication that she was the victim of her husband's fecklessness. There was always a subtler implication in this term, the possibility that she was somehow deserving of this fate. The category 'single mother' did not exist, being at that time a contradiction in terms. Greek families were supportive of their extended kin, but culturally also the category of 'single mother' did not exist, so neither emotional nor material support would be available for such a woman. Education was not considered appropriate for Greek girls, employment opportunities were limited and, in Australia, wages for women were much lower than for men.

In Greece the economic reality for women without men was hopeless and great-grandmother Akrivi, widowed so young and with no sons or brothers to help her, had quite a struggle to raise her girls. Possessed of neither beauty nor assets, she was to spend a poor and lonely life in an isolated corner of a culture which had no use for her. Her mother in turn, my great-great-grandmother Ariadne, had also known sadness and hardship. Ariadne gave birth to twelve children over her lifetime. Eight of them died, four in one week during a diphtheria epidemic which swept the island in the 1850s. Her surviving children were all female, a considerable liability for a poor family, living on a very poor island.

Married and widowed in short succession, great-grandmother Akrivi managed not only to raise her two girls, Koula and Chrissie, but to train them both as skilled seamstresses. Then, when she was 17, grandmother Chrissie (Chrisoula) was married to my widowed grandfather, who was then aged 47. A poor girl, with no dowry, Chrissie was fortunate to be chosen by my grandfather, an ex-patriate Thakian who had established a small business, a fruit shop, in Western Australia. Grandfather's first wife had died giving birth to their third daughter some seven years earlier. Since then, the children had been in the care of the dead woman's sister.

There is a small snapshot of the three young girls who became grandmother's step-children. Ariane, Nina and Ireni are aged 7, 8, and 9, respectively. They are sad little girls, their faces are striking – intense dark eyes, full sad mouths. They've already lost two mothers. After their original mother, grandfather's first wife, died giving birth to Ireni, her sister took over their care until grandfather could arrange his second marriage in Greece and return to Australia with a strong young girl to care for his three daughters. Thus their young aunty had become their new mother until, abruptly, they were removed from her care, although she was the only mother they had known, and were given into the care of their new teenaged stepmother. Poor Chrissie, she was probably most unwelcome to her three young charges and, within five years, she was widowed and had the three teenage step-daughters to care for and two children of her own. Grandmother Chrissie was 23 and my mother, Vickie, was three years old when grandfather died of a stroke. Mother remembers it, he was playing with her on the bed when he suddenly fell to the floor and lay still.

Fortunately, grandmother Chrissie was very skilled at her trade and was able to support herself and her children. My mother, Vickie, was able to stay at school until she was 14 and then she went to business college. This was not only a generous education for the daughter of a widowed migrant during the Depression years, it was for a poor Greek girl, even inappropriate. Both grandmother and mother were always regarded as having rather uppity or deviant values. Mother would pay dearly for this 'deviance'.

As soon as they reached 16 years, the two older girls were hastily married off to Greek men. Being blessed with beauty, they were matched with men who, though middle-aged, were well situated financially. These middle-aged men did not live long, so the sisters were, in turn, widowed at an early age and then left penniless after their estates were 'handled' for them by the male kin of their dead husbands. Widows were pretty much fair game.

The second photo of grandmother is taken only a year after her marriage. It is 1917. Grandmother is plumper still and standing beside grandfather who is proudly holding their infant son.

Spiro's christening, 1917

More elegantly dressed now, it is evident that her status has risen. After all she has performed an important duty, providing grandfather with his first male child, Spiro. The infant boy is wearing an elaborate white frock, much finer than his mother's wedding gown had been. His entry into the world of social identity had been celebrated more extravagantly than had his mother's. The next child, my mother, Vickie, is born two years after Spiro. There is no comparable photo of proud mother and (female) infant.

The next photographic study of grandmother is taken in the 1920s – documenting her next social transition – to that of widow.

Grandmother as a young widow

Aged in her late twenties she is now elegantly dressed in black. She had been a *nifi* for only five years and perhaps she was still hopeful of attracting a younger, more viable partner than grandfather had been, one who might care for her and the five children. But grandmother did not become a bride again, instead there were arranged marriages for the teenage girls.

The first of these weddings is that of the eldest girl, Ariane.

Vickie as flower girl, aged 3

Ariane as a bride, 1922

I pick up the wedding portraits, carefully lifting the fine protective paper. It is 1922 and Ariane, aged 16 and the eldest of the three girls, is a statuesque young bride in an elegant white gown. Her two sisters are bridesmaids. Sitting on either side of her, their dresses too are simple and elegant, their faces serious. All three are tall and in full bloom. Mother, aged 3, is sitting on a chair, legs crossed, ringlets tumbling, her expression strangely solemn. The groom is a good deal older than his bride. There is no father-of-the-bride, only three months have elapsed since grandfather's death. It is for this reason that the bridesmaids are wearing black stockings and that both the bride and the little flower girl have black ribbons trimming their dresses. Ordinarily, Greek weddings are not allowed within a year of a family death, but Ariane's groom is returning to Greece and the opportunity for marriage cannot be postponed. The next wedding portraits are taken only a year later.

Vickie, seated, bride's far left

Nina's wedding, Vickie on bride's left

It is 1923 and Nina, the middle girl, aged 16, is a beautiful dark-eyed bride in a full white gown. Mother, aged 4, is taller but no less solemn than in the previous portrait. She is holding a large basket of flowers, her expression is moody, sullen, too worldly, hinting already of the abandonment and abuse which will mark her life. The groom is another middle-aged man.

Several years later, the third sister, Ireni, is wed. It is a simple ceremony, there are no guests, no wedding breakfast, and only one portrait. Ireni defied tradition and insisted on marrying a man of her choice. It would be nice to report that hers was a happier outcome – but that was not to be.

Ireni's wedding, late 1920s

There are a series of weddings now, mostly documenting mother's girlhood and her regular appearances, first as flower-girl and then as bridesmaid.

Always a bridesmaid . . . Vickie on bride's left

Bridesmaid again, Vickie on bride's left

Vickie, aged 18, seated far left of bride

Always a bridesmaid, never a bride. Poor mother. Is that why her face is sad, her eyes unfocussed? Slim with very dark wavy hair, she wears with grace and poise the clothes which were so beautifully created by grandmother, clothes which were testimony to her remarkable skill as a seamstress.

Chrissie will dress many brides but her own daughter, Vickie, will not be one of them. As gowns were continuously cut and fitted, an endless procession of young brides passed through our little house, to the swishing of white satin and the whirr of the machine, the ceaseless chatter, screams and giggles, the fearful 'oohs' and 'aahs', the passing on of wisdom and the maintaining also of a conspiracy of silence amongst women who never spoke to their daughters of pain and servitude. Our little household revolved around the large central dining room which was grandmother's workroom. Along the length of the room ran an enormous timber table on which she did her cutting. The inevitable Singer pedal machine stood under the window in order to catch the light. I learnt my first words (in Greek) and sewed my first stitches here, at grandmother's feet. I wish I could recall the details of the chatter and the stories and the fears and the confessions which filled that room. How many young Greek girls stood there, filled with excitement, with dread and anticipation, preparing for weddings which were meant to mark great beginnings but which sometimes represented symbolic endings of their lives and their dreams. The dreams would be of homes and families of their own, homes where they might be mistress, where they might experience some freedom, released from the years of chaperoning, the constant vigilance which had been required to protect their major personal asset, their virginity. For some, marriage would become an indenture, servicing husbands and children, and capitulating frequently to demanding mothers-in-law. A strange tyranny of women by women was maintained in this way. Women who had spent a lifetime being controlled and oppressed, first by their families, then by their husbands, were complicit in perpetuating the system, first by idealising their male children and by reinforcing to their daughters that female value was determined entirely by the marriage market and, finally, when their sons married, by tyrannising their daughters-in-law. Divided from each other in this way through service to their men, these Greek women could never free themselves, the slave mentality remained too deeply internalised. The perception of female inferiority and male superiority was not only unquestioned, it was propagated by women. I still remember, as a 20-year-old, in my aunty's house, being instructed to give up my seat to a young male visitor. We Greek girls were taught our place and our value.

The moment when a Greek girl's worth was publicly pronounced was at her betrothal. Whether she married well, whether she was sought after, how much was paid or exchanged between families, these details were avidly exchanged within the oral history groups. Gifts of gold were mandatory. Plain brides or those without important family connections were required to give more. The details were confirmed at the *krevati* (literally, 'the bed', the ceremonial making of the bridal bed) when all was displayed, including the *prika*, the girl's trousseau. This was usually an entire wardrobe and a lifetime supply of manchester and napery and more or less jewellery, according to the financial circumstances of the bride's family.

The *krevati* was ceremonially made, with ritual and song. Five sugared almonds would be thrown onto the bed – these were to represent or invoke fertility. Strange songs were sung by the older women, many of them in widow's weeds. Sad songs, they were, and always brought the mother of the bride to tears, to be followed quickly by the bride herself and then the bridesmaids. It was often as much a dirge as a celebration. Unwilling to tell the truth about the reality of their lives, the older women would weep and exchange sighs whilst the girls twittered about examining beautiful garments. There was no sex education, no mention of the pain of childbirth, the conspiracy was maintained by silence, each girl would have to discover for herself what would become of her dream of marriage. She would be princess for a day as, literally, she and her groom were crowned by the priest with a wreath of blossoms (the *stefania*) during the Greek orthodox wedding ceremony.

Grandmother made not only the wedding gowns, but entire trousseaux, part of the *prika*, for countless brides. These would include the matrimonial nightgown, an assortment of dresses, underwear, even maternity clothes, well in advance of those great events. She stitched and counselled, preparing girls as young as 15 for what lay before them. Most left school at 13, which was then the legal age for school leavers. Even the boys of this generation were taken as soon as possible from school, generally to work in fruit shops, in fish and chip shops, in market gardens, and on fishing boats, helping the family to build up assets. It would be the next generation of boys who would be educated, their fathers having worked hard to accumulate money. Education for girls would be considered unnecessary until another generation again had passed. For most it would be a life much like grandmother's. At 25 she was already a poor widow with no extended family, no income other than that earned by her nimble fingers.

There are no more portraits of grandmother until my birth, in 1943. Grandmother is 47 years old, buxom, matronly, her hair quite white. I turn to study my own reflection in the dusty full-size mirror. My features are so much like hers, yet at 50 I look considerably younger than she did then. I am now the age she was when her life ended. Looking back at the portrait, I can see that her face is both lined with pain yet smiling with pleasure too as she holds me up to the camera. This is to be her last transition, from widow to grandmother. In 1947 she died from uterine cancer.

There is a missing chapter here. How did I arrive without the obligatory wedding? There is no portrait of mother's great day. Each of her sisters is here – Nina is even twice a bride. Widowed six years after her first wedding, she is soon poor after her estate is 'handled' for her by male kin of her former husband. She has two little girls aged 3 and 4, the elder is Angela and the younger is Grandmother's namesake, Chrisoula. Nina is a great beauty so, in spite of her previous marriage, her poverty, and her having two young daughters, she is sought after and is able to secure a second Greek husband. As a bride the second time she is even more beautiful than the first.

Nina's second wedding,
Vickie standing, 1938

Grandmother has excelled herself with this dress of silky white pleats, it is matched with white satin court shoes and a white silk hat which hugs Nina's head and dips deeply over one eye. Those dark damp eyes, rivers of tears will fall from them as they look out over Nina's sorrowful life. There are no portraits to commemorate the funerals, but I remember them vividly – the lamenting, the black dresses, the smell of *buxomathia* (dry biscuits which were baked to serve at the wake), the little liqueur glasses of *krasi* or brandy. There are no portraits of these events, of the deaths of Nina's two mothers, her first husband, her two young daughters, her first son-in-law. We mark their passing only by the increasing sadness of Nina's eyes – portraits reveal only the sudden absences of certain faces, the transition of others into black garments.

Mother is a bridesmaid yet again at Nina's second wedding. Slim and dark-haired, she too is dressed elegantly, her large silky white hat also dipping down over one eye. Sad, like Nina.

There is another portrait, the two little girls of Nina's first marriage. They are quite as beautiful as their mother. Angela was only 20 when she died of scarlet fever. She was buried in a bridal gown made by grandmother for the occasion, one of the last that she was to make. Death was not to rob them of that moment, Angela would be *nifi* for a day. Grandmother died the following year, perhaps better for her not to bear the unbearable when her little namesake, Chrisoula, died too only five years later. Grandmother was not there to make the wedding gown but Chrisoula did have her great day and I am there too, in the portrait, a wide-eyed flower girl, in layers of cherry red tulle. Chrisoula succumbed to illness more slowly and painfully than had her sister, but not before she had to bear the loss of her young husband in an accident. Strange it is to have so much recorded of the weddings and nothing of the funerals.

For Vickie, perennial bridesmaid, there was no bridal gown. How often I would wonder about that and would be given the explanation: 'It was the war.' In the 1940s and 1950s, those words explained many things. It was understandable that there might have been no possibility of wedding ceremonies during those difficult times. 'We were married in a registry office,' mother told me. 'A black velvet dress,' was her whimsical answer to the inevitable question. What became of him? 'It was the war.' This was the explanation in those days for all of life's many mysteries.

It is 1948, I am 5 years old and already appearing in the portraits as a flower girl in a beautiful white satin dress and a large white net hat. We are two flower girls, four bridesmaids, plus four groomsmen. This is a rather new development, the matching set of bridesmaids and groomsmen, earlier weddings had been very much a day for women only.

Carolyn as flower girl, far left of bride, 1948

Grandmother is no longer here, she was never to make one of these gowns for me as I began my rehearsals in this traditional way, first as flower girl, then as bridesmaid. So we prepared ourselves for the great moment, dreaming of our great day, the transition from pre-nuptial seclusion to post-nuptial bliss. We could only hope that our dreams would be realised, that we would be princesses for more than a day.

The weddings come and go, as I progress from flower girl to bridesmaid. Mother's three sisters have twelve children so there are many celebrations as my various cousins marry and have children in turn. I remember the negotiating which preceded so many of these marriages as they were arranged by the families. A fascinating process took place which involved a writing and rewriting of history. The process unfolded in a particular way. There would be preliminary whispers, nods and smiles, then invitations from one family to another to afternoon tea. The respective mothers would examine each other as unobtrusively as possible, the fathers would sit in the back garden drinking small, thick Turkish coffee, small *krasi* (brandy) and eating *kourabiedes* (small shortbreads, covered with icing sugar which were standard fare at social gatherings). The fathers tried to assess and impress each other, the shy, tremulous would-be-bride serving them as graciously as possible, painfully aware that she was being scrutinised. Friends and aunts and cousins would be consulted and extensive data would be collected and analysed. Finally, a handshake between the fathers and the young couple would be allowed to spend some time together – not too much time, and not too far out of sight. The proclamation would be made to friends and family and *logo* (the word or promise) would be given, an official consent and announcement of the nuptials. A date for the *arovouna* would be set (the engagement or betrothal, a ceremony which is officiated by a priest). A series of celebrations would follow and, within weeks, as the couple were observed to smile at each other and to hold hands, the observers announced with pride: 'It's a love match!'

I was always amazed to witness these transformations of narrative. Suddenly all would be convinced that the couple had actually chosen each other, that it was 'true' love! I heard many of those same narratives revised once more when, some years later, trouble and strife were reported and heads were nodded ruefully: 'A bad match.' Too late those reviews. There was no going back, no other course but marriage and children, no economic or social survival for a woman without a husband.

Now there is a series of portraits of me, alone, during my growing-up years. Mother is camera-shy and there is no one else in our little family of two. My final appearance as a bridesmaid is when I am aged 18, and attending a cousin's wedding. It is an arranged wedding of course but this bride, Sofia, was brought to Australia by her older sister some years before and she had had some time to acculturate and to establish a life of her own, albeit in her sister's house. The elder sister had been shipped out in the 1950s and was married immediately to a man whom she clearly detested. A poor, plain woman with questionable family background, she had been betrothed to a man whose (largely unsuccessful) gambling habits were well known. Sofia's wedding seems destined to repeat the pattern of the earlier one. The bride is fearful, reluctant, the groom bemused, embarrassed. 'It will be all right', relatives assure them. But it won't be. I'm puzzled. Why does she resist? Surely she wants to be a bride? Yet I sense that she should not be forced. It is 1961 now. Economic survival for a single woman is no longer impossible. There are jobs, there are opportunities, there is even social security. Sofia can contemplate a life without marriage, without children. She seems to have no interest in men or in marriage. She enjoys her job, earns a little money, invests it wisely, enjoys her female friends. She does not welcome a life of subservience to this man. He's a nice man, but a ne'er-do-well. In his thirties, he has no steady job, no assets, his gambling habits too are well known. She would be expected to wash and to cook and clean and to accept his comings and goings, his late nights, his erratic earnings. She would be expected to meet his sexual needs, to bear him children and hope to survive economically without a steady income from him. No, plainly she would prefer not. But she proceeds with the ceremony anyway. She is bride for a day. Soon Sofia is the first woman in our family to choose divorce. For the elder sister, married in a similar arrangement a decade earlier, that choice had not been possible. Instead, she had endured a lifetime of misery and regret until her death – but my cousin paid dearly as she wreaked what revenge she could in carping and complaining and in sexual withdrawal.

My day arrives! Here I am wrapped in white lace, in a traditional pose, holding forth my white bouquet for the world to see.

Carolyn as a bride, 1965

The message is evident – the white blossoms and I fussily protesting our purity. My little flower girls are wreathed in blossoms too. I turn from the photos to an old trunk, and search for the dress. Here it is, yellowed but still pretty. I stand in front of the dusty mirror and hold it up in front of me. Was I ever that thin! I did it all – the *arovouna*, the *krevati*, the *bombonieras*. Perhaps more than I needed to, perhaps I tried to give my mother the wedding she never had. We are respectable now, mother. We are married.

Now there is another series of wedding portraits – those of my children's generation. These arrangements are different. The days of chaperoning are gone, mostly this generation choose their own partners – although there is still the occasional matchmaking. No one ever talks about it out loud of course, but the question of guaranteed bridal virginity is no longer an issue, the sexual habits of this generation are not much different now from those of their Anglo – Australian peers. Some are divorced and remarried – and at least one couple are *both* previously married. Divorce was a word only whispered in my childhood – 'She's a divorcee' mother's friends would murmur to each other – 'scarlet woman' was a rough interpretation. Only *Englesi* (Anglo – Australians) divorced, Greek people never did, although there was a fairly well-known form of divorce, Mediterranean style, which native Greek (and Italian) men sometimes initiated. It was achieved by emigrating to Australia to find work with the intention of later 'sending for' the wife and children. The man would then simply disappear and bigamously remarry in Australia.

Here is another portrait of a more recent marriage and I remember that the union lasted only three years – and soon after I was buying another wedding gift for the same nephew. I resolved not to spend so much money on wedding gifts for this lot – they don't last! There are now regular 'mixed marriages' (as we used to call them), an Anglo – Australian bride or groom – *Englesi*! (Anglos) – this had once been our equivalent of 'wog'. How ridiculous now seem the family feuds which once took place because someone dared to marry 'out'. To marry 'out' once meant no more than marrying from a different part of the country, or even a different island – let alone a different ethnic group! My own marriage to an Italian would not have been acceptable except for my being such a poor prospect on the marriage market. I had no father, no money, no beauty, no dowry – worst of all – I was educated! This latter actually constituted something of a handicap. An educated girl was deviant, she could hardly marry 'up' since there were too few men of that generation with similar aspirations, and those who did have them were such precious marriage prospects themselves that they could have their pick of the *nifis*, the prettiest and the wealthiest. I certainly did not qualify for that type of marriage. So marrying 'out' as I did was acceptable because it was unlikely that anything else could be arranged for me. Besides I had done my own choosing! (Which of course was only proof of the suspicion that education for girls of my generation would be subversive.)

These stories always bring peals of laughter from my daughter. Her generation are not all that fussed about ethnic or religious requirements, and some are inclined to skip the church altogether. 'De facto', once a rather smutty description, is now more a technical legal term. Lisa's generation don't use the term at all, they prefer the appellation, 'partner'.

I'm confronted now by my own conservatism as my 25-year-old daughter prepares for overseas travel with her 'young man' (I've given up trying to learn whatever is the currently acceptable description). I wonder about the relatives abroad. What will they think? 'Have you thought about it?' I ask her – 'Mother!' She is highly amused (how dare she be amused!), I'm confused. I'm glad that she feels so sure of herself, so indifferent to external judgment. But if it can all be tossed aside so readily, it seems to make a mockery of the struggle and privation which preceded her: the constant chaperoning, the fear of 'talk', anything which might invoke the dreaded '*ntropi*' (shame), the obligatory and arranged marriages, the shame of no marriage, the pain and poverty and the stigma of single motherhood.

Ironically, I regard our lives, mine, those of my mother and foremothers, and that of my daughter who bears our legacy. For great-grandmother, life was blighted by the early loss of a husband/provider, a struggle to raise her daughters and then the unspeakable sadness of parting with them forever. For my grandmother an early marriage to a man thirty years her senior, a stranger who took her from family and culture and soon left her widowed with daughters to be disposed of as best she could. For my mother, a life equally constrained without the haven/prison of marriage and first the struggle but later the solace of keeping a daughter. For me, an enduring and secure marriage, undoubtedly sustained by the vision of those solitary survivors who had preceded me. Marriage has sheltered me from a repetition of their sorrows. I have had my own struggle – and a very different one – that of integrating conflicting and confusing roles, seeking some peaceful coexistence of three separate identities – wife, mother and careerist.

I know that Lisa does not understand this, she stands outside this fractured identity. She asks, 'What's the problem?' There is no dilemma for her – career, partnership, these are not mutually exclusive roles, they are well-integrated aspects of her being. And maternity? That will find its place for her too. There was no integrated identity that I could internalise, there was no role for women of my generation comparable to that of 'breadwinner' for a male. That single description so comfortably subsumes the three roles of worker, father and husband. There is no struggle of three men inside one. For my daughter, hopefully, there will be such integration. She doesn't aspire to be a *nifi* in the traditional sense, but I do believe that she will be a more complete woman.

Fade in daughter, smiling with amusement as she helps return the photos to the hamper. Fade out mother, spotlight daughter.

ACT 2: Lisa is alone, she is putting the photos back into the hamper, and begins her monologue.

I remember this orange hamper and the old photos as well. We had two huge picnic hampers in our old house, one green and one orange. *Yiayia* (Nanna) grew up in a poor family and never fully adjusted to a more affluent life style. I think that is why she bought two of everything, just in case one day the money ran out or the Depression came again. Nanna brought home crystal chandeliers, gilt-edged mirrors, our first colour television set and a fan-forced oven. She really enjoyed extravagance.

Greek grandmothers love to spoil their grandchildren, especially the boys, and our Nanna was maniacally determined not to be outdone in the grandmothering stakes. Thursday was her pay day and also late night shopping, so she would go into Perth to look for presents. There were Barbie dolls, Barbie's swimming pool and camper van for me, Fisher Price towns, airports and aeroplanes for both of us and fire trucks, soldiers and Meccano for my brother. She bought chocolates shaped like pencils, cars and farm animals. When Nanna was late home from work on Thursday we would anxiously wait for her to bring in her parcels.

As children we thought that all grandmothers were exactly like ours, and it never occurred to us that Nanna would ever want to spend money on things for herself. We thought it was only natural that she spent all of her money on things for the house and for her grandchildren. Not that it was much of an investment, we sold the house and both myself and my brother moved interstate. We rarely see her these days.

Sometime in my teenage years I developed a strange compulsion for tidiness and organisation. I started to clean my own room and neatly fold my own clothes, jobs which my Nanna or mother had done for me until then. My tendency to rearrange spices in our spice rack in alphabetical order, and books on the shelf from biggest to smallest was always attributed to no more than a personal quirk. But I think that I was developing the obsessional qualities of a good *nifi*.

Being a fanatical organiser earned me the job of taking care of the family history, and I became custodian of our photos. I loved the old black and white ones of my Nanna and her Greek family. It made me feel as though I was part of a culture which made me more interesting. These pictures hardly ever made me feel depressed, although they would make Mum and Nanna sad. Nanna would sit at the kitchen table with a cup of black tea, and me with a cup of white tea and we would go through the old photos, like two old women. Nanna would tell me who the people were and how they were related, and usually how they died and how many children they had. Most of the women had very bleak lives and often they died very young, they were treated like commodities to be bartered between fathers and husbands. Nanna and I would sigh and shake our heads.

These stories were of terribly hard times, but secretly I thought that they were a little romantic. I regretted that I would never be remembered as having the courage and the strength that these women possessed. They were powerful figures in my life, these stern, grim-looking ancestors, some in large portraits hung in heavy, dark, wooden frames. The strong, serious faces of these women made me think that they were all angry or irritable at the photographer, that perhaps they had been called away from doing some important work to sit in these contrived positions to have their portraits taken. Some of them looked defiantly at the camera – particularly Nanna – others looked distractedly away. I know that some of these women suffered greatly but many of them also challenged and changed their family's values.

Nanna was the first nonconformist in the family, she escaped marriage and was considered a wild one; she smoked cigarettes and moved interstate to work in Melbourne. Nanna was always a great reader and she loved novels of romance, excitement and a little danger. She loved the glamour of Hollywood and films. Nan even dressed like a movie star, in tailored gowns with fur trim and matching shoes and accessories. She probably never thought of herself as a rebel, she was just different. Mother thinks that Nan never remarried because she was unlucky, but I think she chose to have an adventure in the big city instead. So that when Nanna did think about remarrying she was a little bit older, more sophisticated and more independent than most Greek girls. And these qualities, rather than being poor or having a small child, are what made her a bad candidate for marriage.

When I visit Nanna we often talk about marriage, we will watch some old black and white movies and drink cups of tea and eat *halva* and mint-filled chocolates. If we start talking about the men in our lives we will smoke a few cigarettes and shake our heads. Nanna says she is glad she did not have a husband to order her around, and she usually gives me this advice: 'Always be captain of your own ship.'

Mum probably believes in this old saying as well but she would use words like autonomy and individuation to describe it. When Mum told her teachers she wanted to be a doctor, they suggested nursing, but she was stubborn. She worked nights packing crayfish and studied medicine during the day.

In the 1960s Mum married and had two children. My parents designed their own house, and they bought a BMW. Mum took two years off work to have children and then returned to professional life to establish a successful career.

This is almost the Mediterranean – Australian middle-class dream. It would have been perfect if Dad had been the doctor and Mum the one with the nine to five job. Dad worked as a factory manager, he had no great career aspirations, his main ambition was to see that his children did not live as poor and deprived a life as his had once been. Dad was born in Italy in 1931 and lived through the war and the poverty of post-war Europe before emigrating to Australia in 1949. He used to tell us how his mother had to walk up into the mountains to bring water home, even when she was nine months pregnant. Dad wanted my brother and me to have every opportunity that he was denied.

Before I was old enough to go to school Dad would take me to King's Park in the late afternoon where we would wait for Mum to finish work at her office nearby. Nanna would be at home cooking dinner and looking after my brother. I would make Dad push me in the swings as high as he could until it became too dark and cold to stay. We would drive back into the suburbs and we could smell other people's dinner cooking and it usually smelled like chops and mashed potato. Then we would watch TV as we waited for Mum and Nanna to serve dinner.

Dad was always proud of mother's achievements but I think that, as a true Italian, a family oriented *papa*, he must have felt betrayed when her career started taking up more and more of her life. Mum rebelled against the middle-class Mediterranean – Australian dream, she stopped cooking *moussaka* and *lasagne* and making my netball uniforms, she started writing articles for publication in scientific journals and looking for academic postings.

Eventually Mum got her big career break and we moved away from Perth, cutting off the ties with our extended family and our culture. We had never been a nuclear family before and without Nanna around we all had more work to do and Dad had to take over.

Since we left Perth Mum has become more and more successful, although the constraints of family are always going to be her greatest souce of conflict. I think that she feels guilty for not being a 'good mother' in the traditional sense. Dad does most of the housework these days. He is not as good at it as those who have had proper *nifi* training. We are accustomed to the standards set by a Greek grandmother. It has taken Greek women generations to perfect their *nifi* training (to learn how to be a good wife), a man cannot learn all this in just a few years.

Looking at my mother's wedding photographs, I wonder if this is what she hoped for when she was a young girl practising the art of becoming a *nifi*. There is a series of black and white portraits of my parent's wedding, I have one in my bedroom of Mum holding her bouquet. She made a beautiful young bride and my father too looked dashing, very much like a young Dean Martin .

I feel sad to think that there will never be similar photographs of me in a beautiful gown for my daughters and grand daughters to look at and admire. There are separate photo albums from the time we left Perth. Many of the photographs contained in them are of me. I always liked having my picture taken, I think I was scared that I would be forgotten by my family because there were no wedding portraits of me. I feel that if there are no photos of me I will have no place in my family history.

Lisa's graduation, 1994

My recent female ancestors have (fortunately) taught me little about being a good wife, but I hope that I have learned to be as tough as Nanna and as ambitious as my mother. I even get the feeling sometimes, that I am turning into my mother, I have inherited so many of her values. I strive to be an intellectual, an academic, and a professional. What I need to feel connected with my mother is an academic gown rather than a bridal gown. I won't ever wear a white dress and the role of traditional wife and mother is not a serious option for me. I will have no stories to tell any children I may have, like the oral stories that my female ancestors shared. What I have learned is all expressed in written words, in the language of the culture that has provided for my escape from the bleakness of traditional marriage.

My best friend, Paula, is getting married this year. As children we would sneak up to her attic with a glass of milk, laced with a few drops of crème de menthe, and share our fantasies about men and marriage. At 16 I had decided that I would ride down the aisle on a white Harley Davidson wearing a white leather mini-dress. Paula had decided to get married in black. The last time we spoke about it, I had given up on marriage entirely, she was engaged by then and she still wanted to get married in black. Nanna was appalled that a good Greek girl would think of wearing black to her wedding: 'It's not right!' Nanna says it is inappropriate even for the guests at a Greek wedding to wear black. I think it's because they all know, but dare not acknowledge, that 'a wedding is just a funeral where you can smell your flowers'.

I do have one Australian friend who had his wedding at a hillside cemetery, and the bride wore a black lace gown. Nan made a disgusted noise at this too. Her reaction was quite ironic really, when you consider that she had always told us that she was married in a registry office in a black velvet dress.

Paula's family persuaded her of the error of her choice of colours. They compromised, the bridesmaids will have black trim on their dresses – this will be sufficiently outrageous! It is strange to consider that Paula's choice of black trim signifies some partial defiance of tradition – the black trim chosed for *theia* Ariane's wedding so many years ago had a vastly different meaning.

When I rang Paula to congratulate her she said, '*Sta thika sou*!' She assumes that I will eventually get married like all the other girls in my family. It is difficult for her to imagine what I might do if, as Nanna might say, 'my ship never comes in'.

Like many of the women that my mother has told me about I have a glory box at the foot of my bed. It is made of fragrant camphor wood, my father made it by hand and gave it to me on my 24th birthday. A little late. I have collected sheets and towels and a white lace nightie and other junk for my *prika*. While it seems rather ludicrous to continue to store these things, neither does it seem right to use them. When my great-aunt (grandmother Chrissie's sister) became a widow she used her glory box to store brandy for her own wake. She filled the box with tea towels made of red and white checked gingham and doilies and aprons she had made. All of them with labels pinned to them to say who should have them when she died. I grew up in her house, in the musty, strange-smelling house that was so dark and full of memories. Any time we visited she would give us sugared fruit or sugared tomatoes (*glykia*) on tiny crystal plates. These preserves were my favorite sweets but I never learned to make them and when Aunty died we used the crystal plates as ashtrays because we had forgotten what they were for.

These ancestors have taught me about marriage and womanhood and as I establish a home with my partner I can see each of them in the things I do. I love these old photos and their associated memories and the women who have given my life its history.

MARRIAGE CONTRACT

The following agreement sets out the details of the arrangements to be implemented in relation to the marriage of .... and ....

We hereby agree to the following:

1 That we will be married by a celebrant to be chosen by both parties but if agreement cannot be reached, the final decision to be made by .... (the female party).

2 That the words and the duration of the celebration will be determined by both parties but if agreement cannot be reached, the final decision to be made by .... (the female party).

3 That the marriage will be celebrated in a place to be decided by both parties but if agreement cannot be reached, the final decision to be made by .... (the female party).

4 That the invited guests will be limited in number to .... and that each of the parties to the agreement will be entitled to invite an equal number of guests.

5 That because of men's greater earning capacity generally, and women's greater emotional and physical contributions to relationships, all costs associated with the ceremony will be paid for by the male partner.

or

That any costs associated with the ceremony will be shared equally by the parties to the agreement.

Optional clauses:

6 (i) That each of the parties agrees not to arrive at the ceremony inebriated, high or overly affected by drugs of any sort.
(ii) That there be no bucks' night associated with the marriage ceremony.

BIOGRAPHICAL NOTES

DALE SPENDER

Dale Spender is a researcher, writer and broadcaster: she is the author–editor of more than thirty books. On the grounds that it is one of the most honourable and responsible things to be, she is also a feminist.

Since the time she recognised that the voice of authority was male she has been intent on replacing this dominance with a dialogue of equals. To this end she has founded women's presses, journals and women's studies courses. She was a committee member of the First International Feminist Book Fair in London in 1984, the editor of series such as *Mothers of the Novel, Women's Resource Library*, and the *Penguin Australian Women's Library*. Most recently she has – with Cheris Kramarae – become the co-originator of an international data base on women.

She is associated with universities in the United Kingdom and the United States (as well as the University of Queensland) and she has lectured at universities and conferences around the world.

She is aware that women have been able to take charge of their own words in print – but that they now have to start again to counter the dominance of males in the electronic media. *Nattering on the Nets: women, power and cyberspace* (Spinifex Press, Melbourne, 1994) deals with the new communication technologies and their social, political and educational implications.

Her publications include *Man Made Language* and *Feminist Theorists* which, along with selections from *The Writing or the Sex? – or why you don't have to read women's writing to know it's no good*, have been translated into Japanese. *Invisible Women: the schooling scandal* has been translated into German, and *Learning to Lose* was translated into Spanish in 1993.

She has written *Mothers of the Novel: 100 good women writers before Jane Austen* and *The Diary of Elizabeth Pepys*, as well as *For the Record: the making and meaning of feminist scholarship*. Her books, *Writing a New Word: two centuries of Australian women writers* and *There's Always Been a Women's Movement* set out some of the achievements of women. With her sister Lynne Spender she has written *Scribbling Sisters*, and with Sally Cline, *Reflecting Man*.

She has edited *The Anthology of British Women Writers* and *The Penguin Anthology of Australian Women's Writing* as well as *Living by the Pen: early British women writers* and *Heroines: a contemporary anthology of Australian women writers*. With Patricia Clarke she has edited *Life Lines: Australian women's letters and diaries, 1788–1840*; with Kirsten Lees she has edited *Dymphna Cusack, Politics and Pen* and with Cheris Kramarae, *The Knowledge Explosion: generations of feminist scholarship*. She is currently working on her new project, *Brains and Beauty*, which stakes out women's claim for intellectual equality, and authority.

She lectures widely on the possibilities and pitfalls of information technology.

DEBRA ADELAIDE

Debra Adelaide lives in Sydney where she works as a writer, editor, researcher, and mother of two. She has published several books on Australian women writers, and recently co-authored the detective novel, *Headlines* (McPhee Gribble, 1993). Her current projects include more crime fiction and a narrative set in a country hotel, from which 'According to the Book' is an extract.

CAROLINE BAUM

Caroline Baum was born in London in 1958. After studying philosophy and politics at York University she researched cook books and TV arts documentaries. In 1984 she moved to Australia. As a journalist her work has appeared in the *Australian*, the *Bulletin*, *HQ*, *24 Hours* and *Vogue*, where she held the position of features editor.

Today, Caroline Baum is the co-presenter of TVTV on ABC television. She lives in Sydney. 'The Dress' is her first piece of published fiction.

LISA BELLEAR

Lisa Bellear – of the Noonuccal people, Stradbroke Island – was born in the Royal Women's Hospital, Melbourne.

Indigenous Feminist Poet Broadcaster and qualified Social Worker. Recently completed Graduate Diploma in Arts [Women's Studies] and has now commenced an MA in Women's Studies at the University of Melbourne.

For nearly nine years she has done voluntary broadcasting on Melbourne's 3CR Community Radio 'Not Another Koori Show' with Destiny Deacon, Janina Harding and Kimberley Kruger.

Member of the Victorian Aboriginal Child Care Agency, Victorian Aborigines Advancement League Inc, Yuroke Aboriginal Women's Group [University of Melbourne], Australian Labor Party, Deputy Chair of the 6th International Feminist Book Fair and executive member of the Black Women's Action in Education Foundation.

KAZ COOKE

Kaz Cooke is an Australian cartoonist, author and columnist. She is the creator of *Hermione, the Modern Girl* (a cartoon character), 'Keep Yourself Nice' (a weekly tongue-in-cheek etiquette column in the Melbourne *Age* and the *Modern Girl's* series of books and diaries. She is the creator of 'Heartlands' (an exhibition at the

National Gallery of Victoria, 1992) and *The Crocodile Club* (a novel).

She is allergic to cats, the National Party, and that stupid music they play in crystal shops. She is not now, nor has she ever been – married.

ANNA MARIA DELL'OSO

Anna Maria Dell'oso was born in Melbourne of Italian immigrant parents. She works as a writer, essayist, librettist, columnist and film critic. After humanities and violin studies in Victoria and at the Tasmanian Conservatorium of Music (where she studied briefly with Jan Sedivka), she turned to a writing career, winning a cadetship on the *Christchurch Star* in New Zealand. In 1978, she returned to Australia to work on the *Sydney Morning Herald*, where she became best-known for her weekly essays in that paper's *Good Weekend* magazine.

Over the past eight years, Anna Maria Dell'oso has written in a variety of genres, including poetry, short stories, opera and drama. A collection of her essays and stories, *Cats, Cradles and Chamomile Tea*, was published by Random House in 1989. Her short stories have been featured in the anthologies, *Homeland, Harbour, Who Do You Think You Are?* and *Growing Up Italian In Australia*. Dell'oso's libretto to the opera *Bride of Fortune* – about an Italian woman who arrives in Australia in the 1950s to marry a man she has never met – was performed by the Western Australian Opera to great acclaim at the 1991 Festival of Perth. It was Dell'oso's second collaboration with composer Gillian Whitehead. Dell'oso also wrote the mythic-poetic libretto for Whitehead's *The Pirate Moon*, which was performed in Auckland, New Zealand in 1986. Her one-act play, *Tinsel and Ashes*, was performed in 1991 by the Noosa Arts Theatre.

In 1993, Dell'oso was awarded a fellowship from the Literature Board of the Australia Council to write a biography of Australian master musician, Jan Sedivka. She has also completed another libretto, *The Millionaires*, a tragi-comic music-drama about the business dreams and aspirations of three working-class women, set in a pizza franchise in the western suburbs of Sydney. *The Millionaires*, with music by Gillian Whitehead, has been commissioned by the Chamber Made Opera Company in Melbourne.

Anna Maria Dell'oso lives in the inner west of Sydney with her husband David, a violinist, and their two children.

LOIS ELLIS

Lois Ellis trained at NIDA as an actor in the early 1960s. Perversely she has rarely acted but has developed her career as a theatre director. Her directorial work includes the plays of Franca Rame and Dario Fo: *Female Parts, Can't Pay? Won't Pay!*, *Open Couple*, all featuring Evelyn Krape; also *Piaf* with Jeannie Lewis, and *Waiting For Effie* with Mary Coustas. Lois will direct Virginia Woolf's *A Room of One's Own* for a national tour in 1994. She has been bullied into acting the role of Radclyffe Hall in Sara Hardy's play *Radclyffe* and into co-writing, with the same Sara Hardy, *Rosie Fingered Dawn.*

When all this is over she is planning an overseas holiday with the above mentioned . . .

YASMINE GOONERATNE

Yasmine Gooneratne, novelist and poet, teaches English eighteenth century literature and postcolonial literature at Macquarie University, New South Wales, where she holds a Personal Chair in English and the University's first (and to date, only) earned higher doctoral degree of DLitt. Born in Sri Lanka, educated there and at Cambridge, she received the Order of Australia (AO) in 1990 for services to literature and education. Her sixteen books include studies of Jane Austen, Alexander Pope and Ruth Prawer Jhabvala; *Relative Merits* (a family memoir); and *A Change of Skies*, the novel which won the Marjorie Barnard Literary Award in 1992.

KERRY GREENWOOD

Kerry Greenwood was born in the Melbourne suburb of Footscray and still lives there. She has written a number of plays, including *The Troubadours* with Stephen D'Arcy; worked as a director, producer, folk singer and costume-maker. Her first book, *Cocaine*

Blues, was published by McPhee Gribble in 1989: her second, *Flying Too High*, in 1990: her third, *Murder on the Ballarat Train*, in 1991 and her fourth, *Death at Victoria Dock*, in 1992. Her fifth, *The Green Mill Murder*, was published in 1993 and her sixth, *Blood and Circuses*, in 1994. All feature the stylish flapper Phryne Fisher. They have been recorded for Talking Books, and are also published in the United States.

Kerry Greenwood is currently working on her latest Phryne Fisher book. When she is not writing she is a locum solicitor for the Legal Aid Commission and an unpaid curator of a menagerie which includes four cats and a duck called Son of Quark. She has no children and lives with a registered wizard.

KATE GRENVILLE

Kate Grenville was born in Sydney in 1950 and holds an undergraduate degree from the University of Sydney and a masters degree from the University of Colorado. Kate spent seven years in Europe and the USA working and studying. She taught Creative Writing at the University of Colorado. She has worked as film editor, journalist, typist, teacher and sub-titled at SBS.

Her first novel *Lilian's Story* won the Vogel/Australian Award for new writers in 1985 and the Talking Book of the Year Award in 1986. Film rights to the novel are under option.

She has published a collection of short stories, *Bearded Ladies*, and another novel, *Dreamhouse*, with the University of Queensland Press. Her most recent novel *Joan Makes History*, was written with the assistance of a Bi-centennial Writers' Fellowship. Her novels have been published to wide acclaim in the US and UK.

Kate is also the author of a non-fiction work, *The Writing Book*, which was published by Allen & Unwin in 1990. Another book on the craft of writing, *Making Stories*, written in conjunction with Sue Woolfe, was published by Allen & Unwin in 1993. She has recently completed a novel *Dark Places*, which will be published in July 1994.

MARION HALLIGAN

Marion Halligan is the author of three novels, including *Spider Cup* and *Lovers' Knots*, three collections of short stories, of which the latest is *The Worry Box*, and a book of essays about food and related matters called *Eat My Words*. Her work has been short-listed for most of the major prizes and has won some of them.

SARA HARDY

Having acted professionally for several years, Sara finally turned to writing plays. She had decided that, as there were so few good roles for women to perform, she had better write her own. Her first (co-written) play was *Radclyffe*, in which she palyed Una, Lady Troubridge, opposite Lois Ellis' Radclyffe Hall. Next came *Vita! – A Fantasy*, in which she played Vita Sackville-West (and which is published in *Heroines*). *Vita! – A Fantasy* is about a relationship between two married women – namely Mrs. Woolfe and Mrs. Nicolson. Sara is now writing *For a Muse*, a play about Aphra, Artemisia and Ethel – three wonderful Muses.

Having coerced Lois Ellis into co-writing *Rosie Fingered Dawn* (a thoroughly enjoyable process), Sara has now persuaded Lois to co-write a feature film ...

HELEN HODGMAN

Helen Hodgman was born in Aberdeen, Scotland, in 1945 and lived in Colchester, Essex, until 1958 when her family were shipped off to Tasmania by their local Rotary Club as part of the 'Bring Out a Briton' campaign. She eventually returned to England, lived in London for ten years during which time she began writing, and worked at a variety of jobs including bookmaker's clerk and domestic cleaner. She has published three novels, and is working on a fourth. She now lives in Sydney, Australia, and makes her living by writing for film and television.

Publications

1976 *Blue Skies*, Duckworth, London; Penguin, Melbourne, 1981.
1978 *Jack and Jill*, Duckworth, London. (Winner Somerset Maugham Award.) Penguin, Melbourne, 1981.

1988 *Broken Words*, Penguin, Melbourne. (Winner Christina Stead Prize.) Virago, London, 1989. Published as *Ducks*, Harmony Books, New York, 1989.
1989 *Blue Skies* and *Jack and Jill* published in one volume, Virago, London.
1991 *Heroines: A Contemporary Anthology*, Ed. Dale Spender, Penguin, Melbourne.
Theatre:
1981 *Oh Mother, is it worth it?* Waterfront Theatre, Vancouver, Canada.
Film and television:
1984–5 *The Right Hand Man*, feature film, UAA films.
1986–7 *The Silence of Dean Maitland*, mini series, Zarwot Productions.
1988–9 *Giant Freesias*, television adaptation of three Elizabeth Jolley short stories, Zowie Films.
1989–90 *Roundabout*, mini series, SBS.
1990 script editor *The River*, feature film, Hibiscus Films, New Zealand.
1992–3 *Blue Skies*, screenplay, feature film, Cascade Films, Melbourne.
Work in progress:
Novel: *Middleground*
Film: *Looking for Alibrandi*, adaptation of book by Melina Marchetta, M&A Film Corporation P/L.

JACKIE HUGGINS

Jackie Huggins is a freelance writer and Aboriginal historian. She has been an activist for her people for over twenty years. Her first play, *Maakkings*, has toured successfully in Amsterdam, Copenhagen, and other parts of Europe. Currently she is writing three booklets for Queensland Distance Education on urban life styles, a children's book with pupils at West End Primary School (Brisbane), and a text book on Aboriginal women; she is also co-editing a young adult fiction collection by Aboriginal writers. Her biography of her mother, *Aunty Rita*, appears in 1994.

Jackie Huggin's work features prominently in many Women's

Studies journals and her reputation for versatility is well founded. She is the most widely published author on Aboriginal gender and race relations and is determined to show an Aboriginal presence in history.

SUE INGLETON

Sue Ingleton works in the theatre – performing, directing and writing. Acclaimed both here and internationally for her one woman shows, *Strip Jack Naked* and *Near Ms's*, her next major work, *The Passion ... and its deep connection with lemon delicious pudding*, will take us into another dimension in her writing and her search for truth and healing in the public arena.

As a writer Sue was shortlisted for the 'Follow Me' short story competition and later published in *INK*. She has also published *Sue Ingleton's Almaniac, a woman's guide to domestic insanity* (a deeply disturbed book). She was very pleased to be invited to contribute to the ever increasing and valuable editions of Dale Spender.

BARBARA JEFFERIS

Barbara Jefferis is the author of nine widely translated novels, originally published simultaneously in the United States and England. Other publications include a travel book, biographies of three Victorian women, and various publications for the Australian Society of Authors. She began her writing career in Sydney, first in daily and magazine journalism, then in radio, writing more than sixty dramas and documentaries for the ABC as well as scientific series for adults, schools programs, and serials for children.

She's been a tutor at many Adult Education courses for writers, and a judge for numerous literary contests. She travelled to Russia and India on cultural exchange visits, and in 1985 was invited by the Canadian Writers' Union to speak at a symposium in Toronto at which they were exploring means of getting Public Lending Right for Canadian authors.

In 1985 she was made a member of the Order of Australia for services to literature.

JANE MESSER

Jane Messer is a Sydney writer. She completed a BA in Sociology at Macquarie University, and a MA in Writing from The Johns Hopkins University in 1993. Her short stories, poems, reviews and articles have appeared in a range of Australian journals and anthologies. A novel, *Night by Night*, will be published by McPhee Gribble in 1994.

SUSAN MITCHELL

Susan Mitchell is a senior lecturer in the Faculty of Communications at the University of South Australia. She is the author of the best-sellers *Tall Poppies, The Matriarchs* and *Tall Poppies Too*, and the character of Sarah in 'The Wedding' appears in her novel, *Hot Shots*. Her role models are Simone de Beauvoir and Mae West. She is also presenter of *Susan Mitchell: In Conversation* on ABC television.

SARAH NEAL

Sarah Neal was born in Brisbane in 1971 and at a very early age was involved in experimental theatre; writing, directing, constructing and performing for the stage. She became a youth representative and worked on planning committees, conferences and festivals throughout her schooling. Sarah went on to do a BA in Drama and Film at the Queensland University of Technology. She wrote, directed and performed in many productions and became increasingly fascinated by the potential of film – particularly its permanence as opposed to the transient nature of theatre.

In 1992 she set up a film company with a friend, with the aim of writing, directing and producing short films.

The first – *She Won't Tell* – received a post-production grant from Film Queensland and is currently being distributed to film festivals throughout Australia. It will be entered into the New Queensland Filmmakers Awards, among others in 1995.

Sarah has worked in the theatre in the West End of London, travelled through Europe and the Middle East, laboured on a *moshav* in Israel and worked in a sandwich shop. She continues her freelance work in the film industry and intends to undertake further study in film. Currently she plans to travel to Central America and Spain with her film camera and continue to produce more films – including *Daughters and Dilemmas*.

JAN OWEN

Jan Owen is an advocate for children and young people. she has worked in many areas of the human services sector in Australia over the past fifteen years. she has a strong commitment to and involvement in issues which are relevant to women and young women. She was born in Melbourne, grew up in Brisbane and has lived in both Sydney and Adelaide for different periods over the past ten years. Jan currently lives in Brisbane with her partner, David James, and their three children – Joshua, Laura and Alexander.

DOROTHY PORTER

Dorothy Porter was born in 1954. She has published five books of poetry: the most recent is *Akhenaten* (University of Queensland Press, 1992) – a verse novel in the voice of the controversial Pharaoh Akhenaten set in Ancient Egypt. *The Monkey's Mask*, a lesbian detective romance verse thriller, will be published by Hyland House in 1994.

She has also written two novels for adolescents; *Rookwood* (University of Queensland Press, 1991) and *The Witch Number* (University of Queensland Press, 1993).

CAROLYN QUADRIO

Carolyn Quadrio was born in Australia in 1943 and grew up in Western Australia where her family (Mavrokefalos) had immigrated. She attended Highgate Primary School. (Today, 90 per cent of the children at that school are still of non-English speaking background.) She matriculated from Leederville Technical School and entered medical school at the University of Western Australia in 1961, graduating in 1966. She married in 1965 and her children were born in 1967 and 1969. She gained a Diploma in Psychological Medicine in 1970 from the University of Otago, New Zealand (as an extra-mural candidate, child care commitments prevented her from qualifying in Australia at that time). She became a Fellow of the Royal Australian and New Zealand College of Psychiatry in 1973 and moved with her family to Sydney in 1984. She has held academic appointments with the Department of Psychiatry, University of Western Australia (Lecturer, 1970–71 and the School of Psychiatry, University of New South Wales (Senior Lecturer, 1987-1991).

She currently teaches for the Australian Institute of Family Therapy, the New South Wales Institute of Psychiatry, the New South Wales Institute of Psychotherapy and the University of Sydney. Her current research with the Department of Women's Studies at the University of Sydney, concerns the issue of gender in psychiatry.

LISA QUADRIO

Lisa Quadrio is an Anthropology/Women's Studies graduate from Macquarie University where she is currently completing a law degree. She was born in Western Australia in 1967 and went to Perth Girls College before moving to Sydney in 1984 where she completed high school.

ROSIE SCOTT

Rosie Scott is the author of four critically acclaimed novels – *Glory Days*, published in the UK and the USA; *Nights with Grace, Feral City*, (short-listed for the Australian Banjo Paterson Award) and *Lives on Fire.* All are to be published in German. She is also the author of a collection of short stories – *Queen of Love* and a play, *Say Thankyou to the Lady*, which won the Bruce Mason National Award and is the basis of the award winning film, *Redheads.*

LYNNE SPENDER

Lynne Spender completed a BA at Sydney University (1966), then a Diploma in Education (1967) and began teaching English at a time when grammar was still familiar to many Australians. She has subsequently taught, cajoled and lectured in various parts of the world, completed two masters degrees (one in English, one in Sociology – Womens Studies) and a law degree. Her first book *Intruders on the Rights of Men* about women, writing and publishing, was published by Pandora in 1984. She has since published two other books, edited over thirty legal and law related books and is currently the editor of the 980 page 'The Law Handbook'. She received a Literature Board Grant in 1989 and wrote a book on Kylie Tennant which has not yet been accepted by a publisher.

Lynne spent six years as managing editor of Redfern Legal Centre Publishing before a brief stint with the Independent Commission Against Corruption in NSW. She commenced work as Executive Office of the Australian Society of Authors in January 1993.

PAMELA VERRALL

Pamela Verrall grew up in Adelaide. In the 1970s she worked alongside other women developing the Women's Studies Course at Flinders University and establishing the Women's Information Switchboard.

During this period she learned to tap dance, a skill she later demonstrated in *Out of the Frying Pan*, an Adelaide Women's Theatre production. Turning her back on a potentially brilliant performing career, she took herself off to Law School at the University of New South Wales. While cutting a dashing figure in a wig and gown, she knew that dressing up was probably the most fun she'd have as a barrister, so went to work for the ABC making children's television.

From January 1992 to January 1994 she was one of the producers of *The Coming Out Show*, a weekly radio program with a focus on feminist issues.

NADIA WHEATLEY

Nadia Wheatley began writing full-time in 1976, after completing post-graduate work in Australian history. Her first book, *Five Times Dizzy*, received the New South Wales Premier's Special Children's Book Award in 1983 and was later produced as a television series. Her other books include the young adult novels *The House That*

Was Eureka (which received the New South Wales Premier's Children's Book Prize in 1985) and *The Blooding. My Place*, produced in collaboration with Donna Rawlins, was the Australian Children's Book of the Year for Younger Readers in 1988 and also won the Eve Pownall Award for non-fiction. Nadia Wheatley has recently published *Lucy in the Leap Year*, a novel for younger readers. She has also published fiction and non-fiction for adults in publications ranging from *Spare Rib* to *Scripsi*, and has edited two anthologies of essays by Charmian Clift.

Acknowledgements

Many people have contributed to this volume – some of them indirectly. (I have not been averse to studying the weddings and wifely habits of relatives and friends.) But I would particularly like to thank my own parents, Ivy and Harry Spender, for the marital model they have provided: it has changed with the times.

On behalf of women authors, I would also like to acknowledge a debt to Susan Hawthorne and Renate Klein, for their dedication to women's books and women's writing; their efforts have helped to make the literary climate a much healthier and more exciting place.

Despite the pressure of her own work, Kirsten Lees has been more than helpful in providing insights – as has Chloe Bryce. Janet Irwin has been wise and wonderful and Colleen Forrester – a marriage celebrant, and a supportive friend – has given me the benefit of her wealth of experience. And Katy Steenstrup has enlightened me on more than one occasion.

From a well-established vantage point Carolyn Mason read the manuscript and offered sound advice: Sarah Neal acted as chauffeur, secretary, chef and a refreshing stimulus. And Helen Thomson is the best long-distance fax-critic and colleague an editor could have.

Carolyn Quadrio has been more than a personal psychiatrist – and has even let me counsel her as my therapy.

From Barbara Jefferis and Ray Koppe I received reassurance, replenishment, and a reference point for dealing with authors. I am grateful for their example, and friendship. Margaret Mittleheuser and Cathryn Mittleheuser have extended my horizons.

Cheris Kramarae is an inspirational model for all who know her and Jeanie Taylor has been there every day – on my e-mail. Robyn Daniels is also an e-mail-pal, and a source of invaluable feedback.

My thanks to Quentin Bryce for her walking and talking companionship, and to Jill Hickson for constant encouragement, and commitment.

Lynne Spender has provided professional and personal advice and has modified her own contribution to accommodate the whole; she is the one with whom I have talked late at night about change, authors, print, feminism, families – and weddings and wives.

And Ted Brown is testimony to the fact that statistics do not tell the full story.

I wish to acknowledge also the contributions of Jessie Bernard, Germaine Greer, Hugh McKay and others whose work has informed much of the discussion. Thanks to Cascade Films who hold copyright in the film *Blue Skies* by Helen Hodgman. Lines from the song 'Satin Sheets', as sung by Jeanne Pruett, are reproduced by kind permission of MCA Music Australia Pty Limited.